Balthild of Francia

WOMEN IN ANTIQUITY

Series Editors: Ronnie Ancona and Sarah B. Pomeroy

This book series provides compact and accessible introductions to the life and historical times of women from the ancient world. Approaching ancient history and culture broadly, the series selects figures from the earliest of times to late antiquity.

Cleopatra
A Biography
Duane W. Roller

Clodia Metelli
The Tribune's Sister
Marilyn B. Skinner

Galla Placidia
The Last Roman Empress
Hagith Sivan

Arsinoë of Egypt and Macedon
A Royal Life
Elizabeth Donnelly Carney

Berenice II and the Golden Age of Ptolemaic Egypt
Dee L. Clayman

Faustina I and II
Imperial Women of the Golden Age
Barbara M. Levick

Turia
A Roman Woman's Civil War
Josiah Osgood

Monica
An Ordinary Saint
Gillian Clark

Theodora
Actress, Empress, Saint
David Potter

Hypatia
The Life and Legend of an Ancient Philosopher
Edward Watts

Boudica
Warrior Woman of Roman Britain
Caitlin C. Gillespie

Sabina Augusta
An Imperial Journey
T. Corey Brennan

Cleopatra's Daughter
And Other Royal Woman of the Augustan Era
Duane W. Roller

Perpetua
Athlete of God
Barbara K. Gold

Zenobia
Shooting Star of Palmyra
Nathanael Andrade

Eurydice and the Birth of Macedonian Power
Elizabeth Donnelly Carney

Melania the Younger
From Rome to Jerusalem
Elizabeth A. Clark

Sosipatra of Pergamum
Philosopher and Oracle
Heidi Marx

Helena Augusta
Mother of the Empire
Julia Hillner

Radegund
The Trials and Triumphs of a Merovingian Queen
E. T. Dailey

Balthild of Francia
Anglo-Saxon Slave, Merovingian Queen, and Abolitionist Saint
Isabel Moreira

Balthild of Francia

Anglo-Saxon Slave, Merovingian Queen, and Abolitionist Saint

ISABEL MOREIRA

OXFORD
UNIVERSITY PRESS

Oxford University Press is a department of the University of Oxford.
It furthers the University's objective of excellence in research, scholarship,
and education by publishing worldwide. Oxford is a registered trade mark of
Oxford University Press in the UK and in certain other countries.

Published in the United States of America by Oxford University Press
198 Madison Avenue, New York, NY 10016, United States of America.

© Oxford University Press 2024

All rights reserved. No part of this publication may be reproduced,
stored in a retrieval system, or transmitted, in any form or by any means,
without the prior permission in writing of Oxford University Press,
or as expressly permitted by law, by license, or under terms agreed with
the appropriate reprographics rights organization. Inquiries concerning
reproduction outside the scope of the above should be sent to
the Rights Department, Oxford University Press, at the address above.

You must not circulate this work in any other form
and you must impose this same condition on any acquirer

Library of Congress Cataloging-in-Publication Data
Names: Moreira, Isabel, author.
Title: Balthild of Francia : Anglo-Saxon slave, Merovingian queen, and
abolitionist saint / Isabel Moreira.
Description: First edition. | [New York, NY] : Oxford University Press, [2024]
Identifiers: LCCN 2024024851 (print) | LCCN 2024024852 (ebook) |
ISBN 9780197792612 (paperback) | ISBN 9780197518663 (hardback) |
ISBN 9780197518687 (epub)
Subjects: LCSH: Bathildis, Queen, consort of Clovis II, King of the Franks,
-approximately 680 | Queens—France—Biography. | France—Kings and
rulers—Biography. | Christian women saints—France—Biography. |
Franks—Queens—Biography. | Merovingians—Queens—Biography. |
Enslaved persons—France—Biography. | Anglo-Saxons—France—Biography.
Classification: LCC DC69.8.B35 M67 2024 (print) | LCC DC69.8.B35 (ebook)
| DDC 944/.013092 [B]—dc23/eng/20240603
LC record available at https://lccn.loc.gov/2024024851
LC ebook record available at https://lccn.loc.gov/2024024852

DOI: 10.1093/oso/9780197518663.001.0001

Sheridan Books, Inc., United States of America

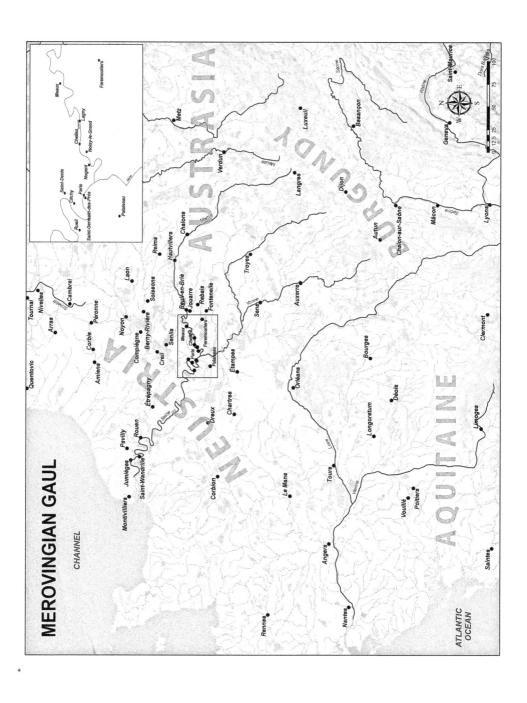

Simplified Family Tree

Some dates are approximations

Contents

Acknowledgments   xiii
Preface   xv
Abbreviations   xxii
List of Figures   xxiii

1. Finding her Story   1
2. Trafficked Slave   16
3. Marriage Makes a Queen   29
4. Regent, Reformer, and Rescuer of Slaves   55
5. Life and Death at the Convent of Chelles   88
6. Mother, Mutilator—and Murderer?   122
7. Abolitionist Icon   140

Appendix: The Baldehildis Seal Matrix   177
Endnotes   179
Bibliography   197
Index   211

Acknowledgments

The writing of this book straddled the Covid-19 years. Just before the pandemic hit, I was immensely fortunate to be able to undertake in-person research on the project in France in the summer of 2019 with the support of an NEH Summer Stipend. (Any views, findings, conclusions, or recommendations expressed in this book do not necessarily reflect those of the NEH.) By 2020, like everyone else, I was scrambling to find all the free online resources that research institutions and other organizations were providing. I could not have completed the book without access to the digitized collections on *Gallica* and the *Internet Archive*. A Kickstart Grant from the College of Humanities at the University of Utah provided additional funds, and the two-year James Clayton Research Professorship provided time to write during which time Balthild became a demanding member of our Covid bubble.

I would like to thank the librarians and archivists who provided help accessing sources at various stages of this project. Staff at the *Bibliothèque nationale de France*, at the François-Mitterand and Arsenal sites, and at the *Archives nationales* at Pierrefitte-sur-Seine helped me navigate the catalogues. I am especially grateful to Pauline Darleguy at the *Bibliothèque historique de la Ville de Paris*, and Pascal Piviale for help identifying archival dossiers. Director Christian Charamond and Madame Patricia Mittard at the *Musée Alfred-Bonno* in Chelles provided access to their collection of items associated with Balthild even while the Museum was closed for renovations; I thank them for their time and expertise. As ever, I am thankful for the efficiency with which the staff, and especially the interlibrary loan staff, at the Willard J. Marriott Library at the University of Utah, tracked down necessary sources, and thanks to Justin Sorenson (GIS services) who translated my messy dots into a map.

This project has benefitted greatly from conversations with friends and colleagues. Bonnie Effros, Alan Bernstein, Jim Lehning, Megan Armstrong, Lisa Bailey, Chris Jones, Eric Herschthal, Benjamin Cohen, and Hollis Robbins have either read chapters or discussed issues related to the project. The students in my *Biography as History* senior seminar classes have been companions in the arts and perils of biographic writing—I owe them more than they know.

A special thanks goes to my editor Stefan Vranka for suggesting the Women in Antiquity series for the work, and to Ronnie Ancona and Sarah Pomeroy for bringing Balthild into the fold. Stefan's thoughtful reading of the manuscript alongside the comments of the anonymous reviewers for the press greatly improved the manuscript. Any errors of fact or interpretation are my own.

A special thanks goes to friends and colleagues, especially Eric and Carrie Hinderaker, Rebecca Horn, Kay and Mike Ringwood, Margaret Toscano, Katharina Gerstenberger, Anne Christie, Anne Johnston, and Tina Burton, a constant companion when trails got tough. Finally, and most importantly, my wonderful family: Robert, Laura, and Julia—always.

Preface

> Another of these obscure queens! What's the point?
>
> Pierre-Armand Malitourne, critic

The sour critic of the marble statue of Queen Balthild destined for the Luxembourg Gardens in Paris goaded his mid-nineteenth-century readers with questions that must still be answered today. Who was this seventh-century queen? What was the point of her? And we can add, why is she obscure? One of the reasons for her obscurity relative to other historical queens is that the Merovingian era itself is not very well known to general readers of history. Balthild is not obscure to Merovingianists, of course. Nor was she obscure to the Catholic population living in the Paris region up to the nineteenth century. In the Luxembourg Gardens she stood as one among twenty marble queens. Should she have a place alongside the other famous queens of history? I would argue that she should and that both her existence as a seventh-century queen who was once a slave, and her role as an icon of abolition in the early modern era, earns our attention.

Biography is the oldest way to tell a story, but it can be an odd way to do history. To think in modern biographic terms, a reader wants a mental image of a person—how they lived, what their environment looked like, what their thinking was, and what their ambitions were. Likewise, a biographer wants to stop the clock and imagine a person who occupies space, looks around them, smells the air, sees a landscape, and walks through a crowd. There is a desire for conjuration. In the past, the aim of religious edification provided sufficient reason for authors to preserve and retell the story of religious figures of the past. Today, we are not only more curious about how people really lived, but thanks to scientific advances in archaeology we have more resources to reconstruct a distant environment and perhaps more fully immerse ourselves in the past. Balthild's story as told by her hagiographer has attracted many iterations over the centuries. But what was it like to be a Merovingian woman? What was her physical and cultural environment like? How did she live? What was her cultural milieu? Six years immersed in a broad scope of the history and archaeology of the

Merovingian world editing the *OHMW* convinced me that it was worth a try to see a Merovingian person in the round by means of a cultural biography.[1] The final two and a half centuries of the ancient world are still obscure to the general reader of history in large part because there is not a strong sense, in Anglophone literature at least, of the individuals who inhabited this world. How many people can name a Merovingian? This may change as more translations of the Latin texts that told their lives are made available and bring some of these individuals into better view. Fortunately, there are good English translations of Balthild's Merovingian and her Carolingian Life that are readily accessible; I have used them alongside the Latin text.[2] Balthild is someone whose life and name is worth better knowing.

The notion that biography truly brings us close to the lived experience of its subject is an illusion, of course. Yet it is possible to feel sympathy and curiosity about a subject whose life was so different from our own. As shrouded as Balthild's lived life must remain, she was a person who experienced first-hand one of the most harrowing aspects of seventh-century life: forcible relocation. Encased as she is in the conventional virtues of a Merovingian saint, Balthild's life story was nevertheless unconventional for a seventh-century saint. And yet, as unconventional as it was, it was also a life experience that contemporaries recognized and understood. As tenuous as our connection to her is, there is a core internal consistency in the way she deployed social and political reform to address a cluster of problems that had social distress at its core. She had her supporters and her detractors but that was the price she had to pay. She did things; she existed as a meaningful force in her time.

We never hear Balthild's spoken voice directly in the sources. In the first account of her life no political opinions are directly expressed as her own. Rather, she is an observed figure, who inhabits a narrative determined by others. Yet a closer acquaintance with Balthild's story instills one with the sense of an intelligent force—a woman who survived a cutthroat system, made her bargain with the world, enjoyed the exercise of power, suffered reversals, yet somehow was able to be both socially engaged and politically astute. Balthild's actions, ambitions, and her hard-policy objectives are etched on a life that must not have been easy, even when it became materially comfortable. At first sight she seems to embody a sanitized version of the great sixth-century Byzantine empress Theodora who was also active in addressing the social issues—especially of women—activated by poverty and circumstance. Indeed, the "real" Balthild, whoever she was, may have found inspiration in the empress. The two women faced some issues in remarkably similar ways.

There is some irony in the fact that an era that saw such a great flourishing of saintly biographies (hagiographies) is also an era that has attracted so little attention from modern biographers: indeed, these circumstances may be linked. The Lives of the Saints written in the sixth and seventh centuries were often well-crafted, informative, and useful. Over the centuries religious authors copied and revised them, popularizing them first in manuscript copies, and then in print. In the early modern period, in the hands of their first critical editors, Merovingian saints and monastic founders became honorary Benedictines. Later still, the legends that grew around these saints and their monasteries became the stuff of romance and antiquarian curiosity.

Unsurprisingly, Balthild's story attracted the attention of pious biographers over the centuries. Whether it is the fanciful medieval legend of her God-inspired decision to maim her rebellious sons, or the idea that she rid France of the scourge of slavery (all French are born free!), Balthild's story has spun out centuries of fascinating fiction. Her first anonymous biographer was a hagiographer, a writer whose task it was to portray her as a saint, but who was nevertheless wise to the strangeness of her life path and who did not attempt to erase entirely the presence of her detractors. This hagiographer's narrative voice—respectful and succinct—worked within the Merovingian convention that a saint's life history was predetermined, which meant that her life and her ambitions were depicted as virtuous from the start. The hagiography is chronological and for this reason its structure and focal points are powerful determinants in the way her life can be told today, even while other sources for her activities exist. Later biographers generally followed the first hagiographer's chronological lead. Yet there were always embellishments to the tale reflecting new priorities. The Carolingian version of her life turned her into an indisputably royal figure. In an era of strong regencies, seventeenth-century biographers chronicled her virtues as queen-regent of France. In the Napoleonic era her early life trended gothic. In the later nineteenth century, she was the gentle queen, often stripped of her role as liberator, who joined the list of queens and princesses of France whose anodyne lives were considered appropriate models for the instruction of schoolgirls. Two biographers of the modern era have filled out the stark narrative of the original. Mathieu Couturier's

1909 biography of the queen broadened the scope of her story by interweaving it with the presence of the many political and religious men who surrounded her and by chronicling the history and success of monastic institutions founded and supported by her.[3] In keeping with the convention of religious biographies, Couturier included essential cultic information for the devotee: brief information on her relics and the text of hymns and offices associated with her cult. André Bellessort's 1941 biography is closely centered on Balthild herself and it ends with her death. His work is embedded in competing historiographic images of early medieval France, and there are still wearisome speculations on Balthild's "very white skin," good eyes, and elongated features.[4]

Today, scientific advances in archaeology and a generation of scholars who have crafted critical approaches to seventh-century sources have changed our perspective on what can and cannot be done. This biography combines a close reading of the sources for her life with a wider lens on what Balthild has meant to the communities, artists, and writers who embraced her story. This account of her life and afterlife extends Balthild's story further, into the nineteenth century, to capture and examine the explicit claims made for Balthild in early modern sources, namely that she "abolished" slavery. This claim for Balthild deserves attention both for our understanding of what she confronted in the seventh century and how she emerged as a political icon in the nineteenth century. This biography is not a comprehensive cultural history of the mid-seventh century, nor is it a full account of Balthild's presence in all the sources and debates of subsequent centuries; even less is it a history of slavery. Rather, by thinking about a seventh-century life, and diving into a sampling of the rich materials of the early modern and modern era, I hope to put a name to a Merovingian woman who lived in the final century of the ancient world and whose life story resonated in the minds of later generations.

A Note on Names, Dates, and Ages

Merovingian sources do not render personal names consistently. The name spelling-conventions in this book are those used in the *Oxford Handbook of the Merovingian World*. The names of the kings, queens, and saints who figure in this biography are rendered variously in different European languages, and they changed considerably in French sources over time. I have used the anglicized versions that English readers are familiar with. "Balthild" is used throughout; the modern French rendition of her name, *Bathilde*, is still a given name in France.

When essential details such as dates, the ages of protagonists, and even the sequence of events, are sometimes unknown, I made choices so that the narrative would not become too cluttered with qualifiers. We do not know Balthild's exact age at any point in this story. Therefore, I have assumed that Balthild was about the same age as her husband, Clovis II. She was marriageable when he was available to marry at about fifteen, and while it is possible that she was a little older, it is unlikely that she was much younger. Her death at about forty-five years of age in 680 fits the osteological appraisal made of her remains in 1983. Age ranges are thus based on the supposition that Balthild was born around 635. Another challenge is that contemporary sources disagreed on the birth order of her sons. I use the birth order that was traditionally used in French histories based on the *Liber Historiae Francorum* chapter 44: Chlothar III, Childeric II, and Theuderic III.

A Note on Terminology and Concepts

Balthild is described as Anglo-Saxon throughout this book. Strictly speaking, neither the term nor the political, social, or ethnic identity it sometimes implies can be traced in sources of this early date. Her first hagiographer described her as a Saxon from overseas, "de partibus transmarinis…ex genere Saxonum." Her political connections and those of her convent were with England (which also did not yet exist as a political unit).[5] The term is used for convenience to reflect the geography, and cultural and religious milieu, in which contemporary sources situated her.

Modern concepts of slavery and slave-systems do not map well onto late antique sources. During the period Balthild lived, the Merovingian Franks governed and exploited territories that depended on slave labor. However, while retaining much of the framework and language of the Roman legal system that distinguished sharply between servile status and the free, by the seventh century Roman-style slavery and slave status had slipped into something more fluid and negotiable than before. Although historians today propose the term "unfree" in recognition of these changes, there remained a fundamental difference between soil-bound servile laborers and those who were captured or sold into slavery. The slave crisis that Balthild represented as a trafficked woman, and against which she militated when in power, was a trade in dislocated and vulnerable people who were not integrated into a local community where free and unfree mingled and where they had some protection. The calamity faced by transported slaves, and the debates they occasioned among churchmen in particular, are analogous in some ways to the way slave transportations to the western hemisphere were discussed in sources from the seventeenth century onward where the trade in Christian slaves formed the basis for reflections on the role of slavery within the Christian religion.[6]

Throughout this book I use the word "slave" to denote Balthild's status. It is the correct term. Balthild was described as a *puella*, a low-status servant-girl, and as *ancilla*, a slave or servant. Historians recognize these terms as indicators of female slave status, and Merovingian sources refer to these women using these terms. In Balthild's case, we are told explicitly that she was traded and sold for a low price. That said, Balthild was a particular type of slave—one who had been captured and transported to Neustria from overseas. Her status was thus different and recognized as different from that of the slave and servile population that formed much of the laboring class in Frankish territories. The sources that discussed traded slaves used the same vocabulary they used for home slave laborers, but the tone is different. The outrage at the enslavement and trafficking of Christian slaves was directed at slaves like Balthild and not at the local enslaved population of Francia. Indeed, as queen, Balthild would herself have owned domestic slaves, and slave labor tilled the lands of the royal fisc and the lands she granted to religious institutions.

This brings me to another term: "abolition." Although the word "abolition" existed as a Latin word, it was not part of the seventh-century vocabulary for the freeing of slaves; *manumissio* was the term most often used. The term "abolition" entered accounts of Balthild's policy in 1664 when it replaced, for French readers, the Latin "prohibited" of the original. Thereafter, Balthild's policy was understood in terms of abolition: "car ce fut elle qui abolit cet abus," wrote Arnaud D'Andilly.[7] In modern connotations, abolition contains the idea that the entire institution of slavery will be challenged and eradicated; in practice historical abolitionism was often directed at the slave trade, and in European sources this was certainly the case. Likewise, Balthild's reforms examined in this book aimed at freeing slaves, were not directed at the eradication of servile status for all, but rather, in a way analogous to eighteenth- and nineteenth-century concerns, her reforms were targeted at an inhuman trade in which one polity benefitted from the new enslavement of the population of another. Balthild's reforms and her solutions for trafficked slaves were important in that they were a recognition that a distressed and displaced population, forcibly relocated from one country to another, constituted a religious, social—and perhaps humanitarian (?)—crisis. In any event, in the seventh century, freeing trafficked slaves was an activity upon which a reputation for piety could be built. Balthild's prohibition of slave trafficking in Frankish territories contributed to the early modern fiction that she had abolished slavery in France. It was a convenient modern fiction that overlooked the predatory labor systems of seventeenth-century France as much as it did those of seventh-century Neustria. Does Balthild merit the soubriquet: "abolitionist"? That is debatable. However, the case for her importance in the long history of emancipation is made here, both in her person as an embodiment of the trafficked slave and as a figurehead for those who were willing to see the elimination of slavery as both a religious and a royal virtue. Insofar as modern abolition and abolitionist movements lurch from success to failure to success again, Balthild's identification of the slave trade as an immediate social problem, and her efforts and those of her allies to engineer a 'humane' solution for the displaced and vulnerable, was a significant—and very early—articulation of a problem that abolitionists in every age would face: how to get started. The views expressed in Balthild's time, and which she embodied as a freed slave, sink below the surface of European sources until centuries later. Balthild's time in power in the middle decade of the seventh century was a moment in time when a new idea could be expressed; that the slave trade was a horror that had to be confronted and mitigated at the highest levels of government. It was a seed from which later abolitionist sentiment could grow. That seed was embedded in her policies, but also in her biography. As later generations preserved, copied, modified, translated, fictionalized, and monumentalized her person, her life story as much as her policies allowed her name, and her mission, to survive into the modern era and in the public imagination.

Abbreviations

AASS	Johannes Bollandus (Jean Bolland) et al., eds. *Acta sanctorum quotquot toto orbe coluntur*....Antwerp and Brussels, 1643–.
AASS, OSB	Jean Mabillon, ed. *Acta sanctorum. Ordinis sancti Benedicti.*
AN	Archives nationales de France.
CSEL	*Corpus scriptorium ecclesiasticorum latinorum.* Vienna.
F&G *LMF*	Paul Fouracre and Richard Gerberding. *Late Merovingian France.* Manchester: Manchester University Press, 1996.
HF	Gregory of Tours. *History of the Franks.* Trans. Lewis Thorpe. London: Penguin Books, 1974. La Neustrie La Neustrie. Le pays du nord de la Loire de 650 à 850. Colloque historique international. Ed. Hartmut Atsma. 2 vols. Sigmaringen: Jan Thorbecke Verlag, 1989.
LHF	Bruno Krusch, ed. *Liber historiae Francorum. MGH, SRM* II (1888), pp. 215–328. Ed. and trans. Bernard S. Bachrach, *Liber Historiae Francorum*, Lawrence, Kan: Coronado Press, 1973.
MGH, SRM	*Monumenta Germaniae historica, Scriptores rerum Merovingicarum.* Hanover, 1826–.
OHMW	Bonnie Effros and Isabel Moreira, eds. *The Oxford Handbook of the Merovingian World.* New York: Oxford University Press, 2020.
PL	Jacques-Paul, Migne, ed. *Patrologiae cursus completus: Series Latina.* Paris, 1844–64.
VB I	Bruno Krusch, ed. Life of Balthild ("A"). *Vita sanctae Balthildis. MGH, SRM* II (1888), pp. 475–508.
VB II	Bruno Krusch, ed. Life of Balthild ("B"). *Vita sanctae Balthildis. MGH, SRM* II (1888), pp. 475–508.
VE I and II	Bruno Krusch, ed. Audoin, Life of Eligius of Noyon. *Vita Eligii episcopi Noviomagensis. MGH, SRM* IV (1902), pp. 634–761.

List of Figures

1.1 The earliest manuscript image of Queen Balthild? From an eleventh-century manuscript of saints' lives thought to be from Saint-Arnoul de Crépy. Balthild is nested in the letter V of Verba Regis, the opening words of the prologue to the Carolingian version of her Life. BnF Ms. Latin 18300 fol. 33r.   8

2.1 A portion of Balthild's hair now in the collection of the Alfred-Bonno Museum, Ville de Chelles, shows signs of hair dye.   26

2.2 Balthild's extant skeletal remains, shown here shaded in black, illustrate how much of her body was gifted to other monastic institutions over the centuries. Laporte and Boyer, *Trésors de Chelles*, p. 23.   27

5.1 Balthild's vision of a ladder. Prefatory image to Étienne Binet, *La vie excellente de sainte Bathilde* (1624). The image is based on a block cut by Alexius Lindt (1517), print by Leonhard Beck (British Museum #1920,0430.7). However, in this image we see how the convent looked in the seventeenth century when Binet's work was dedicated to Abbess Marie de Lorraine. Balthild is shown praying in front of the altar where she sees a vision of a ladder and her soul being carried to heaven.   107

5.2 Fringed shawl after restoration. Alfred-Bonno Museum, Ville de Chelles. Laporte, *Le Trésor des Saints de Chelles*, Plate III.   116

5.3 Balthild's "chasuble" or "chemise." 117 × 84 cm (3.8 × 2.75 feet). Linen with silk embroidery. Alfred-Bonno Museum, Ville de Chelles.   117

6.1 A color sketch of the tomb of the two princes made in 1828 by Espérance Langlois, daughter of Eustache-Hyacinthe Langlois who wrote a history of the monastery of Jumièges. Archives départementales de la Seine-Maritime (6Fi02/76).   134

6.2 Évariste Vital Luminais, "Les Énervées de Jumièges." Now in the Gallery of New South Wales, Australia with the title "The Sons of Clovis II. 1880." Accession number 712. A copy of this painting with minor modifications was made by Luminais, now in the Musée des Beaux Arts, Rouen.   138

xxiv LIST OF FIGURES

7.1 Seventeenth-century view of the Royal Abbey of Chelles, in Dom Germain, *Monasticon Gallicanum*. Matériaux du Monasticon Gallicanum de Dom Germain. BnF. Latin 11820.   142

7.2 Pierre Gobert's portrait of Louise Adélaïde d'Orléans, abbess of Chelles. Her name in religion was "Soeur Bathilde," Sister Balthild.   146

7.3 Victor Thérasse, "Sainte Balthilde." Luxembourg Gardens, Paris.   163

A.1 Gold seal matrix found near Norwich. It bears the name of Baldehildis. There has been much speculation as to whether this could have belonged to Queen Balthild or an associate. On the reverse side is an image of a naked man and a naked woman.   178

1
Finding her Story

We do not know where Balthild's story started, but we do know where it ended—at the convent she had founded in the small community at Chelles. By the time she died on January 30, 679 or 680, Balthild had lived at the convent for sixteen years as a retiree. Perched on a small bluff on the right bank of the river Marne, a tributary of the Seine, thirty miles east of Paris, and defined to the north by a minor arm of the Marne, the small community of Chelles was situated in a pleasant spot that in the Merovingian era could still be called an island. The woods around had long been prized by the Merovingian kings as hunting grounds, and a royal palace in Chelles was a favored residence, a leafy retreat from the heat of Paris. Balthild must have loved the spot because she chose Chelles as the place to found her convent. A small church dedicated to Saint George had been located there over a century before by King Clovis I' wife, Chlothild, no doubt to serve the needs of the court when it was in residence. Balthild did much to expand and improve the site, recruiting an abbess and establishing a regular life for women.

Balthild had situated her convent well. The river provided easy access to Paris and her sons and friends were frequent visitors. Sitting in her convent, Balthild had much to look back on: a career that had taken her from England to northern France as a slave, and then to the royal court as queen. She was the mother of kings and she exercised power for some years as queen-regent. It was a public life that she had given up unwillingly, and she was forced to watch on the sidelines as two of her three sons ruled and then died, first Chlothar III in 673, seemingly of natural causes, and then her son Childeric II who was assassinated in 675 in a year of devastating unrest. Her third son, Theuderic III, lived on as king.[1]

Balthild's story would be remarkable in any age. A slave who became a queen was not a common career, and contemporaries took note of her. The basic outline of her story can be reconstructed from surviving documents. Born sometime in the 630s in England, a Saxon from lands across the sea, Balthild arrived in the Merovingian kingdom of Neustria in northern

Balthild of Francia: Anglo-Saxon Slave, Merovingian Queen, and Abolitionist Saint. Isabel Moreira,
Oxford University Press. © Oxford University Press 2024. DOI: 10.1093/oso/9780197518663.003.0001

France as a slave.[2] There she was bought by Erchinoald, mayor of the Neustrian palace, and entered his household. Subsequently, she was married to the young Merovingian king Clovis II. She bore him three male sons that we know of and, on her husband's death, she was regent for their underage sons. As queen, and later as regent, she used the vast resources of the Merovingian royal coffers to undertake public projects close to her heart. Alongside her husband, she founded and endowed convents and monasteries, a land-based philanthropy that secured powerful political allies. As regent she pursued social policies, such as the freeing of trafficked slaves and the prohibition of infanticide, that would resonate down the centuries. As a key political figure among many noble contenders, Balthild managed to navigate the fraught politics of the 660s and 670s, with extraordinary success. But as a political figure she also attracted opposition and bad press. Her reputation and her legacy were important to her, no doubt, but also to the convent and the royal house, and her cult appears to have been carefully managed by her community. At her death, her body was placed in a tomb along with fine clothing, and deposited under the monastery's own church, dedicated to the Holy Cross. She had lived an extraordinary life until her death at the age of about forty-five and after her death miracles were recorded to attest to her sanctity. Soon after, a biography affirmed just how holy her life had been, and she was honored as a saint.

The kingdom of Neustria in what is now northern France, was centered around the cities of Paris, Soissons, and Reims where Frankish tribes had settled in the waning years of Roman control. In the seventh century, the Merovingian royal dynasty controlled most of modern-day France and parts of Switzerland and Germany, but they did not settle in great numbers in the south. Even in northern France the Franks comprised a small elite that dominated and governed the Romano-Gallic population of the late Roman provinces of France. While family conflict had determined which branch of the Merovingian dynasty was in power in the sixth century, and which parts of France they controlled, from the time of Dagobert I (d. 639), the father of Balthild's husband Clovis II, the Frankish kingdom was controlled from Paris, with a son of the dynasty sent east to Austrasia to rule until, periodically, the kingdoms would be united again. The kingdom of Neustria was the area of greatest Frankish settlement density west of the Rhine and one of four great land tracts that each had a distinct character derived from both distant and recent history. The kingdom of Austrasia to the east of Neustria and centered on the Rhineland was both older in terms of Frankish presence and more militarized than the Seine basin. The Austrasian region was also more dynamic militarily in terms of continuing expansion east of the Rhine. Aquitaine, former Roman province and Visigothic kingdom until it was taken by Clovis in 507, did not form a separate Frankish kingdom but was controlled by Merovingian kings. And Burgundy, a post-Roman kingdom centered on the Rhône valley and the Lake Geneva hinterland was annexed by the Franks in the 530s. Burgundy and Aquitaine were alike in being heavily Roman in population and environment, governed by laws that respected both locals and newcomers. Burgundy was under Neustrian control in the seventh century, and Aquitaine maintained historical ties with Austrasia, although it could be hived off with Gascony when necessary.[3] Seventh-century Merovingian rulers had inherited a network of bishoprics centered on the old imperial cities, although increasingly Frankish and Romano-Frankish bishops joined the episcopal cadre, while older Gallo-Roman clerical families who tried to assert their rights to be elected from their communities were, in fact, appointed from the Neustrian court.

The Merovingian kings were late Roman rulers more than they were post-Roman rulers. The remnants of Roman Gaul were all around them, they lived in cities that were once controlled by Rome and then briefly by late Roman "kings." The fields, pastures, and vineyards continued production in many places from Roman times, although agricultural patterns also adapted and changed. In the sixth and seventh centuries Merovingian kings had expanded their territorial reach, but they continued to exploit as best they could the resources that had been available to the late Roman state. Taxes were assessed from tax registers in the sixth century based on periodic censuses, but they were criticized as inaccurate and gradually gave way in the seventh century to other revenue streams. Still, a key element in Balthild's social program had to do with the problem of punitive taxes. Landed estates brought in produce and revenues that found their way directly and indirectly into the royal fisc. Booty in the form of treasure and human labor provided kings with a lucrative if sometimes ephemeral form of wealth as mobile resources could be as easily lost as gained. Nevertheless, treasure looms large in the written sources as a source of prestige and bragging rights among royal contenders. The balance of political power radiated increasingly from northern Francia, but the Merovingian kings, bishops, and population at large were not entirely detached from the economic pull of Mediterranean trade and Mediterranean politics, especially in matters related to religion.

Merovingian connections with territories to the north were also strong. The Neustrian court under Queen Brunhild had been instrumental in fostering papal efforts in the Christianization of Anglo-Saxon England in the late sixth century. By the mid-seventh century when Balthild left its shores, much of England was ruled by Christian kings, although reversals and holdouts like Raedwald of Mercia were still in play. Merovingian magnates and bishops were closely interested in events going on across the Channel and, as the richer and more sophisticated neighbor, the Merovingians had their fingers in many Anglo-Saxon pies. The Channel was a thoroughfare for northern Franks, and the Neustrian mayor Erchinoald, Balthild's master, had strong connections to those in power in Kent. It was probably no coincidence that slaves from England, and perhaps from further afield, found their way to Erchinoald's lands. It is only because of Balthild's extraordinary history that we know of the name or story even of one of these.

Balthild's Saintly Tale

Even as a queen, little would have been preserved of her story had Balthild not also been venerated as a saint. Indeed, it is fortuitous for our knowledge of her that she ended her career in a convent. No purely secular Merovingian queen of the seventh century was provided a biography. Biography was the preserve of saints. Most of the fine detail of our view of Balthild comes from a holy biography—a hagiography—that was written within a decade of her death.[4] Some scholars have argued that the author must have been a nun at Chelles.[5] If so, the author gave little detail about her convent and her life there.[6] The work's central focus is on Balthild's public life and policies. Unlike the Life of Saint Radegund by the nun Baudonivia that reported tales told by the nuns, information on Balthild's life in the convent is sparse. Furthermore, the version in which we have the work is addressed to an audience of monastic brothers. While a female author cannot be ruled out, and women were certainly capable of undertaking such commissions, on balance, it seems most likely that the author was a monk or cleric, perhaps commissioned by the abbess of Chelles, Bertilla, to secure the queen's cult. Indeed, it is possible that the author was a cleric attached to one of Balthild's own monastic foundations, at Chelles or at Corbie in the 680s. Such a connection would explain the author's interest in her, and also his willingness to see her extraordinary career as something that was divinely ordained. However, although the author was Balthild's contemporary, we do not know if he had ever met her. He was certainly well informed about some aspects of her public life, and he viewed her policies in a positive light. A royal monastery in the third quarter of the seventh century would have been a hotbed of information and gossip about the political events raging outside its walls. Even if he was not personally acquainted with Balthild, he would certainly have known about her activities in the public sphere. Her son Theuderic III was still in power and the Neustrian royal house was the center of politics at the time he was writing. For the personal details of Balthild's life, and how her life was conducted within the convent, he could have sought information from the abbess of Chelles, but the biography provides scant information on these issues. The abbess Bertilla, especially, could have been an excellent source of information and indeed she may have commissioned the work. Still, there are aspects of Balthild's life which were glossed over such as her childhood, her time in the household of Erchinoald, and her daily life in the convent. Given the availability of contemporary sources, one cannot escape the impression that the author's silence in places was intentional. Succinct and detailed in those parts of her biography that were political, his prose is particularly elusive and fanciful when describing her personal life. His biography of the queen, the *Vita Sanctae Balthildis* (Life of the Holy Balthild; hereafter *VB* I), is a work of hagiography in that it is crafted to present her as a saint. However, it is also the portrait of a queen who had been very much involved in the high politics of the day and whose reputation was still alive to his readers and listeners. He included specific political reforms that were associated with her. In this sense his work has some of the excellent and sober qualities of a political biography.[7]

In the Merovingian age, when slavery was all too common, the biographer took something of a risk in shaping Balthild's story so fully and so fancifully around her early slave status. Recent history did not provide the biographer with an exact model to follow when describing a low-born queen saint—earlier kings had slave consorts, but their destinies were not as illustrious as Balthild's. Instead, the author looked to the bible and to earlier female hagiographic models. From the Old Testament the author drew inspiration from the story of Queen Esther. Like Esther, Balthild was chosen as the king's bride for her beauty.[8] Like Esther, she was counseled by a venerable man who became the king's advisor. Like Esther, there was a darker side to Balthild's partisan position towards her enemies. The two biographies of Queen Radegund of Poitiers provided another model for the hagiographer in shaping his story of a foreign woman who married into the Merovingian dynasty. There were substantial differences between Radegund and Balthild's circumstances, but behind both lay the scintillating figure of the relic-chasing Helena, mother of Constantine.[9] The hagiographer knew that in Balthild he had the makings of a good story—a rags to riches tale, a Cinderella fable, in which a young girl was rewarded for her virtue, beauty, and cleverness by being married to a young king who made her his queen. For those who were aware of the turbulent events of the 660s, the author explained how Balthild survived to live through a coup and retire in peace to her convent, how she died a venerated member of that community, again, aided by divine power. For an audience that still lived under one of her sons, the hagiographer portrayed Balthild as a saintly queen who had been able, briefly, to stabilize a kingdom that was often rent by factionalism.[10] For the monks and nuns who would read Balthild's story and draw inspiration from it, he related how a divine vision illuminated her final days and how, after she was honorably buried, petitioners at her tomb were healed, demonstrating her sanctity and supernatural power. There was a Balthild for everyone.

These essential episodes crafted by her first biographer became an enduring point of reference for those who wanted a story in which they could marvel at God's power to change the destiny of even the lowest of his servants. Balthild became a creative muse for future writers and artists who encountered her story. Much of what made the story appealing was its upbeat, positive, even romantic take on a woman who started as a slave and who achieved her goals in a world of male political power through her pleasing presence, nurturing qualities, diplomatic know-how, peacemaking capabilities, and her fecundity. It was a story that appealed to seventh-century and to nineteenth-century readers alike. Balthild's biographer knew exactly what to make of such a case of stratospheric personal advancement: God had exerted himself to raise a humble woman to the highest peaks. With God as prime mover in her story, any personal ambition, desire, or political activity, was modestly subsumed to a greater historical force. Yet as Balthild's contemporary, the biographer did not, or could not, entirely efface the queen's personal influence in the actions and policies of her regency. Nor were his efforts sufficient to quash salacious stories told about his heroine within a few short years of her death.

Fortunately for us, our knowledge of Balthild's story does not rely entirely on this single account. Balthild's appearance in other contemporary histories and documents, and a small pack of biographies of the churchmen she worked with, allow us to gain a relatively rounded view of her circle and their priorities. Seventh- and eighth-century chroniclers mention her, her husband, and children.[11] The section of the Fredegar *Chronicle* written by an author writing around 660 provides information on Merovingian doings up to 642, thus covering the deeds of Clovis II's father Dagobert and the regency of his mother, Nantechild. The years of Balthild's marriage to Clovis and Grimoald's coup in Austrasia, are described in the *Liber historiae Francorum* (*LHF*), a work from the Paris region completed in 727; it provides a Neustrian perspective on the events of those years. Then, the first Fredegar continuator used the *LHF* for those same years, with some small refinements to suit Austrasian interests, and provided moreover information beyond the years covered by the *LHF*. Thus, for the crucial years of Balthild and Clovis II's marriage, two versions exist: the *LHF*, and the slightly modified reprise of the *LHF* in chapters 1–10 of the first continuator of Fredegar's *Chronicle*. In both works, Balthild is praised and Clovis II's deeds are decried. The *LHF* for example, indicates that Balthild was "beautiful, clever, and of strong character," while her husband was "a seducer and a debaser of women, a glutton and a drunk." This cue was taken up by a continuator of Fredegar's *Chronicle*, who also praised her as a "sensible and attractive woman" while stating that her husband was '*amens*,' "out of his mind."[12]

Beyond the histories, Balthild makes a brief appearance, or is alluded to, in some other sources. She also a presence in the hagiographic lives of the bishops and abbots of her time: of Bishop Eligius of Noyon (in a work written by another episcopal associate Bishop Audoin of Rouen), the martyred Bishop Leudegar of Autun, Bishop Aunemund of Lyon, and Abbot Philibert of Jumièges and Noirmoutier. She is also mentioned in the Life of Bertilla, abbess of Chelles, in Jonas' Life of John of Réomé as a benefactor, and in the Life of Bishop Ansbert of Rouen.[13] In the early eighth century, Wilfrid of York's biographer Stephan of Ripon was peddling quite a different view of the queen in northern England, accusing her of being a "Jezebel," that is, a whore and a murderer; Bede drew on this latter description for his *History*.[14] Yet Balthild's importance as a queen, saint, and healer was widely recognized by the Carolingians. Charlemagne's own sister Gisela was an abbess of Chelles. In 833 Balthild's remains were moved ('translated') to a place of greater honor in the convent church. It seems likely that this elevation was prompted by a second biography (*VB* II) which, expanding on the first, gave greater weight to Balthild's royal status and more information on the site of the convent; indeed, the author claimed that Balthild's will was preserved in their archive. This second biography went so far as to assert that Balthild was of royal descent (*erat ex regali progeniae*).[15] This version of her life was copied and included in collections of saints' narratives throughout the Middle Ages (see Fig. 1.1). Importantly, it was this second, more royal, biography that was translated into French vernacular in the seventeenth century and as such it was the most accessible version of Balthild's life for French readers in subsequent centuries (see Chapter 7, pp. 140–75).[16]

Whether for good or for ill, Balthild's story would always be shaped by the writers who drew inspiration from her vita. However, in Balthild's case,

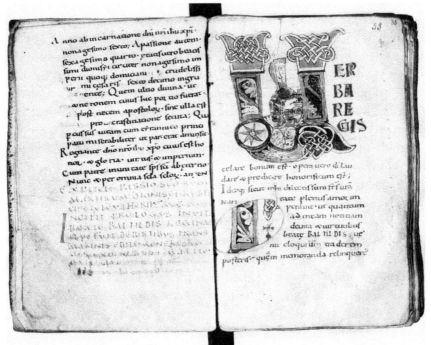

Source gallica.bnf.fr / Bibliothèque nationale de France. Département des Manuscrits. Latin 18300

Fig. 1.1 The earliest manuscript image of Queen Balthild? From an eleventh-century manuscript of saints' lives thought to be from Saint-Arnoul de Crépy. Balthild is nested in the letter V of Verba Regis, the opening words of the prologue to the Carolingian version of her Life. BnF Ms. Latin 18300 fol. 33r.

this was not the end of the matter as her human and material remains were preserved by the nuns of Chelles. Up to the French Revolution, the location of Balthild's relics had always been known. Successive generations of the curious had opened her grave and taken out objects and bones to use as personal relics or distribute as institutional gifts. Many of these occasions were documented, and it is a long list (see chapter 7, pp. 140–75). Her remains were scattered during the French Revolution, divided up among the nuns, but once things had calmed down, many of them were recovered, ending up in the Église de Saint André, the parish church of Chelles, where they remain to this day, displayed in seventeenth-century coffers. In the nineteenth century, the relics continued to be gifted. At the turn of the twentieth century, the local priest, antiquarian, and religious entrepreneur, the abbé Alfred Bonno, took out her embroidered "chemise" and nailed it to a wooden frame, parading it as a devotional object through the streets of Chelles. But it was in 1983 that modern archaeologists discovered that many more of the items in which she had been buried had survived in the coffers of the parish church. Alongside her bodily remains, hair, and clothing, the coffers also held the remains and clothing of the abbess Bertilla. Alongside the relics and fabrics of some other early medieval saints, these were scrutinized, analyzed, and, in the case of the textiles, preserved and reconstructed, so that what emerged from the fragments and remains was powerful evidence of the long reach of Balthild's cultural environment. Here was evidence of the Merovingian connections to the resources of the Mediterranean world and beyond. Balthild's story gained a new lease of life.

What emerged from the analysis of the relics at Chelles in the 1980s was that the remains of Balthild and her companions provided a means to access new information not only about an unusual and important figure of the seventh century but also of the connections of Francia with Mediterranean kingdoms and empires through trade and diplomatic gift. Since that time, new research trajectories and new scientific methods have expanded our view even further. Thanks to scientific advances in archaeology such as use of infrared and ramen spectroscopy for gemstones, isotopic analysis of teeth and bones, DNA analysis, archaeozoology, and archaeobotany, the story of Balthild's world and that of her contemporaries can be told today in a way that would have been impossible even a decade ago. As a result of such research, we know more about the environment than was the case in the past. We know which plants were grown for food and the weed varieties that infested the fields. We know what the climate was like (generally, a period of cooling in the northern hemisphere termed the "late-antique little ice age"), where the garnets in her accessories came from, how much traffic there was on the rivers that brought wares from near and far, and the vessels that her wine came in. From archaeozoology we can learn about Frankish food preferences and how they changed over the Merovingian centuries.[17] It is therefore possible to write a richly textured biography of Balthild's life and times, including situating the Merovingians within a global context of trade and consumption, showing the importance of contact with outside influences, both medical and spiritual. Balthild's lifetime has become important in ways not fully appreciated before.

So, there are sources beyond the literary to reconstruct Balthild's world. However, this does not mean that we know all we could want to know about her. There are large gaps about her life that are missing in the sources, not least the vexed question of her childhood origins. Childhood has always been regarded as important to biographers. Even ancient biographers recognized this. Childhood was a canvas upon which the earliest etchings of character could be detected, and whether as a story of continuous piety, or of damascene conversion, childhood stories served to root the biographer's subject in their time. Increasingly, archaeologists seek out evidence for childhood experiences of the past. In the written sources, Balthild's story starts with her arrival in France. It is testimony to her seventh-century biographer's care that he did not invent a childhood for Balthild, to hide what was missing or what was hidden from his gaze. But this did not stop later biographers from wondering what her life in England may have been like. Nineteenth-century writers, especially, were enchanted by the opportunities presented by the story of a beautiful slave girl abducted from her home to become the sexual partner of a king. Balthild's life inspired many works of historical imagination in France; a selection of these are mentioned here as they reflect early attempts to fill in biographical gaps.

Today scientific methods present new opportunities to fill biographic gaps, especially about disease, health, and diet. In Balthild's case, our best evidence comes from the archaeological investigations conducted in the 1980s under the careful eye of Jean-Pierre Laporte. His publications on the relics and history of Chelles are still the most important resource on the finds.[18] But until the next time that Balthild's bones are removed from their coffin, newer scientific methods of investigation will have to wait.

The problem of biographic gaps, and in Balthild's case the mystery of her Anglo-Saxon origins, raises a larger issue about the responsibility of the modern biographer and historian to fill them. Can a reconstruction of a childhood that is unsourced add something materially to the enterprise of biography for a modern reader? Should the modern biographer do what ancient hagiographers are often accused of doing—filling in gaps with suppositions based on their understanding of their subject? In some respects, it is precisely in the imaginative filling of gaps that commentators on Balthild historically have left their mark. We will encounter some of their more imaginative musings along our way. However, it would be remiss to ignore entirely the advances in science that indicate the potential for reconstructing Balthild's childhood in the future.

Reconstructing a Lost Childhood

With the investigation of Balthild's remains in the 1980s, and new insights into the population of early medieval England drawn from the scientific investigation of graves, there is new potential to fill the gap in our knowledge of Balthild's childhood if, in the future, her remains once again become available for analysis. For the moment such speculations are in the realm of "what if." Can modern archaeological methods and scientific inquiry help us insert Balthild into her natal environment given the regional differences within Britain, and the fact that we do not know exactly where she came from? The picture that emerges is mixed.

Perhaps the most intriguing possibility for understanding Balthild's natal environment from a future analysis of her remains arises from the use of isotope analysis of bones and teeth found in archaeological context since this can reveal the diet of the individual and their community. Ratios of stable carbon and nitrogen isotopes in bone collagen can provide information on protein in the diet, even to the extent of distinguishing between dairy, meat, and fish.[19] It would be interesting to know more about the kind of diet the young Balthild might have had.[20] Most recently, archaeologists have started to look at dental enamel since teeth often survives better than porous bone. Essentially, dentine is laid down on the tooth in a kind of dental dendrochronology, revealing information about diet and disease over time. For example, teeth preserve evidence of childhood health stressors in the form of dental hypoplasia—irregularities in the enamel. Dental enamel can also reveal the region in which a person was born and spent their childhood; strontium and oxygen isotopes in teeth can indicate the geological area ("geological fingerprint") from which an individual drew food and water in their earliest years.[21] If we had Balthild's teeth (we do not) such analysis could help solve the riddle of Balthild's origins. We do not know if her bones would yield viable DNA for analysis.

Isotope analysis of bones and teeth can also tell us interesting *social* information such as the age at which an individual had been weaned from breast milk. An analysis of remains from the late Anglo-Saxon cemetery at Raunds indicated that children in that community moved from exclusive breastfeeding to complementary breastfeeding before the age of two (1.75), and breastfeeding ceased by age three.[22] This aligns with burial and legal evidence for a change in a child's status around age three. A cemetery in which children's burials reveals early weaning may indicate a resource-rich environment. On the other hand, breastfeeding is advantageous to the child's long-term health, and so may indicate generally healthier children. Since the weaning pattern seems quite consistent across Anglo-Saxon sites, we can imagine that Balthild the toddler would have been entirely weaned by age three at which point she would have participated in varied protein adult diet. The point is that in Balthild's case, her physical remains could yet provide a window onto her early, childhood environment in England, even though she died in her mid-forties in France.

Could bone and tooth analysis also help solve the discrepancies in the written sources about her status in England prior to capture? If we had access to her bones and teeth, what could be deduced? Analysis of children's graves in Anglo-Saxon cemeteries reveals that geographic location more than status and wealth determined health. An investigation of her teeth could tell us about her personal health as a child and adult, and this would be helpful, but this analysis would not necessarily help us to determine her status since most recent works on seventh-century cemeteries in England reveal no strong correlation between wealth and dietary choice.[23] Unfortunately, Balthild's teeth have not survived, or at any rate not at Chelles. The archaeologist's reconstruction of her remaining skeleton in 1983 shows that part of her jawbone survives, but no teeth. Teeth would have been particularly easy to detach from their sockets and given away as gifts. There is a better chance that something could be done with her hair since that survives and it belongs to the museum collection rather than the parish church. However, hair analysis provides information on diet only for the last ten years of life, so an analysis would tell us about Merovingian diet in the latter half of the seventh century (which would be very interesting) but not about her childhood diet in England.

What we can say about Balthild is that she lived into her mid-forties and that she appears to have been in good health until the last year of her life. The sources describe her as beautiful and appealing, perhaps an indirect testimony to her general health. She produced three healthy boys and survived. Her skeleton—what remains of it—shows no obvious signs of disease or stress caused by carrying heavy weights (vertebral spondylosis). Only two fragments of her skull survive,[24] so it is not possible to check for *cribra orbitalia*, a sign of anemia caused by iron deficiency often associated with women at this time. The direct scientific approach is intriguing but for the moment beset with insuperable problems, not least of which is that her remains are considered relics and therefore not readily available for forensic analysis.

It is possible, of course, to make some more general points about the environment in which Balthild would have been raised through analysis of children's graves.[25] However, this too turns out to be quite a challenge. Children are disproportionately absent from burial sites, a problem the archaeological community has been grappling with for thirty years. And, while childhood experience is recognized as being integral to understanding adult health and personality, modern scholarship on childhood insists that age-related classifications are especially problematic. Furthermore, there is now greater awareness of the fact that children in the past were participants in social life and work life in ways that differ significantly from modern western patterns.[26]

Still, situating an individual within a general framework of a known archaeological context may yield some general insights about Balthild's health in childhood. We can observe that she survived in an era when infant and childhood mortality was high. It is estimated that in Anglo-Saxon England about half of the population died before the age of seventeen. If they lived in buildings that used organic material, or if they lived in the cramped environments of early medieval towns, Anglo-Saxons were prone to the parasites and diseases that such close contact brought. Robin Fleming points out that medieval towns were "astonishingly filthy," but also observes that the gap in health between the rich and poor was not as pronounced in the pre-urban sixth and seventh centuries as it was to be in subsequent centuries.[27] Life in a rural hamlet may have been healthier than it was for those living in a more crowded environment. If Balthild came from a noble family's environment, she would not have suffered food scarcity as food consumption was important to noble display. Judging by two landlocked seventh-century cemeteries in Kent (Polhill) and Cambridgeshire (Melbourn), individuals across social ranks ate plants, meat, dairy, and possibly fresh water fish. Moreover, there was no striking sex differentiation in the findings for adults at the two sites, and only a slight difference for children at one site.[28] If Balthild came from a lower status, food may have been scarce—or not, if she came from a prosperous village. If she came from slave stock her nutrition, health, and life experience would have depended on the kind of slave she was: Aethelberht's Law Code, c. 10–11, recognizes three types of female dependent: a king's maid, a grinding slave, and a third kind, unspecified. Much work has been done to extract information about childhood pathologies from children's graves, but there is no way to reliably identify the condition of slavery in the archaeological record. Most pertinently, Balthild was healthy enough to not end up in an Anglo-Saxon grave.

In short, any reconstruction of Balthild's childhood is dogged by the greater problem of ascertaining her status in England. If she was from a noble family, and if she had a connection with court activities, her life experience could have been quite different to that of a peasant girl. If she came from noble stock, she may even have received some basic education within the home, and she could have learned the forms of religious observance that were the backbone of seventh-century female piety. If she was of lower, even unfree status, how different would her life have been? Under Anglo-Saxon law, whether born free or a slave, children were equally viewed as property and within the household their activities would have been equally controlled by physical punishment. Their lives may have been similar in other ways. They would have been expected to contribute in some way to the family economy. Anglo-Saxon hagiographies reveal that children, even from noble families, were expected to do work of some sort. St. Cuthbert of Lindisfarne, for example, tended sheep as a youth. Girls probably learned domestic tasks in the home. But slave work often included sex work and the law codes indicate that children became adults quickly. Analogies with the modern sex trade would suggest this could happen as early as nine or ten years of age. Anglo-Saxon law codes reveal that children were considered adults at the ages of between ten and twelve and they could be enslaved for theft. Ine's lawcode [7.2] specifies that "A ten-year-old child can be [regarded as] accessory to theft" and thus enslaved.[29] Nineteenth-century biographies imagined Balthild as an adolescent, wrested precipitously from a secure domestic environment, suggesting that her captivity was of short duration. This view is implicit in the "noble Balthild" hypothesis and it was likely bundled with the notion that Balthild maintained her virginity. Statistically speaking, this is the least likely scenario. This was a slave-owning society and in the seventh century slave labor was in demand in Merovingian Gaul. Women and children were particularly valuable as domestic labor, and to men for sexual gratification. Anglo-Saxon slave-captives (as well as Welsh and other groups) supplied that demand. It is not until the turn of the eighth century that we see Anglo-Saxon legislation prohibiting the sale of "countryman" slaves abroad.[30]

Some nineteenth-century biographers wanted to fill the childhood gap in Balthild's biography. Absent modern scientific methods, they did this by employing their imagination, developing backstories and characters that lent color to her life in England and the drama of her capture and removal from her former life. In the short story penned in 1853 by Alfred Des Essarts in *Le Correspondant*,[31] he imagined a scene in which "Bathilde" was riding to the royal palace at Chelles with her husband when she recognized a very old slave throwing roses in front of the horses' hooves. The slave's name was Arwold and we learn that it was he who had trafficked her in return for gold, until he himself had been taken into slavery. Bathilde asks him whether her parents are still alive. She learns from him that her parents are dead, having never forgotten their lost child. We also learn that Bathilde was a descendant of Saxon kings. Showing husbandly outrage, Clovis orders the old man to be taken prisoner, but on learning that Arwold has a young daughter who will be left fatherless, Bathilde intercedes for him with her royal husband and forgives her former slaver. Essart's imagined scenario of pious forgiveness reads tritely in a modern light. However, in imagining what Balthild's thoughts must have been about lost parents and a lost childhood, he has drawn our attention to other gaps in Balthild's story. Loss of family, dislocation, these were human consequences of slavery that even her closest observers did not choose to observe.

In the end, if we consider what constituted the most formative experience of Balthild's youth, it is less likely to have been the diseases and diet of her earliest years than it was the trauma of her removal from family and homeland and transportation as a slave to a new environment. Indeed, the policies of her regency were directly aimed at ending the trade in slaves from England to northern Gaul and providing shelter for rescued girls.

It is time for Balthild to step off the boat.

2
Trafficked Slave

When Balthild arrived on the shores of northern France sometime in the 640s, her situation was dire. Whatever her circumstances had been back home in England, she was now a slave. As such, she was part of a regular traffic of commodities across the Channel between England and France, arriving in a shipment destined for sale. She was probably in her early teens, and aside from the other slaves destined for the slave market, she was probably alone; no family members are mentioned in any sources.

Her arrival was an unremarkable event because seventh-century Europe traded in slaves; slavery was a simple fact of life for many.[1] It was an institution recognized in law and social practice and it could involve long-distance relocation, physical abuse, and sexual vulnerability. Furthermore, slavery thrived in Christian society. High-status clerics owned slaves to provide for their personal comfort, and as labor on church lands.[2] The slaves they owned were probably Christian, although as a result of the slave trade it was possible that this was not always the case. The practice of taking captives as war booty meant that a supply of slaves was available. In arriving in northern France as a slave, Balthild was a casualty of circumstance that fed this trade in human labor.

Yet, unlike slavery in some modern societies, in the seventh century slavery was a condition that was not always permanent, and the slave's experience could vary greatly according to the individual's status and environment. For example, self-sale into slavery—for protection or for debt—was a decision individuals and families could make in a calculated bid for preferment or survival.[3] In some circumstances, slave status could be reversed. Others might be set free at their owner's death. Change of status was recognized in a public ritual and supported by documentation recorded in the archives, municipal or ecclesiastical.[4] But manumission was probably rare, and in any case the economic fate of the freed slave was not necessarily better than it was in servitude. Young women especially were valuable as domestic servants in Christian households. They were also prized as sexual partners.

This was the future that Balthild faced when we first encounter her as a member of the Christian household of Erchinoald, the Neustrian mayor of the palace, and his wife. Her hagiographer states that she was sold to Erchinoald for a "low price" a detail supplied to illuminate the irony that she was, in fact, "a precious and best pearl of God."[5] Recognizing the common assumption that a pretty young slave might be targeted by her master, we are told that Erchinoald indeed developed an interest in her as a companion, and that on the death of his wife he wished to marry her. The problematic timeline of this episode is discussed in this chapter. Whatever the facts of the case, the author of the first Life of Balthild had a delicate task before him—to explain how a slave as beautiful and clever as Balthild could survive as a virgin and as an honored servant in the household of the forceful Erchinoald.[6]

What Was Balthild's Status?

We know nothing of Balthild's background or status before she was transported to France. This is a fundamental and intractable question about Balthild that cannot at present be resolved. This has not stopped speculation on her status not just in modern scholarship but also by authors over the centuries. Was she an ordinary slave trafficked like so many others at this time, a free women caught up in a raid, or a noblewoman sold in the wake of a political or military disaster? In short, was she raided or traded? We will probably never know. The essence of the evidence is this: her Merovingian hagiographer writing within a decade of her death informs us that she was a slave, transported to France from overseas, with no mention of family background, and sold for a low price; a revised hagiography from the Carolingian period, and a Carolingian-era annal, the *LHF*, claimed that she was a slave but from a royal background. The Merovingian account was written soon after Balthild's death while Balthild's younger son ruled as king and there were people who could have read the work who had known the queen. There is a high chance that the hagiographer's portrayal reflected prevailing opinion. One has to wonder how well her royal son would have received a biography of his mother that cast her as a common slave if she was in fact nobly born. It seems an unlikely circumstance. I am inclined to accept Balthild's non-illustrious birth because it fits both with the biographer's account and with what we know of some other royal marriages at this time. By contrast the Carolingian life was written in an era when Balthild's cult was being promoted by the imperial family under the direction of Gisela, the sister of Charlemagne.

The claim that it was the Carolingian Life that preserved her true "noble" status has had its supporters over the years. The convent that depended on the successful cult of their saintly founder pressed the Carolingian claim that Balthild was nobly born. And this has been the most consistent interpretation of Balthild's status over the centuries, eventually enshrined in French memory through French language translations of the Carolingian Life (see Chapter 7, pp. 140–75). Arguments in favor of Balthild's royal birth have been offered in modern scholarship too, and this view has achieved some measure of acceptance. In this interpretation Balthild may have been a high-born woman whose status had changed for the worse, perhaps the result of her capture after a military defeat.[7] The context for such a reversal may align with known political disruptions in England at that time.[8] Such a scenario would help to explain her position of honor in Erchinoald's household, and also the heights she attained when, perhaps, she experienced another reversal of fortune through her Anglo-Saxon kin and this enabled her to marry a king. High birth might go some way to explain how she came to have a visible and honorable position in Erchinoald's household, performing the role of cupbearer that kept her in close contact with the family. It might also help explain Erchinoald's desire to marry her on the death of his wife since he and his family had entrenched connections with Anglo-Saxon rulers. Noble origins would also fit with the later account in *LHF* and the Carolingian Life, but as already noted, this was written at a later time when the political landscape in France had changed. In summary, there would have to be a lot of presently undocumented, circumstantial evidence to make this case strong.

The counter argument requires us to take the most contemporary account seriously when it states that she was a slave, making no further claims for her heritage. Indeed, her first hagiographer was adamant on this point, stressing that she was sold to the Neustrian mayor Erchinoald for a low price. Of course, a noble captive could also be sold for a low price, but this does not seem to be the point that the hagiographer is trying to make. Rather, the opposite. It is Balthild's low status and humble origins that make God's will to elevate her so remarkable. Hagiographers were wordsmiths. They framed their holy subjects according to traditional narrative patterns in order to convince readers of their subject's sanctity. In this case, there was no immediate example of a low-born slave-saint to draw on, so the hagiographer carefully employed biblical references to indicate that indeed, in special circumstances, lowly people could be raised by God to fulfill a divine destiny; Balthild was like the poor man raised from the dunghill (1 Samuel 2:8; Psalm 113:7–8). Was this low-born slave status entirely a pious fiction perpetrated by her hagiographer, or even Balthild herself? It is a hard leap to make given the strong association of nobility with piety in the seventh century and the fact that her royal son was still on the throne. Furthermore, within hagiographic convention, if Balthild had come from an illustrious, or even simply a respectable family, it would have been conventional to mention it. Not all saints came from an aristocratic background even in the Merovingian era. The Life of Eligius, later bishop of Noyon, clearly states that he came from a respectable but not illustrious family, and his parents are named. So it is a problem that when the claim for Balthild's noble status was made in the Carolingian era, no details concerning her family or connections were provided to support this. Authors in subsequent centuries were more creative, however, linking her with the Northumbrian royal house.[9]

In fact, if we put aside the attempt to make her into something other than how she is represented in the first Life, we find that her hagiographer's claim that she was a slave, with no caveat about alternative circumstances, fits well with what the sources tell us about the social mobility of some slaves within the Merovingian royal family and, indeed, further afield. Across the Mediterranean world it is possible to find examples of low-born women, including slaves, becoming consorts and mothers of rulers. The example of Theodora of Byzantium, Justinian's empress, is well known.[10] In early Islam, slave women were often the mothers of caliphs.[11] And if she was a lowly slave girl, Balthild would not have been the first captive slave to become a Merovingian queen. In 608, barely half a century before Balthild's marriage, another Merovingian king, Theudebert, had married a woman whom his mother, Queen Brunhild, had bought "from merchants." The slave Bilichild was queen for only two years before she was murdered by her husband. Unlike Balthild, she had not produced a son to bolster her status. Furthermore, it had not helped that she had alienated her mother-in-law, who did not take kindly to her former servant taking on new airs since, we are told, Bilichild "thought herself in no way inferior to Brunhild. Brunhild for her part reproached her with having been her slave."[12] Bilichild's untimely death is recorded with little comment by the annalist as it was more important to record that Theuderic took as wife another low-born woman, "a slave girl (*puella*) named Theudechildis."[13] Kings were surrounded by lower-status women with whom they could associate or even marry. Indeed, marrying low-born women is better attested for Merovingian kings than royal pairings. Queens held little status beyond what their husbands chose to give them, unless they ended up as regent for underage male heirs. Furthermore, capture-marriages are better attested for high-born women than for low-born captives. In the fifth century, the imperial princess Galla Placidia had been captured and then married to the Visigothic leader Athaulf.[14] The patrician Hector of Marseille had abducted his heiress bride.[15] In the mid-sixth century, Queen Radegund, a Thuringian princess and captive of war, was claimed by one of the victors, King Chlothar, who raised, educated, and then married her. Chlothar's motives in this were clear: Through marriage with Radegund he maintained a connection with the remnants of the Thuringian tribe, and in killing her brother and other family members who might one day challenge him, he removed his enemies. Small wonder that Radegund despised her royal life and fled to the protection of the church as soon as she could.[16]

One further reason to consider the value of an ordinary slave as a queen was that in the seventh century there seems to have been a pattern in which slaves were married to feeble-minded Merovingian kings. The ill-fated Bilichild was married to a king who was openly described as such, and she was initially procured for him by his mother, who then strove to continue her control over the king. It is possible that slaves were viewed in some quarters as optimal partners for weak kings, put in place by people who sought to control them and avoid the complication of intermarriage with an ambitious noble family. Although Balthild's fate was better than Bilichild's, both were viewed as exceptional women by contemporaries in contrast to their husbands. Bilichild was described as "a woman of spirit and much loved by all the Austrasians because she bore with nobility the simple-mindedness of Theudebert (*simplicitatem Teudeberti*)," and Balthild was described as "kind," "honorable," and "a sensible and attractive woman." For such women, the nature of the bargain was probably clear.

Interestingly, both Bilichild and Balthild have Merovingian-style names, which one would not immediately expect of someone who had been a foreign slave. Her name is rendered "Baldechildis" in Fredegar's *Chronicle* and "Baltechildis" in the Life of Bertila.[17] These women may have been given, or adopted, names that reflected their new connections and status on marriage. A name change would make sense for a low-born woman and, in fact, one can find examples of this practice even among later queens of noble background. For example, King Aethelred I of England's Norman wife Emma was known as Aelfgifu in Anglo-Saxon sources, and so, rather confusingly, was his other wife. In short, Balthild's Merovingian-style name may not be her pre-marital name or indicate her status.

One of the more unusual and striking aspects of Balthild's biography is the way her hagiographer describes her body. Balthild's personal attributes are described in a rather frank, appraising manner more suited to the assessment of a slave than a noblewoman: "the form of her body was pleasing, very slender, and beautiful to see. Her expression was cheerful, and her gait dignified. And since she was thus, [quoting Esther 7:3] she was exceedingly pleasing to the prince and she found favor in his eyes." If Balthild was of royal blood, such a frank gaze would not have been appropriate. Hagiographic convention allowed that all saints were beautiful in the sight of God, and a woman's complexion was often described in accordance with classical norms of beauty, but it is rare to have the kind of intrusive, sensual appraisal that her hagiographer gives her entire body in this description. These details were supposed to explain how it was that she aroused the interest of her master, and ultimately of the king. Her piety as a youth in Erchinoald's household is stressed, but so too is her pleasing body and her close contact with her master. One of her jobs in Erchinoald's household was to serve wine as cupbearer. In this era, a cupbearer could be a high-ranking servant whose position brought them into close contact with their master and whose legal status was tied to the master's rank.[18] The honorable nature of this job is stressed by the hagiographer, who may have had other less honorable associations in mind since in the ancient world female cupbearers could also be available women.[19] She was undoubtedly a servant (she "stood" in his service, thus maintaining the distinction of rank that divided those who stood from those who sat) yet she was evidently in a quite intimate and privileged station since we are told that her position did not lead her to lord it over her fellow servants. And when Erchinoald's wife died, we are told that "he decided to join the most honorable virgin, Balthild, to himself in the matrimonial bed" and she was summoned to his chamber. Balthild fled from this proposition, an impulse her hagiographer attributed to her humility. We are then told a convoluted story about how Balthild was able to hide under some rags until Erchinoald turned his nuptial inclinations to another woman, introducing a "chastity plot" to signal

Balthild's virtue.[20] But given her slave status and her personal attributes, and the privileged contact she had with her master, matrimony may not have been on Erchinoald's mind or even possible while Balthild was under his roof. In fact, since the date of Balthild's marriage is not certain, Erchinoald's wife may have died after Balthild was married to King Clovis; this would put this entire episode in a rather different light.[21]

Whatever the precise nature of their relationship, it does seem that Erchinoald and Balthild were political allies, at least at first. It was undoubtedly he who arranged or smoothed her marriage to the king, and he remained an important figure in her life over many years during which he served the king as mayor of the palace. He continued to support her as queen through her regency until his death in 659. Their connection was thus public, and her time as a slave in his household was well known. It may have been important to assert Balthild's purity in view of the obvious inference that she could have been his concubine. Erchinoald is lauded as "a man of illustrious standing" whose intentions towards her were honorable, and they may have been so. But, as noted above, the chronology of these events is unclear. So why introduce the story of hiding in the rags at all? The answer may lie in a desire to offset accusations by her "detractors" mentioned in the first Life. In the context of disputed succession, her enemies may have used an accusation of sexual impurity against her—an accusation that would reflect on the legitimacy of her children also.

The hagiographic convention of a virgin saint repudiating the advances of a lustful suitor does not seem to fully justify the attention given to Balthild's relations with Erchinoald in this hagiography. It is also interesting that the description of her body and her beauty is explored in the chapters dealing with Erchinoald, not in the chapter describing her marriage to the king. Indeed, there is a kind of displacement of the king by Erchinoald in the work that unsettles the conventions of the genre. One gets the sense that Balthild's relationship with Erchinoald was far more important to her and her hagiographer than her relationship with the king, who is hardly mentioned in this work. This may not represent the true situation, but the relationship of master and servant dominates the early part of the vita.

The hagiographer's skill in describing Balthild's life is evident throughout this work, but nowhere did he have to work harder than in the story he told of a slave girl who did not succumb to the sexual overtures of her master. This is not to say that there was a sexual liaison that was being hidden, but rather that the chastity of a slave was a claim that had to be made, not assumed. His use of scripture, especially a glancing allusion to the Old Testament figure of Esther, points to a desire to shape an improbable and perhaps uncomfortable narrative. His response to Balthild's origins and possibly compromised position in Erchinoald's household was to "double down" on the slavery motif, developing a rags-to-riches story of a slave girl Balthild who first repudiated an earthly suitor (Erchinoald) in favor of Christ, and then went on to marry a king. Alongside the many positive attributes which he ascribes to her is a cheerful countenance: *vultu hilaris*. It is a positive quality that masks the poignancy of her early predicament. Like so much in this work, this "cheer" has its precedents in hagiographic literature, but it is also in keeping with the uplifting tenor of the work as a whole. The reader learns that God's intervention in saving Balthild for noble purpose singles her out as unusual and special. Hers is not the ordinary lot of slaves because her piety and humility will reap the ultimate reward.

Balthild's slave status was a legal yoke that had to be resolved before marriage.[22] A slave could not engage in a legal marriage, and since the offspring of a slave woman inherited her servile status, freedom was required for her to bear legitimate children. It was Balthild's slave status that had enabled her transportation from overseas, and that allowed Erchinoald to purchase her. Whether in preparation for his own marriage, or marriage to the king, Erchinoald would have had to grant Balthild legal freedom, an act that would be public and recorded in writing. Masters who freed slaves had the right to expect continued obligations from those whom they freed. In freeing her, Erchinoald lost little since he now provided the king with a queen who had ties of obligation to him, just as a daughter would have to a father. In Balthild, Erchinoald gained a symbolic daughter to tie him even more tightly to the royal family. Indeed, the choice of an Anglo-Saxon for this role may have been a long-term strategy envisioned by Clovis' mother, the Anglo-Saxon regent Nantechild, and eventually carried out by Erchinoald. They both had connections to Anglo-Saxon England.[23]

While the sources do not allow firm answers to many questions about Balthild's condition on her arrival in France, there is no reason to doubt that Balthild arrived as a slave or that she achieved her new station through happenstance. Her personal qualities may have appealed to the young king; by all measures, theirs was a successful, if short, marriage. The road from slave to queen was viable in the seventh century.

Personal Appearance

One of the challenges of this era is that very few portrait images survive to convey a sense of what people looked like or how they wanted to present themselves. Coins, seal rings, and wax seals provide portrait busts that convey little information beyond hairstyle, and sometimes the clothing, of an individual. Of course, we have no way of knowing whether the images even on these items were attempts to represent the features of a real person rather than generic symbols of authority. Literary sources are more forthcoming, but they, too, are often conventional in their description of beauty or the grotesque. In Balthild's case, we have two ways of approaching an imaginative reconstruction of her person. One is to see her through the eyes of her contemporaneous hagiographer who, as noted earlier, took a frankly appraising note of some of her features. The other is to seek a reconstruction of her appearance based on the physical remains of Balthild's body and associated items preserved by her convent of Chelles, now in the Ville de Chelles' museum.

Balthild was said to be very beautiful. Her hagiographer described her as *aspectu decora*, "beautiful to see." More than was the case with most biographies, Balthild's kindly temperament and public affect informed the literary portrait: this "best pearl of God" was kind of heart, modest in speech, loving and obedient, friendly to all, and generous. Such beauty would explain her appeal to a slave captor; it would explain why her master, Erchinoald, wanted to bed her; and it would explain how she ultimately made the most prestigious match of all—to the young king Clovis II. God's providence had a hand in this, her hagiographer insisted, but the reader is left in no doubt that nature had prepared her in other ways for her future role. In the Merovingian era biographers of queens and saints could be counted on to flatter their subjects while at the same time insisting that their rejection of personal vanity was a remarkable symbol and a model for contemporary observers. Consequently, male and female saints alike were routinely described as paragons of their sex, good to look at, and shining with divine luminescence. Drawing on motifs inherited from late antique aesthetics, hagiographers particularly flattered female saints by comparing their complexion to lilies and roses and lauded their persons as well formed and appealing. The idea behind this was that perfection of the body in this world foreshadowed perfection of the soul in heaven, a phenomenon admired by all who viewed it. Yet Balthild is described in a less conventional way; her beauty encompassed an active intelligence. Her hagiographer notes that she was "astute" or "shrewd."[24] The author of the *LHF* notes that Balthild was "beautiful and exceedingly clever (or capable)" while her husband Clovis was a fornicator, glutton, and defiler of women.[25] The adjective used by the author of the *LHF* to describe Balthild's intelligence is *strenua*, a term usually used to describe warrior strength; indeed, it is the term used by the Fredegar continuator to describe Erchinoald.[26] The term may have been mistakenly appropriated by the author of the *LHF* for Balthild from Fredegar's description of Erchinoald, but it is an interesting elision of the two individuals nevertheless. Balthild's intelligence or cleverness, often seen as a military attribute, seems an appropriate description, underscored by the direct connection of Balthild's intellectual qualities with those of Erchinoald. The sense we get is that Balthild and Erchinoald were alike in some essential ways and that they worked as a team.

Fortunately, Balthild's bodily remains and some items associated with her person were preserved at the convent of Chelles. Together with a little imagination, they can help us penetrate literary convention and reach some way to an image of Balthild as a living person who might enter a room and hold court.

To be sure, we cannot know for certain that Balthild was beautiful. But, thanks to the preservation of part of her body and the material objects that have survived, we can construct an impression of how she might have appeared in her prime. Standing at just under 5 foot 2 inches, she was of average height. Her body was well proportioned as far as can be deduced from her skeletal remains. The examiners of 1983 saw no visible sign of disease or stress associated with hard labor. Much of her natural beauty would have been in her hair, which we know from her remains to have been strawberry blond (Fig. 2.1). At the time of her death her hair was very long and tied with ribbons that wound around her hair in a crisscross pattern to secure her loose braids. These covered plaits could be worn long or serve as an anchor for hair pins allowing her to arrange her hair high on her head, or alternatively so that it framed her face. As a married woman, Balthild's head would have been topped by a veil, but as a young woman, and in private settings, her hair and its ribbons would have been visible. We know that in her later years she covered her white hairs with dye that blended with her natural color, suggesting that her hair was at least partly, or occasionally, visible even in the convent.

26 BALTHILD OF FRANCIA

Fig. 2.1 A portion of Balthild's hair now in the collection of the Alfred-Bonno Museum, Ville de Chelles, shows signs of hair dye.

Hair was a symbol of status and honor for women as for men in the seventh century and law codes exacted heavy penalties for those who assaulted or killed women, or boys, with long hair. Long hair was also a symbol of royal status for Merovingian kings, who were known as the "long-haired kings." Long tresses distinguished male Merovingian royals from the rest of the population; cutting the hair of a Merovingian prince removed him from consideration for kingship; if he was already a king, he was effectively deposed, as was the case with the last Merovingian king, Childeric III. We can be sure that Balthild's husband Clovis would have displayed his long hair with its central parting as a sign of his authority to rule. Hair care was thus important for the royal couple.

As far as we know, Balthild was healthy. Her hagiographer indicates no ongoing debility before the last year of her life. Her skeleton shows no visible signs of trauma or disease, although it is far from intact (Fig. 2.2). She successfully bore three sons (and perhaps other children unrecorded) and lived some years into retirement from public life. Only one illness is mentioned by her biographer, occurring shortly before her death: an abdominal sickness had caused her distress but was at first treated successfully. Based on the analysis of her surviving bones reported by Jean-Pierre Laporte in 1983, Balthild was probably in her forties when she died, which aligns well with what we know from other sources. She probably died at the age of forty-five.[27]

We may not know as much as we would like about her appearance, but we do know from her grave that she prized her royal status even into retirement to the convent, and in her preparations for death. Balthild appears not

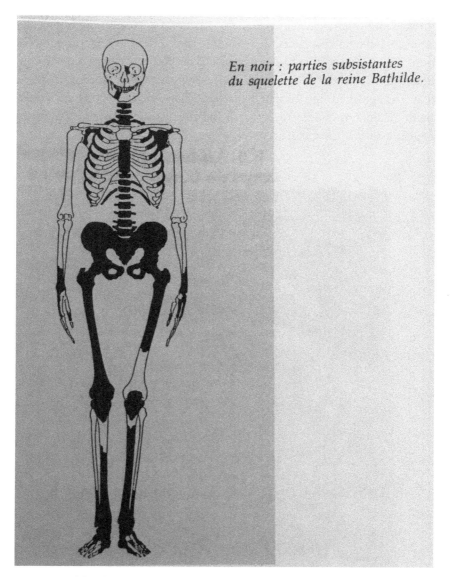

Fig. 2.2 Balthild's extant skeletal remains, shown here shaded in black, illustrate how much of her body was gifted to other monastic institutions over the centuries. Laporte and Boyer, *Trésors de Chelles*, p. 23.

to have taken the monastic habit when she entered the convent: her hair dye and burial clothes suggest that she maintained a secular appearance even in her retreat until, perhaps, close to the end (discussed further in Chapter 5, pp. 88–121). Perhaps she hoped for yet another reversal of fortune that would see her back at the court of her son. Perhaps a founder who still looked like a queen was useful to the convent as it recruited noble nuns. Balthild may have had to accept her forcible retirement but she continued to care about her external appearance and maintained it in a way that distinguished her from those around her. For as long as she could, Balthild did not choose to embrace the monastic clothing and outward appearance of a "slave of God."

3
Marriage Makes a Queen

Sometime around 650 Balthild was married to King Clovis II. Clovis was probably between fifteen and seventeen years of age and Balthild was probably about the same age. By the time of his marriage Clovis II had been ruling Neustria nominally for about eleven years with his mother Nantechild as queen-regent, until her death in 642. The mayors of the palace during Clovis' minority were first Aega and then Erchinoald, both of whom are mentioned as working alongside Nantechild.[1] Once Clovis neared his majority and was of marriageable age, Erchinoald may have been an important influence in arranging his marriage to Balthild.[2] With a wife and the children she bore, a new royal household came into being centered on Clovis and Balthild as a royal couple. Erchinoald continued as mayor of the palace in the first years of the marriage, and we can imagine that mentorship was an important element in his relationship to the young couple and how they configured their court.[3] Although we never hear of Balthild's family, her marriage to Clovis brought her new relations. As was the case with Merovingian kings before him, Clovis' father Dagobert had had multiple marriages and children by different women. Clovis' older half-brother Sigibert III, Dagobert's son by a woman named Ragnetrude, had been ruling in Austrasia for almost twenty years. Sigibert had a wife named Chimnechild, and two children that we know of, a daughter named Bilichild and a son, Dagobert, named for his grandfather. Sigibert III died in 651, soon after Balthild's marriage, after which there was a time when the Austrasian kingdom was ruled by a usurper, "Childebert," the "adopted" son of the Austrasian mayor, Grimoald.[4] It is not recorded that Balthild met her brother-in-law, or his wife Chimnechild, but Balthild's second son, Childeric would eventually marry his first cousin, Bilichild, Chimnechild's daughter, which speaks to shared political interests. But this was in the future. At the time of Balthild's marriage to Clovis, it was the people and policies of Dagobert's court, the memory of Nantechild's regency, and the direction of the "forceful and intelligent" mayor Erchinoald that determined the configurations of Neustrian power into which Balthild married.

Neustria

Balthild's marriage catapulted her to the center of an important Frankish kingdom: Neustria. Merovingian princes might fight among themselves for dominance, and they were not immune to assassination or coup attempts, but their rule as a family dynasty was broadly acknowledged by the nobility. The Merovingians were the "long-haired kings," the *reges criniti*; their status as kings was signaled by their distinctive long hair. By the mid-seventh century when Balthild was married, the basic outline of the Frankish kingdom comprised most of what is now modern France together with territories on its eastern border: parts of modern Belgium, Luxembourg, Rhineland Germany, and Switzerland.[5] In the seventh century, the Neustrian kingdom was centered on Paris. The Austrasian kingdom to the east was in a continuous process of negotiating its eastern border. During Balthild's time as queen the ancient kingdom of Burgundy no longer had its own king but was dependent on the Neustrian kingdom to the north. Elsewhere Franks ruled over territories whose Romano-Gallic population tried to hold on to their Roman administrative structures and cultural norms. The south-eastern territories of Aquitaine and Gascony were part of the Frankish kingdom but governed by dukes (*duces*) who retained significant autonomy in practice. Aquitanian interests were often aligned with Austrasian interests. Provence came under Frankish rule from 536 and was governed by patricians. Septimania, whose lands bordered the Mediterranean Sea from west of the Rhône River to the Pyrenees, did not come under Frankish control until the Carolingian period: it was part of the Visigothic kingdom. The Merovingian sphere of influence extended beyond its borders and at times their kings exacted tribute from the Lombards and Visigoths, and their dominance over parts of Anglo-Saxon England ran deeper than that.[6]

It was in northern France in the Frankish kingdoms of Neustria and Austrasia that the bulk of the Frankish population resided, creating a culture that was an amalgam of late Roman and Frankish practices, and from the time of Clovis I they were governed by some form of the Salic Law. Although Frankish customs and practices meant that the northern kingdoms of Neustria and Austrasia were more Frankish than other parts of the Merovingian kingdoms, they retained nevertheless a strong Roman Christian culture. The Franks had been settled in formerly Roman territories for a couple of centuries before they took royal control; they were Romanized before they were Christianized.

Queenship through Marriage

Balthild was Clovis II's sole wife and acknowledged queen. This was clearly in her favor. Early Merovingian kings practiced serial polygyny.[7] This was made possible by a secular, legal notion of marriage that accommodated changing political circumstances and alliances. A Merovingian prince could marry a woman, have children with her, put her aside (divorce), remarry, and start a new family. In addition to the acknowledged wife, some Merovingian kings had concubines or "secondary wives" as well as women who did not attain even such reduced status. Merovingian rule descended through the male line. A king's acknowledged sons were eligible for rule irrespective of the social status of their mothers provided their royal paternity was accepted and there was political will to advance them in this role. The legitimacy of heirs begot on concubines was notably challenged by Columbanus, an Irish missionary who attempted to "reform" religion in Francia at the turn of the seventh century, but he was not completely successful in eradicating Frankish royal marriage customs.

Serial polygyny continued into the seventh century. The king usually had an acknowledged wife whose children were princes and princesses, and whose boys were eligible to be elevated to kingship. Both Dagobert and Clovis II were accused of debauchery in some sources which meant that they had relationships, and perhaps children, outside of marriage. However, when a king died leaving an underage son who was the acknowledged heir, it was that son's mother who became regent. Dagobert had at least five wives in succession (and numerous other women, we are told). After Dagobert's death, his queen Nantechild's regency for her young son Clovis II was acknowledged by the nobility and we see her actively working alongside the mayor of the Neustrian palace. Clovis' earliest years, therefore, saw a female regency of the sort he would eventually bequeath to Balthild and his own underage sons. Balthild's marriage to Clovis II was arranged to produce heirs for the dynasty and her status depended on her relationship to the king and to her success in providing sons. If her husband had died later in life, Balthild's fate might have been quite different. As it was, no other woman with sons was in the running for the regency and Balthild's marriage and rights with respect to her sons appears to have been acknowledged.

Mayors of the Palace

Merovingian kings did not rule without help. Although King Clovis I (d. 511) had eliminated his political rivals to establish his sole control over Frankish territories, the Frankish nobles, the old Romano-Gallic landowning classes, and church magnates were powerful and influential in governance. Military leaders (*duces*) had power that was readily apparent. In the cities, counts exacted taxes and made themselves generally unpopular. Town "opinion" could be expressed even if we cannot be sure that town councils in the late Roman fashion were still fully functional.[8] Prominent churchmen often claimed to speak on behalf of their cities, although cities and towns could be hotbeds of dissent and factionalism and bishops sometimes fell afoul of their flocks. In the seventh century the most prominent political actor in a kingdom was the mayor of the palace (*maior domus*) who advised the king, ran the palace and thus the court, saw to the execution of the king's will, or shaped it, and probably to some degree controlled access to the royal person. The mayor of the palace was second only to the king in power, and sometimes in practice more powerful. In the early seventh century the office had come to represent the interests of the secular and religious nobility, and the mayor was elected from their number.[9] From the time of Chlothar II the post became de facto hereditary, and noble families vied with each other to benefit from connections to the person of the mayor as well as to the king and queen.

The mayors of the palace in Balthild's time were powerful men. As already noted, Balthild benefitted from being connected to the mayor Erchinoald who held competing powers in check in the interests of a stable political life. When he died, he was succeeded not by his son Leudesius, who may have been too young at that juncture (but who later became mayor), but by another powerful figure, Ebroin, whose plans and alliances differed from what had gone before.

Clovis II's Parents: Dagobert and Nantechild

When Clovis became king at the age of four or five, he inherited from his grandfather Chlothar II (d. 629) and from his father Dagobert (d. 639) the kingdoms of Neustria and Burgundy.[10] Dagobert, especially, was a larger than life figure whose deeds supplied chroniclers with much to write about.

During Chlothar II's reign, Dagobert had been placed as king over the Austrasians. On Chlothar's death in 629 Dagobert was able to shunt aside his brother Charibert to consolidate the kingdoms of Austrasia, Neustria, and Burgundy under his sole control. Charibert was given lands in Aquitaine and Gascony to rule; on his death his lands also passed to Dagobert.

King Dagobert's reign started propitiously. Guided by Arnulf, bishop of Metz, and Pippin, mayor of the palace, we are told that "he ruled Austrasia so prosperously that he earned unlimited praise of all peoples."[11] The chronicler dates his first marriages to his time in Austrasia. First, he married Gomatrude on his father's orders, but then put her aside to marry Nantechild, "a maiden of the bed-chamber," making her queen. This was Clovis II's mother. But Dagobert was polyamorous and we are told that while making a royal circuit of his realm, he took a girl (*quadam puella*) named Ragnetrude and had a son by her named Sigibert.[12] This Ragnetrude did not displace Nantechild, who remained queen, and when Nantechild's son Clovis was born, it was he who succeeded to his father's Neustrian and Burgundian kingdoms. There were other women associated with Dagobert, such as Wulfegund and Berchild who were both given the title of queen by Fredegar, but the chronicler continued that "the names of his mistresses it would be wearisome to insert in this chronicle; there were too many of them."[13] In any case, none of these women dislodged Nantechild in Neustria. So it was that although Clovis was Dagobert's youngest son, it was Clovis who was designated as his father's heir for the combined kingdoms of Neustria and Burgundy.

As for Sigibert, Dagobert had already provided for his eldest son in a ceremony in the Austrasian city of Metz. Dagobert had agreed to raise his son to the kingship of Austrasia with the support of Chunibert of Köln and Duke Adalgisel "to control the palace and the kingdom."[14] Fredegar's *Chronicle* tells us that Dagobert had some work to get Sigebert and the Austrasian nobles on board with this arrangement but that they acquiesced out of fear of the king.[15] In placing Sigibert in Austrasia Dagobert replicated the pattern of his father in which the older son was assigned to Austrasia during his father's lifetime, but it also possible that Sigibert had ties to Austrasia through his mother, Ragnetrude.[16] The immediate context for Sigibert's early elevation was the war that the Franks were fighting against the Wends who continued to raid the eastern frontier. By setting up his son as king in that region, Dagobert was able to provide the beleaguered population of Austrasia with a Merovingian royal presence, demonstrating his commitment to the region and providing a figurehead for resistance to Samo, the Frankish king of the Wends.[17] Dagobert supplied Sigibert with "sufficient treasure" for this new role.[18]

With his eldest son entrenched in Austrasia, toward the end of his reign Dagobert designated Clovis, his son by his queen Nantechild, as his heir for the kingdoms of Neustria and Burgundy. Fredegar attempted to explain the reasoning behind this decision by remarking that Sigibert III and Clovis II's respective kingdoms were comparable in terms of territorial extent and population.

Two years later, as Dagobert lay dying of dysentery just outside of Paris at the villa of Épinay-sur-Seine, he called for his wife and mayor to finalize the succession. The Neustrian mayor, Aega, was to protect his wife Nantechild and their young son and govern the kingdom until Clovis was of an age to rule. This Aega proceeded to do, ruling with queen Nantechild for just over two years. Thus, Clovis' early years were spent under the care of his regent mother and the mayor of the palace, the latter receiving a generally good press in Neustrian sources.[19] Aega's death from a fever at the royal villa at Clichy ushered in the appointment of a new mayor, Erchinoald. It was he who had purchased the slave girl Balthild. Fredegar tells us that Erchinoald was related to Dagobert's mother and was thus an uncle of some sort to the young Clovis. In his capacity as mayor, Erchinoald was furthering the cause of his own family, especially the future of his son Leudesius who would briefly assume the position of Neustrian mayor some years later. Erchinoald may have had a daughter who married into the Kentish royal family although this connection is not at all certain. In arranging Balthild's marriage to the young Clovis, Erchinoald may have been positioning Balthild as a kind of adoptive daughter to further extend his political reach.

Marriage to a Young King

As the bride and groom were in their mid- to late teens they were at an age when their married life could start immediately. We know nothing about their first meeting, but it is likely that it was not by chance and that Erchinoald had a direct role in getting them together. At some point Balthild had attained her freedom. Her marriage to the king would have been public, witnessed by nobles and churchmen, and thus legitimate; she was expected to produce legitimate children.[20] Presumably, Erchinoald stood in loco parentis and negotiated the settlement (*dos*) that the king would give to his wife. Although we do not know Balthild's views on the alliance, or whether she had a choice in the matter, her hagiographer told a particular kind of story: about how she expressed her will in escaping marriage to the mayor, how it was her destiny to marry the king, and her own reputed "cheer." We can only suppose that at some level this was a marriage Balthild was able to accept.

How did Balthild's life change as a result of her marriage? The sources provide us with little certain knowledge of how Merovingian marriages were arranged and carried out. Those details that have been preserved reveal that marriage in the Merovingian period was an amalgam of Roman and Germanic practices.[21] Throughout the Merovingian period, men married women who they could later divorce, as was the Roman custom. Merovingians male elites, like Roman elites before them, could maintain concubines and other women if they could afford to keep them. But whereas the children of concubines were not considered legal heirs to their fathers' patrimony under Roman law (and some distinctions of status were also made in the Merovingian period), the children of Merovingian kings bore the royal bloodline regardless of the status of their mother and provided the king with heirs that he could acknowledge if he wished, or that others might acknowledge even if he did not.[22]

As marriage was a community affair, and royal marriage was also a political affair, Balthild's marriage to Clovis would have been witnessed by the secular and ecclesiastical elite. We do not know if the marriage was controversial in any way, or if Erchinoald's role in engineering the match was viewed as patently self-serving. Church representatives would have attended the ceremony, and indeed, as an elite marriage, it is likely that it was accompanied by liturgical prayers and blessings. If the marriage was conducted in Paris we are out of luck since we do not know who the bishop of Paris was at the time of Balthild's wedding. However, there would have been celebration and feasting. Any transfer of property on their marriage would be witnessed, recorded, and preserved in archives. There is no account of Clovis and Balthild's betrothal or marriage ceremony. However, the ceremony need not have been elaborate. As already noted, some Merovingian kings took women as their wives and then disposed of them which, suggests that some marriage ceremonies might have been perfunctory.[23] However, marriage created legitimate heirs even though not all wives were recognized queens. The attention given to the royal nuptials a century earlier, when Sigibert married the Visigothic princess Brunhild, was highly unusual and intentionally classical in in spirit.[24] In Germanic tradition the groom endowed his bride with a dowry (*dos*) and a *morgengabe*—a gift to the woman of lands, revenue, treasure, and other moveable goods, on the consummation of the marriage. This was an arena where the family practices of the Frankish kings departed from the practices of their Roman predecessors. In Roman marriages, the woman's family provided a dowry to her husband. In Merovingian royal marriages, it was the husband who endowed his bride with property and goods which she would keep even if he divorced her. This meant that kings could marry women of any background and their wives were provided with the wealth needed to fulfill their role as benefactors and patrons should they be recognized with the status of queen. As we have seen, Dagobert had married one of his chamber maids, Nantechild, and now their son, Clovis, married Balthild, a former slave. Both women were recognized as queens.

What Kind of Man Was Clovis?

Sources written soon after his death were not kind to Clovis II. By the time he died, he had been ruling in name for about nineteen years, the last eight years as king regnant. A disruptive tendency in his nature exacerbated by self-indulgence had alienated the observers who mattered. But at the time of his marriage there was much good to hope for, especially when Balthild started to bear him sons, thus securing the succession. There is no indication in any sources that married life was unwelcome to Balthild or that she desired a different kind of life. Her hagiographer attempted the idea that Balthild wanted to save herself for a heavenly groom when she was evading Erchinoald's advances, but marriage to the king appears not to have elicited such concerns. Indeed, as her hagiographer explained, her evasion of Erchinoald was divinely designed so that she would later have Clovis as her husband so that God "could thus raise her to a higher station through the merit of her humility." Pragmatically, God's purpose in this was to ensure that she would produce future kings and that "from her, royal progeny might come forth."[25]

At least at the beginning, Balthild was no Saint Radegund aching to be rid of her mortal husband so that she could dedicate herself to the religious life. Rather, the contrary appears to be the case. As we shall see, Balthild seems to have quickly found her footing, seeking ways to integrate herself within the web of power at court, and dedicating herself to increasing her earthly family from whom she maintained her prominent position. Even with the preparation she received in Erchinoald's household, Balthild's marriage catapulted her into a very different world from the one she was brought up in. Merovingian Neustria was far more sophisticated than anything Balthild would have known in Anglo-Saxon England. While Neustria was not as Romanized as the southern provinces of Gaul, it would have looked very Roman compared to anything in England, even with its surviving Roman structures. The Neustrian kingdom was speckled with ancient Roman cities: Paris, Soissons, Rouen, Sens, Reims, Tournai, Cambrai; further afield in northern Aquitaine and Burgundy, there were the Roman cities of Orléans, Lyon, and Tours, among others. Paris was the Neustrian capital city, but it was also a Roman city. It was a large city in comparison with others, and operated as a cultural center. Balthild spent much of her time in places tied to Paris and within the Seine Basin region; her visual frame of reference would have been that of Roman cities with stone used for public buildings, mosaic floors, roads, and other amenities. She would also have spent time at the countryside compounds that Merovingian kings favored for hunting. She must have looked upon her new home and environment with awe.

Balthild Cultivates Relationships at the Neustrian Court

When Balthild joined the household of the mayor, she was already at a center of power. When mayor Erchinoald promoted her and saw her married to the king, Balthild benefitted from a rare convergence of luck and strategy. With the mayor as her patron and the king as her husband, Balthild started her marriage and career at court in a position of strength. Her hagiographer observed that she actively strove to maintain and expand this advantage. Balthild entrenched herself with court constituents: "she obeyed her king as her lord, and to the princes she showed herself a mother, to the priests as a daughter, and to the young and the adolescents as the best possible nurse."[26] Her hagiographer's emphasis on her humility is nowhere so much on show as when describing her relationship to her seniors. "And she was friendly to all, loving the priests as fathers, the monks as brothers, the poor as a faithful nurse does, and giving to each generous alms. She preserved the honor of the princes and kept their fitting counsel, always exhorting the young to religious studies and humbly and steadfastly petitioning the king for the churches and the poor."[27] This paean to womanly power through studied subservience adhered to a purposeful religious tone, but it also described a pathway for an astute woman to navigate between competing interests, bolster her position, and gain powerful supporters. The hagiographer's comment about her generosity in giving alms points to an intrinsic way Merovingian queens could integrate themselves into patronage networks that did not openly compete with male power. (Founding and endowing monasteries was more competitive.) The church had always looked to queens as potential allies in exerting Christian values and influence within the royal family. In Balthild's case, churchmen were the kind of allies that could both protect her position as a legitimate wife and provide her with a vehicle for patronage. In late antiquity, piety in the rich required giving alms to the poor. Since the church had co-opted "the poor," as their clients, Balthild's generosity was handled by her almoner, Abbot Genesius, and "through his hands she served the priests and the poor, fed the hungry, clothed the naked with garments, and conscientiously arranged for the burial of the dead."[28]

In recent years we have become more aware of the canvas of "the poor" and the careful distinction that is to be made between the "poor" as a rhetorical device, and the impoverished who received vital support from the church. In the eyes of the clergy, the list of deserving poor might include indigent clergy.[29] Be that as it may, churchmen were among the grateful and loyal recipients of Balthild's patronage.

Abbot Genesius was the public face of Balthild's civic and religious charity. Balthild's hagiographer is clear that this appointment was made by her husband Clovis to aid her. This is an indication that Clovis supported his queen in her public role; it may also indicate that they worked together. In Genesius we encounter a person whose position brought him as close as anyone to the queen, with a responsibility to promote Balthild's reputation as a benefactor, and he remained associated with her even after his death. Genesius was an abbot without a monastery—an abbot attached to the court. Eventually, Balthild promoted him to the bishopric of Lyon. The kind of poor relief described by Balthild's hagiographer was the public display of charity expected of kings and queens and it came out of the royal purse. Balthild was thus a partner with the king, and later with her son in establishing and supporting religious institutions.

Balthild's hagiographer ascribed Balthild's success as queen to her humility and her relationship to the princes, clerics, monks, and the poor. However, we must imagine that Balthild relied on a host of other individuals to support her in her new role. Sadly, unless they were major political figures, the sources are silent on who these people may have been. We have seen that the instrumentality of the mayors of the palace (Erchinoald, and later Ebroin) were highlighted. But it is worth pausing here to consider who we do not hear about. For example, Balthild's natal family members are never mentioned. The Life portrays her as a lone figure. Were her parents alive? Did she have siblings? Did other womenfolk accompany her into servitude and then to the court? Silence about family and any ties to England that might have survived threw into relief her presence as a foreigner at the court. Yet we hear nothing of linguistic challenges or personal relations with the female members of the court.

The women who surrounded Balthild in her early years are not credited with any part of her success; her circle of female friends and servants eludes us. Did Ragnoberta, the mayor Flaochad's widow, return to Paris after his death to be part of the court? Were the wives of other magnates milling around? Were any of Dagobert's other women still in public life? Did Balthild inherit some remnants of Nantechild's female circle? A woman who has three live births, and possibly other pregnancies, would have been surrounded by women.

Aside from Erchinoald, Balthild's young husband could also have been a source of support. It was from him that she gained her three sons, and the financial wherewithal and personal authority that enabled her to secure her position at his side and to survive his death. We are not poorly informed on Clovis' political life—he was the figurehead trotted out at the age of about six or seven during Nantechild's forays into Burgundy with her newly appointed mayors, and his activities during his years of sole rule are attested in the annals and in charters. But besides the obvious results of their intimacy (their sons), we are presented with an image of a happy court rather than a happy marriage. Perhaps the unfavorable descriptions of Clovis as a vicious young man, "a debaser of women, a glutton and a drunk" were somewhat close to the truth—a young king was hardly expected to live the life of a monk. But this is not the Clovis we see briefly in Balthild's Life: there he is represented as helping her with her public role. How far Clovis' poor behavior was the sour judgment of clerics on a youthful king, or how much could be attributed to mental instability as both Fredegar's *Chronicle* and the *LHF* claim, is impossible to ascertain. One shocking deed was laid at his door by the *LHF*: the torture of the Austrasian usurper Grimoald, a nobleman. This was viewed as heinous and transgressive of social norms, as we shall see at the end of this chapter.

Life in Paris and at the Royal Villas

With a population possibly as large as 20,000, Paris was a major city in the seventh century.[30] From 508, the dynasty's first Christian king, Clovis I, had declared the city as his royal seat. Although in subsequent years kings clustered around other cities in their realms, such as Soissons, Orléans, and Tournai, Paris retained an abiding role as a capital city for the dynasty and a kind of neutral space when relationships between the kings were fraught. In Balthild's time, Paris was still recognized as the prime city of the Neustrian kingdom and the center of royal and political activity.

Much of Paris' appeal as a capital city for the Merovingians was its defensible position, as it had been for the Romans and the ancient tribe of the Parisi before them. The largest island in the Seine, the Île de la Cité, gave the city's inhabitants the natural defenses of the river, and the island was further fortified to withstand assault. However, from the earliest times there were settlements and cemeteries on the left (south) bank of the Seine, and eventually, as a Roman city, the hilly rise on the left bank provided the space needed for major public and civic buildings: the Forum, Baths, theater, and large Amphitheatre (Arènes de Lutèce) with a capacity of 15,000. The left and right banks were linked to the Île de la Cité by a bridge, and the route to the expanding city on the left bank was a major road, the *cardo maximus* (today Boulevard St. Jacques). East-west roads cut across the cardo from the Seine up to the site of the Forum, with the *decumanus*, the principal road, leading from the Forum to the Arena. The left bank was supplied with water via an aqueduct on the south side.

There was probably a Christian presence in Paris earlier than our sources indicate. The earliest attested bishop was Victurinus in the fourth century.[31] There was a cult of another bishop, Marcellus, whose cemetery is attested in the fifth century, and a cult around Saint Genovefa (Geneviève) whose prayers were said to have averted the city's sack by Attila the Hun. However, there were also legends of earlier martyrs such as Saint Denis. With Clovis I' public conversion to Christianity, Paris became a focus for a spate of new religious building. An early church and baptistry dedicated to Saint Stephen was already located on the Île de la Cité, at a site where a temple to Jupiter had once stood, close to the future site of the cathedral of Notre Dame. In the cemetery to the south, cults had arisen around the tombs of Marcellus and Crescentia. On the rise east of the Forum, on the "mountain" of the current Panthéon, a funerary church dedicated to Genovefa (Geneviève) was expanded by Clovis I and Queen Chlothild and dedicated to the Holy Apostles. Clovis was buried there in 511, and in time the church was the burial place for Chlothild and other members of the dynasty. In addition to the church on the Île de la Cité. we learn from Gregory of Tours that Paris had six suburban churches by the late sixth century.[32] By the end of the Merovingian period, Paris had at least seventeen churches, testament to a vigorous religious building and refurbishment program.

In the seventh century Merovingian kings were particularly active in founding churches and collecting holy relics. Burial close to the remains of saints, known as burial *ad sanctos*, was supposed to encourage the saints to protect the nearby Christians in the afterlife. From Clovis I's time forward, Merovingian kings and queens arranged for their own burials and those of family members within the holy precincts of churches that they favored. In the early seventh century Saint Denis outside of Paris was elevated to become a royal necropolis, but even before that time Merovingian kings were buried in the churches that they had founded and beautified in Paris. In addition to the church of the Holy Apostles where Clovis and Chlothild were buried, another great church was built by Clovis' son Childebert, dedicated to Saint Vincent and the Holy Cross. Situated in field west of the city, this church was eventually renamed for Germanus, a saintly bishop of Paris, to become known as Saint-Germain-des-Prés. The church became a major burial site for early Merovingian kings. One of Clovis' sons, Childebert (d. 558) and his wife Ultrogotha, and two of Clovis' grandsons, Charibert (d. 567), and Chilperic (d. 584) and his wife Fredegund, and their son Chlothar II (d. 629) and his wife Beretrude were buried there. Eventually, Clovis II's second son Childeric II and his wife Bilichild, both murdered, would be buried in the royal necropolis. This formidable pile of dead Merovingian royals meant that the church had great prominence on the physical and mental space of Paris in Balthild's time. On the right side of the Seine, visible downstream from the Île-de-la-Cité was a new church (*basilica nova*) built by Chilperic I. And further north, at a location outside of Paris, was the church of Saint Denis built by Dagobert, Balthild's father-in-law, and used as his resting place.

One can only imagine the impression that such a city would have had on an Anglo-Saxon visitor, whatever her social station. With its already long history of habitation, its fine Roman buildings, many of which would have been visible and functional in the seventh century, and some which will have been adapted and still in use, and the great dynastic churches built by earlier Merovingians, Balthild was introduced to a busy city with a grid of stone-paved roads, an urban landscape, a port, beautiful churches, municipal buildings, palaces, and private dwellings. There were also areas of squalor, no doubt.

From Dagobert's time, an international market attracted wares into the city for further distribution. The river Seine provided transportation up and down the river, and its flow was also a means of sanitation. The hills provided vistas of the river, distant churches, and dense forests beyond. Although clerical sources tell us about the new churches erected in Paris, Roman roads and some of the stone buildings were repaired and maintained. Indeed, it is now thought that Paris was not devastated during the "barbarian" invasions as was maintained in older sources, but rather that we should think of Paris as a battered but resilient late Roman city. While it is true that some dilapidated buildings were quarried for stone, and that already in the third century the great arena had been plundered by the inhabitants to shore up the fortification on the east side of the Île de la Cité, the casual comment by Gregory of Tours that King Chilperic repaired the city's amphitheater in 577 and held performances there indicates that monumental public buildings of Roman construction could be used and valued, and that stonemasonry skills were sufficiently competent for the ambitious restoration of an enormous building.[33] As yet, no evidence has been found of city walls around the left bank; the ability to retreat to the fortified Île de la Cité may have continued to present the population with the best option in the Merovingian period before the ninth-century Viking raids prompted authorities to build a fortified enclosure on the right bank.[34] Indeed, at any one time, we can be sure that the Paris that Balthild knew was a place of ongoing construction and that Parisians would have felt they were living in a flourishing and expanding city.

Cities like Paris, Rouen, and Soissons could be impressive in their fading late Roman grandeur. By the time Balthild married into the Neustrian royal family, its members were often—perhaps mostly—spending time in royal villas outside of the cities, sometimes termed a *palatium* if it was a royal seat of government.[35] During her time at court Balthild must have spent much of her time at the royal villa of Chelles outside of Paris, or at Clichy, and perhaps at Nogent, Palaiseau, or Rueil. To the north-west of Paris, there was a royal villa outside Rouen at Le Vaudreuil that was important in the late sixth century. And the royal villas of Berny and Compiègne, outside of Soissons, are mentioned regularly in the sources. During the reign of Clovis II's grandfather, Chlothar II, the royal villa and complex at Clichy had risen to special prominence by virtue of its proximity to, and cultic association with, the church of Saint Denis. Indeed, Chlothar II lived his final years exclusively at Clichy, a villa which continued to be important through the seventh century until it was abandoned during the reign of Balthild's third reigning son, Theuderic III (673/75–690). As important as Clichy was, the location of this villa is today unknown, a symbol of the problem that besets historians interested in knowing more about the centers of secular power in these centuries. Over time, country villas may have become less important as centers for affairs of state, but that did not necessarily mean that they were totally abandoned. How long did a royal site hold on as a symbolic or economic center beyond the patchy view we get from written sources? With little or nothing remaining of them, we are left to wonder what a royal villa site would have looked like in the seventh century. Would a Merovingian villa be recognizable to a Gallo-Roman of the previous century? It seems likely that it would. Unless the royal site was centered on an old Roman *castrum*, which would provide defensive walls, Merovingian villas appear to have been residences without fortification, built of stone with roof tiles and with interiors in which it was possible to conduct a late Roman style of life.[36] Although many villa sites were destroyed in the fifth century, and they had been less concentrated in northern Gaul than in the south to begin with, Merovingian sources continue to mention villa sites, in which the amenities for luxury would have persisted and could be improved upon.

The small community of Chelles, where Balthild would later establish her convent, had been favored by Merovingian kings since the time of the first Clovis, the first Christian king of the dynasty. In addition to the villa structures that constituted the royal "palace," queen Clothild had been instrumental in setting up a church there dedicated to Saint George, ensuring that the royal entourage had the benefit of clerical services as would have been necessary for a stay of any duration. In Balthild's time Chelles was a place with a history but also a place that was prized and loved.

Over the course of the seventh century, tensions between Neustria and Austrasia encouraged Neustrian kings to locate royal residences further east in the kingdom in places that were strategic for the oversight of all three kingdoms. During Balthild and Clovis' marriage, Clichy (outside Paris) and Compiègne (outside Soissons) were the most important royal centers of government. But during Balthild's regency and then rule of her sons, Clichy was progressively abandoned in favor of Compiègne to the east.[37] Balthild's residence at Chelles and the convent she had founded, together with its proximity to Paris and its excellent hunting grounds, secured the continued importance of Chelles when other royal sites faded from view. The importance of royal villas to the Merovingian kings, queens, and the court, shows a desire to accommodate life-style preferences that privileged access to the outdoors, recreation, hunting, and space to expand. However, none of these sites were very far distant from fortified cities and their bishops, and we know that kings continued to occupy Paris on occasion throughout this period.

Dress, Food, and Abundance: The Splendor of a Merovingian Court

The Merovingian court was itinerant in the sense that it was in session wherever the king and his advisors were residing at any given moment. For the most part the court was in residence in one the major cities of the Neustrian kingdom or close to whichever royal villa where the king was resident. Royal residences in the countryside were considered to be "palaces" wherever they were held, and with the sizeable personnel needed to run a royal center effectively, buildings must have included public spaces, and the palace complex would have had rooms in which secretaries and other personnel could work. Bishops seem to have spent considerable time at royal palaces and were evidently able to conduct business from there. A few even died at royal villas, presumably because they were in attendance on the king.

The physical appearance of the rooms in which royal activities took place is unknown to us as above-grade evidence of palaces and villas has not survived. Archaeology can provide us with some insight into the fabric of elite buildings of this era, as can the few remaining Merovingian structures of ecclesiastical buildings, such as crypts. Still, we can imagine that court members enjoyed any means of comfort available to them. Merovingian writings offer glimpses of comfortable living, often in the context of all the nice things that ascetics were expected to renounce. The impression overall is of a court environment infused with color, ornamentation, and luxury.

The Merovingian nobility relished personal finery. Fine clothing communicated wealth, identity, the king's favor, international connections, family connections and affiliation, and religious status. Although the court was influenced by the austere monastic movement of Columbanus and his disciples, as was Balthild herself, at court the king and queen would have dressed in the finest textiles; silks imported or gifted from Byzantium were prized, used, and copied by local artisans. The embroidered bejeweled necklace on the linen "chasuble" or "grand chemise" among Balthild's relics reveals the desirability of Byzantine design in high status jewelry.[38] And like so many women of this era, Balthild will have worn finger rings with precious gems and possibly also a signet ring to seal her correspondence and her belongings.[39]

Courtiers, especially those holding some form of office, would have dressed in a manner that reflected and enhanced the general splendor of the court. Cutting a good figure and attention to personal grooming was important. We are told that in his youth, Eligius' manly beauty enhanced the court: "He was tall with a rosy face. He had a pretty head of hair with curly locks. His hands were honest and his fingers long. He had the face of an angel and a prudent look."[40] He was also clean-shaven, evidently court style for those in secular as well as religious life, and when it was later discovered that some of his hair clippings had supernatural power, it was reported it was scented, "aromatic as with pungent unguents."[41]

The wealthy wore clothes made of linen, silk, and wool, with linen undergarments as a breathable and protective base-layer. Robes were dyed, with yellow and red as favored colors. Tunics could be trimmed with gold thread, worn belted with a finely wrought silver buckle encrusted with precious gems, even if, as was said of both Audoin and Eligius, they wore hair-shirts beneath their finery, even during their secular career.[42] In public life hair-shirts were not for show. As goldsmith-courtier, Eligius cut a dashing figure: "At first, he was used to wear gold and gems on his clothes having belts composed of gold and gems and elegantly jeweled purses, linens covered with red metal and golden sacs hemmed with gold and all of the most precious fabrics including all of silk." But this was a facade according to his biographer, because "as he proceeded to perfection, he gave the ornaments for the needs of the poor. Then you would see him, whom you had once seen gleaming with the weight of the gold and gems that covered him, go covered in the vilest clothing with a rope for a belt."[43] In Europe, hairshirts were generally made of horsehair, but camel hair was favored by ascetics who craved a closer connection with the storied privations of the desert fathers of the Mediterranean world; we know of at least one camel in northern Gaul that could have provided this itchy essential![44]

Belts encrusted with jewels were worn by women as well as by men and following the example of Queen Radegund, the gift of a royal belt was seen as a particularly significant and generous donation to a church or monastery. Balthild is said to have given one of her belts to the monastery of Corbion.[45]

Royal residences would have been splendid, but with only fragments and decorated crypts to guide us, there is nothing above ground to give us a direct view of how Merovingians lived at court. However, we will probably not go too far wrong if we suppose that the luxuries of previous centuries continued in some form. We also have clues if we consider that secular buildings and religious buildings may have expressed a similar aesthetic, and we know that monasteries built in this period boasted cloisters and porticos, rooms to conduct business, cellars, and areas for communal dining. Columns with decorated capitals and decorated bases were still used as decorative items in stone buildings. Smaller than their monumental Roman counterparts, but wonderfully carved with exuberant and eclectic irregularity, these columns seem to be a deliberate and playful disruption of classical uniformity in service of a distinctive late Merovingian aesthetic.[46] Favored designs from antiquity continued in popularity: acanthus leaves, serpents, anchors, and palm leaves. Molded tiles decorated the floors and perhaps the walls and ceilings of public rooms and stucco panels enhanced walls. The columns of the crypt of Jouarre were sourced from quarries in the Pyrenees, which must have supplied other building materials as well.[47] Mosaic and glass fragments suggest that some buildings at least retained the late antique jeweled-style aesthetic. The use of plaster on walls also continued as it was abundant in the Paris region. Plaster walls could be painted and decorated with natural and religious images. Tile roofs were still part of the cityscape, with antefix decorations attested in large numbers, continuing the Roman tradition of roof decoration, although now with faces of the saints.[48]

Is it too far a stretch to imagine that some interior rooms looked more like the rooms of Pompeii than a Germanic hunting lodge? Reliquaries gifted to the royal couple may have surrounded them as we know from the

Life of Eligius that relics were sometimes hung on the walls to aid private devotion. Diplomatic gifts of tableware of the sort unearthed at Sutton-Hoo would have been expected to adorn the tables on state occasions. Illuminated manuscripts with decorative book covers with gems set in wood, ivory, and precious metal, brought Byzantine and Coptic designs to the heart of Neustria. Beautiful objects such as agate and onyx vases were heirlooms, and like jewelry, included older Roman forms together with newer pieces.[49] In leaving England, Balthild left behind a relatively rustic, wood-bound world of the Anglo-Saxons to live in late Roman palaces of marble, tile, and painted stucco.

Soft furnishings must have been common and easily transported when the court moved. They made a palace into a home. In late antiquity, embroidered and woven curtains divided rooms into living spaces, and insulated against drafts. Cushions were used for comfort when reclining on couches around a dining table, at least in geographical areas where Roman cultural preferences continued, such as in Clermont.[50] Feather beds were rejected by ascetics precisely because it was a sacrifice to renounce them; their modest beds became relics after their deaths.[51]

Food consumption and feasting at court drew on the best produce to be found in town and country. Meat was a prized protein on a table and would have included beef, pork, and to a lesser extent lamb and goat.[52] Tender young animals would have been favored at court, especially in the consumption of veal and suckling-pig which could be boiled, steamed, or roasted, then dipped in a honey-vinegar sauce.[53] Chicken, fattened goose, and mallard duck was available, and even the occasional peacock (preferably hung for five or six days) adorned the table of the rich on special occasions according to Anthimus, the dietician at the sixth-century Frankish court. The Franks learned to eat from the Romans and for as long as the elite could draw on the bounty of their estates and the long-distance trade routes that continued to bring spices from the east, as they still as late as Balthild's time, food preparation would be used to showcase both exotic and local delicacies. Game animals such as stags and boar were prized for meat and for the hunting experience that had acquired them; hare was a lesser game animal but also important to a well-furnished table. Concern for meat-providing breeds can be seen in attention to animal husbandry which extended to the introduction of new breeds into northern Gaul, for example, the many-horned sheep that were introduced into northern France from Britain.[54] Salted pork was reputedly a Frankish favorite. Beans, legumes, and root vegetables were staples although opinions diverged on how healthy these items were, and their preparation might need to be more carefully managed than the preparation of meat. Soft-boiled eggs from a variety of fowl, were appreciated with a little salt for seasoning. Bread, wine, and beer would fill out a meal and were considered healthy in moderation. Ocean fish (sturgeon was favored by the rich) and shellfish were largely confined to elite tables, and river fish, or fish raised in a fish-tank (*vivarium*) ensured that fish was available for holy days.[55] All food could be seasoned with salt and with herbs such as coriander, dill, and leek (known to us mainly from lists of monastic gardens and from Anthimus' dietary work), and for the rich and well connected, pepper was the ultimate luxury. Olives and olive oil were a cooking essential into the seventh century and were also used to add flavor to boiled foods. Although writing in the previous century, Anthimus' description of a dish of lentils enlivened by sumac shows how imported spices could deliver a robust flavor profile even to the simplest of dishes.[56] Fresh cheeses could be sourced locally, and ripened cheeses were brought in from further afield. Seasonal fruit such as apples, pears, plums, peaches, cherries, and quinces could be paired with honey to add sweet elements to the table. Fresh figs and forest fruits such as blackberries were prized as well as a variety of nuts. Dried fruits such as dried figs, dates, and raisins and sultanas added sweetness to savory as well as sweet dishes.[57] There were plenty of delicacies available to tempt the palates of a hungry court.

Food consumption could also be dangerous, especially when available in some abundance. Stomach ailments afflicted those whom Anthimus sought to advise in the sixth century. Boiling and blanching foods went some way to mitigating the worst effects of natural poisons in food, and wine and oil was prescribed for those who had eaten wild turtle doves that had feasted on hellebore since this poison could be transmitted to the hapless consumer causing vomiting and diarrhea.[58] Religious observances such as Lenten fasts and a preference for plain foods would also have been expected at court on occasion, following the lead of the clergy in residence. In Merovingian texts, food abundance and scarcity was made the subject of holy miracles, making the rhythms of feasting and fasting at court and elsewhere part of the religious life for all sectors of society.[59]

One advantage of a moveable court installed periodically in countryside villas was the diminished presence of the rats that had plagued the dense urban environments of late Roman towns. Domestic cats and dogs, both well attested in northern Gaul, must also have helped keep rat numbers at bay.[60] Merovingian court life with its protein-rich diet and regular activity had the potential to provide a healthy environment relative to ordinary city life in late antiquity. Balthild bore her children and thrived. And some people, like Bishop Eligius and Bishop Leudegar, lived into venerable old age.

The People of a Merovingian Court

Wherever it was held, the court was the administrative center of the kingdom and was populated by busy officials. The court was also the most cosmopolitan hub in the kingdom. Envoys and ambassadors with their entourages brought gifts, hostages, and petitioners.[61] Closer to home, the court was the "melting pot for the Frankish provincial elite."[62]

The king was the indispensable center of governance. Around him were the many officials and advisors who consulted with him and carried out his dictates. Royal cities, the *sedes regiae*, were still the administrative centers of the realm, but by Balthild and Clovis II's time, royal villa-palaces in the countryside were also equipped to handle essential functions. The individual closest to the king in power was the mayor of the palace who oversaw both executive and judicial realms in the name of the king. Around them both was the steady buzz of people necessary to the smooth running of government: major and minor functionaries, the chancellor (referendary) in charge of the chancery, treasury employees including tax-collectors, and the king's retinue composed of friends and counselors, bodyguards and members of the military, bishops and clerics, and young boys and men being trained up to serve the next generation.[63] Tutors trained the boys who Balthild befriended at court as a "nurturer." We rarely hear of armed personnel at court, but they were there. Bodyguards (*antrustiones*) protected the king and his family, and since men in secular life were generally armed, there were many around the royal family to provide protection. As Laury Sarti explains, "the military elite was involved to a significant extent in the core functionalities of Merovingian governance."[64] We hear of an armed group being present as part of Balthild's retinue when she attended Eligius' funeral with her young son in 660.[65] Finally, Merovingian kings could rely on the continuity of an administrative cadre that, like the modern civil service, kept the business of government moving. The Merovingian court was also the center of a legal and documentary culture that relied on scribes producing charters, wills, judgments, edicts, and all the "papyrus work" that was needed on a day-to-day basis.

A foreign queen could provide cultural diversity to a court. From the beginning of the Merovingian dynasty, some kings had married foreign queens who brought their own experiences and customs from foreign courts: Childeric I married Basina whose natal origins are unknown but who was said to have come from Thuringia; Clovis I had married a Burgundian, Chlothild; Chlothar I married the Thuringian Radegund; Sigibert I married the Visigothic princess Brunhild, and his brother Chilperic I married Galswinth, her sister. The latter marriage was spectacularly unsuccessful as Galswinth was murdered by her husband, apparently at the instigation of Fredegund, the low-born queen she had temporarily displaced. In the seventh century royal wives are less visible to us, and while they might be foreigners like Bilichild, Nantechild, and Balthild, they were either not from royal stock, or their natal status went unrecorded by contemporary authors. Cross-Channel marital connections also went in the other direction: at the end of the sixth century the Frankish princess Bertha was married to King Aethelbert of Kent.

We have already noted the importance of the mayor of the palace. Alongside the mayor, many bishops with their clerical retinues spent time at court to further the interests of their flocks, and perhaps their own. The influence of Eligius of Noyon (examined in Chapter 4, pp. 55–87) on the royal couple, and on Balthild during her regency, appears to have been profound and consequential. It was the power of bishops and clerics that we see Balthild cultivating in the Life. Yet this was also a dangerous time for bishops whose political ambitions exposed them to removal, and in some cases assassination. More bishops were killed in Merovingian Francia in the seventh century than in any other part of Europe at this time, a vulnerability attributed to their close integration into high politics.[66] As we will see in Chapter 6 (pp. 122–39), Balthild was herself accused of playing a part in the murder of bishops.

Merchants, pilgrims, and foreign travelers passed through Frankish towns. France lay at the geographic center of Christian Europe. Saxons are occasionally named in Merovingian texts, such as Aeghynan who attended the Council of Clichy in 626/27, and Thille, Eligius' assistant.[67] Indeed, from the Life of Eligius we get the sense of a society bustling with the movement of people, great and small. We learn of Roman, Italian, and Gothic "legates" who visited Eligius in preparation for visiting the king. Foreign royals also came through the court. We know of one visit by King Suinthila of the Visigoths to Dagobert's court.[68] Irish and Anglo-Saxon missionaries found their religious "exile" in the monasteries of Gaul.[69] Retired princess-abbesses crossed the Channel on their way to Chelles, and royal pilgrims and political exiles made their way to, or through, Frankish territories. Wilfrid of Ripon, for example, spent extended periods in Frankish territories and chose to be ordained as bishop of York while still resident in Gaul: the opulence of episcopal ordination ritual in Lyon was flamboyant, at least as described by his hagiographer Stephen of Ripon who noted that the bishop was carried aloft on a golden chair.[70] Whether there was any truth to the elevated episcopal chair, Wilfrid was keen, it seems, to tap into the magnificence that Merovingian episcopal rituals could provide, and which he viewed as a ritual worthy of the great office he now held.

Above all, the Merovingian court presented itself as a bastion of orthodoxy. Non-Christian inhabitants, "gentiles," and those who held to different practices, were often viewed with suspicion. In the sixth century we hear of Jews at court, probably visitors from southern Gaul where the Jewish communities we know of were concentrated, but such references are gone by the seventh century.[71] Irish missionaries were by now indelibly part of the northern spiritual landscape, but they were also sometimes suspected of marginal views that needed to be kept in check.[72]

Alongside those present voluntarily, there were others who were constrained by circumstance to be there. We hear of hostages taken, and ransomed, but they are not strongly present in the sources. However, the court was teeming with domestic servants and slaves. There were kitchens and wine stores overseen by cellarers, and cooks prepared and preserved the food. Servants served, including cupbearers such as Balthild had herself been in Erchinoald's household. Slaves did the dirty work of keeping the rooms of the elite clean, including serving the queen in her bedchamber. Balthild had been able to shed her servile condition, but she was surrounded by those who could not and, as we have seen, in the reigns of some kings, ladies of the bedchamber ended up in the king's bed.

In short, the Merovingian court was a busy and diverse place. It must have also been a place where many languages could be heard spoken: ambassadors and legates did not travel alone, and language interpreters are mentioned in contemporary sources.

How Prepared Was Balthild for her Role?

As a foreigner at court, how prepared was Balthild for her new role? Sadly, while it is possible to learn something of the educational attainment of seventh-century aristocratic woman in Merovingian Gaul, our sources for female education in England outside of monastic institutions are nonexistent. Tellingly, perhaps, Balthild's Life does not indicate whether she was well educated or even educated at all; it is her piety that is always stressed. The absence of any comment about her education is notable when set alongside the claims made for noble women and other holy queens of the time. However, she may have learned to read and write in Erchinoald's household, if not before, and during her regency she lent her name to donation documents alongside that of her son, although this could have been accomplished with a seal. When her hagiographer described her life at court, she was praised as "best nurturer" (*optima nutrix*) of the young and adolescents, "exhorting the young to religious studies." *Nutrix* is a term that encompasses the maternal sense of a nurse but also one who encourages, guides, and nurtures the young. But there is no claim that she undertook their education herself. Unlike Queen Radegund in the sixth century who, we are told, imitated priestly processions as a child and composed poems, or the aristocrat Aldegund of Maubeuge, who is said to have received elements of a classical education (the *trivium*), Bathild is never described in this way. She is never described as reading, even in the convent—rather she attended the divine reading.[73] During her secular career she was instrumental in initiating major policies, but these achievements are described as taking place in an oral environment—through the help of churchmen and from personally petitioning her husband. In brief, it is possible that even if she were a high-status Anglo-Saxon, Balthild may have joined the sophisticated court of Clovis II at an educational disadvantage to those around her.

Balthild's Sons

Balthild's most important role in her marriage was to bear healthy sons. A large part of her ability to become a figure of power was her success in doing this. The birth of her first son, Chlothar, would have been great cause for celebration and a personal relief for her. Her hagiographer, laconic on any personal details of his subject, merely comments that it was God's will that "royal progeny might come forth" and that "this has now come to pass."[74]

However, Balthild's first pregnancy assumes an importance in some sources that suggests that the stakes were high. Indeed, it was the subject of a prophecy, and in this context we are told a rather touching tale about Balthild's very realistic anxieties about securing a male heir.[75] Bishop Eligius reassured her, predicting that she would indeed produce a boy:

> For when he was still in the womb and the queen was greatly afraid that she might have a daughter and the realm succumb because of it, Eligius came to her and reassured her. In the presence of the pregnant woman, he predicted a male birth to all and foretold her son from the mystery of regeneration. He then named the child in the womb and promised certain pieces of work that a child could use and had them made and ordered them to be kept against the birth. And all happened as he predicted which at last was attested by the king. For the queen brought forth a son and he was like a little son to Eligius. And the king called him by the name Chlothar which Eligius had bestowed upon him. After this, God multiplied his progeny and he sired two more sons.[76]

Balthild's anxiety was understandable as her position was entirely dependent on her husband and on her ability to produce heirs. She would also have known that servant girls who married Merovingian kings did not secure their status unless they provided sons, and if Bilichild's fate was anything to go by, far worse things could happen.

The story in which Eligius allayed Balthild's pregnancy fears was penned by Audoin of Rouen who was Eligius' friend and was, like him, a courtier before he became bishop. Both were bishops at the time of this first royal birth, and Eligius' calming role was easily viewed, in hindsight, as prophetic. Pregnancy visions were the most common stories told about secular women in religious sources, invariably in the form of a prophecy for the birth of a holy son or daughter.[77] Eligius' prophesy is examined further in Chapter 6 (pp. 122–39), but note here the touching detail that Eligius prepared items (toys?) for the child, a reassurance for the mother that the child would live.

Although we do not have exact dates for the birth of her sons, Chlothar was likely born around 650; her second son in 653, and her third son in 654. In short, in her twenties, Balthild managed to produce three healthy sons within five years. However, while Balthild was protecting the succession in Neustria, events were taking a darker turn in Austrasia on the death of Clovis' half-brother, Sigibert.

Grimoald's Coup

When King Clovis II died in 657, Balthild assumed the position of queen-regent with the mayor of the palace, Ebroin, governing alongside. One of the ongoing tasks of her regency was to deal with the aftermath of the "Grimoald affair." The catalyst for this crisis was the death of Balthild's brother-in-law, Sigibert of Austrasia, on February 1, 651 (or possibly in 656). Sigibert's death had opened an opportunity for Grimoald, mayor of the Austrasian palace, to intervene in the royal succession, placing his "adopted" son on the throne and sending Sigibert's son and heir, Dagobert II, on an extended tour of Ireland.[78] The details of the coup are obscure and scholars have reached no consensus on when the coup started or how long the "coup" had lasted.[79] The coup may have started in 651 or in 656, both dates before Clovis II's death had made Balthild regent. But the uncertainty of the dates makes it unclear whether a particularly shocking accusation against Clovis II should be legitimately attributed to him.

Grimoald had been finally brought down by an ambush of Neustrian Franks. He was handed over to Clovis in Paris where he was imprisoned. "His death came with a great deal of torture," states the *LHF*.[80] Accusations of torture within the nobility are not common, and the assault on Grimoald the kingmaker was shocking enough to be notable. However, if the dates of the coup were on the later side, it may have been Ebroin, not Clovis, who was responsible for Grimoald's tortured death.

The crisis of Grimoald's coup was finally resolved when Balthild's second son, Childeric II was placed on the Austrasian throne and married to Bilichild, his first cousin, daughter of Sigibert III of Austrasia. The early years of Childeric and Bilichild's reign in Austrasia fell under the regency of Bilichild's mother (Sigibert's widow) Chimnechild. Thus, for a brief period, both Neustria and Austrasia were governed by queen-regents. The two women, Balthild and Chimnechild, must have worked together to secure the marriage that brought peace to the Austrasian kingdom.[81]

It has been argued that the Grimoald affair had a wider context in Frankish-Byzantine relations at this time, and that the resolution of the situation strengthened Balthild's position alongside her mayor, Ebroin, and that this was related to a purge of bishops by exile or execution in 663.[82] As we shall see, this purge of bishops was consequential for Balthild's hold on power and for her reputation.

4
Regent, Reformer, and Rescuer of Slaves

Clovis II died in October 657.[1] Balthild was now a widow with three young sons: Chlothar, Childeric, and Theuderic. Unlike Dagobert, who was ill long enough before his death to appoint his wife as regent, Clovis II's death in 657 seems to have come suddenly. The *Liber historiae Francorum* relates that Clovis had reigned sixteen years, suggesting that his death came at age twenty, but the Fredegar *Chronicle* continuator recorded his reign as eighteen years, which would have made him twenty-two or twenty-three, which accords better with a birth date around 635. Balthild's age can only be estimated as being about the same, so she became a widow in her early twenties. The *LHF* and the Fredegar continuator perfunctorily records Clovis' death, stating merely that "The Franks thereupon made (*statuunt*) his eldest boy, Chlothar, king, with his queen-mother by his side."[2] Thus, it was the Frankish nobles that ensured the succession of the young king and affirmed Balthild's regency. The term "regent" and "regency" was not used until the early modern period, but it conveys the essence of how her power was enacted. In her seven years as queen-regent, Balthild, like Nantechild before her, proved politically active.

As we consider Balthild's term as regent it is worth reflecting on how her mother-in-law, Nantechild, had exercised her own power as regent during Clovis' minority. Like Balthild, Nantechild was described as a servant girl, *puella*.[3] She was also likely Anglo-Saxon. Nantechild may have been a *puella* when her husband married her, but she gained all the authority of a queen by her marriage to Dagobert and birth of a son. According to Fredegar's *Chronicle*, before Dagobert died he commended Nantechild to the mayor of the palace, Aega, who supported her in her regency and who was reported to have ruled worthily alongside her.[4] Mayors were appointed with the agreement of the Frankish nobles and the queen-regent. When Aega died, Erchinoald was appointed as mayor to succeed him. Nantechild appointed Flaochad as mayor to the dependent kingdom of Burgundy, working with Erchinoald.[5] Significantly, both Flaochad and Erchinoald were related to Nantechild. Erchinoald was related by blood to Dagobert's mother,

Balthild of Francia: Anglo-Saxon Slave, Merovingian Queen, and Abolitionist Saint. Isabel Moreira,
Oxford University Press. © Oxford University Press 2024. DOI: 10.1093/oso/9780197518663.003.0004

and Flaochad, her appointee as mayor of Burgundy, was married to Nantechild's niece, Ragnoberta. We do not know how directly the niece was related to Nantechild, but Fredegar depicts the marriage as part of the project to install Flaochad in Burgundy, stating that Nantechild and Flaochad were co-conspirators in matters contrary to God's will. Nantechild evidently chose to rule through family connections and in Erchinoald she had a mayor who, like herself, had Anglo-Saxon connections.[6] Erchinoald's mayoralty spanned Nantechild's regency, Clovis' and Balthild's marriage, and the early years of Balthild's regency. With Erchinoald at the helm, guiding the regency of two Anglo-Saxon queens in turn, the Neustrian court was a place with strong cross-channel connections and cultural affinity. First as queen, then as queen-regent, Balthild was in a court that understood the role and stability offered by a well-tuned regency.

Even with the succession arranged so quickly, and the example of Nantechild within memory, there was much that Balthild needed to do to secure her position and influence. For one thing, after Flaochad had ended his mayoralty and life ignobly, he was not replaced, and Erchinoald served as sole mayor for the remainder of Clovis II's reign, an act that was touted as a sign that the "Burgundians and the Neustrians were united."[7] This merger continued under the regency so that Balthild had only to deal with a single mayor at a time, but she also inherited political discontent in Burgundy. When Erchinoald died a new mayor took power, a man from an opposing Neustrian faction named Ebroin. Although it seems she consented to this appointment, and worked with the mayor during her time as regent, the discontents and machinations that swirled around Ebroin colored the end of her time in power.

Balthild may have been a regent, but she was also a widow. Widows with sons were better positioned to succeed than those without, but it was a condition that left a male vacuum that could be filled by remarriage, or in Balthild's case, the male influence of the mayor of the palace, Frankish nobles, and prominent churchmen. Balthild's hagiographer provides us with important insight into the transition that saw her become a regent for her young son. After noting Clovis's death, the hagiographer continued: "In his place after him, his son, the late King Chlothar, took the throne of the Franks and then also with the excellent princes, Chrodebert, bishop of Paris, Lord Audoin, and Ebroin, mayor of the palace, along with the other great magnates and very many of the rest."[8] Here we see a trifecta of power: the mayor of the Neustrian palace Ebroin who was Erchinoald's successor,

Chrodebert, the bishop of Paris, Neustria's capital city where Balthild and her son were based, and finally, Audoin, bishop of the important Roman city of Rouen, a man who had been part of the famous court circle of Chlothar II and Dagobert, and who was friend and eventual biographer of another important figure in Balthild's life, Eligius, bishop of Noyon. Audoin was now quite aged, being in his early to mid-sixties during Balthild's regency. Churchmen and secular potentates were the advisors to a young king, alongside his mother. This was how the Franks ruled during a minority. The hagiographer wanted this point to be made explicit: "And, indeed, the kingdom of the Franks was maintained in peace."[9] When Balthild's middle son, Childeric, was made king of Austrasia, "by the arrangement of Lady Balthild and, indeed, through the advice of the great magnates," we are incidentally informed of the way royal mothers were instrumental in the successful completion of dynastic marriages: she must have had a role in making the match between her son and Bilichild, the daughter of the Austrasian queen Chimnechild. Balthild's task was to keep the competing interests of powerful men in check.[10] Her hagiographer continues: "As we believe that, with God guiding, and in accordance with the great faith of Lady Balthild, these three kingdoms kept harmony of peace among themselves."[11] Disagreements there may have been, but the importance of the queen as a figurehead was understood by contemporary observers, and all continental accounts are consistent in their praise of her diplomatic abilities. Balthild was active in the political life of the realm, but she was also wise to maintain the balance of male power that was essential for political stability and that secured her sons' successions.

"A Great Award Awaits Her": Balthild's Social and Religious Projects

If Balthild's story had been left only to the chroniclers, we would know nothing of her political interests. It is fortunate that her contemporary hagiographer gave considerable space to them. His information fits with what we know of the conversations that were guiding high politics at this time. The list of her projects is impressive and they sit at the intersection of political power, religious mission, and humanitarian need. She was instrumental in freeing trafficked slaves and prohibiting Christian trafficking in her kingdom, a prohibition of infanticide, and the compassionate burial of the dead.

She was also active in promoting new religious trends in her realm, seen especially in her promotion of monastic spirituality, monastic building, and the internal regulation of existing religious communities. All these activities made her a force for good in the eyes of her biographer. While the author made it clear that these policies were enacted with the support and encouragement of the mayors of the palace and the clergy, there is no reason to doubt her personal agency in these matters or to suppose that these were not policies very close to her heart. Indeed, the careful list of policies and enactments in the hagiographer's account may well have originated in Balthild's own desire to be remembered for these things. Her final years in her convent at Chelles, host to the slave girls she had rescued, must also have provided an ongoing identification with these policies. If slaves entered monasteries in any great number, then in Balthild's time, Chelles, and the other monastic institutions patronized by her, were engaged in a radical social experiment that disrupted the entrenched structures of unfree labor. Furthermore, Balthild's concern for the enslaved, which surely arose at least in part from her own experience, was ahead of its time both in terms of its public expression and policy enactment.

In view of her reputation as an abolitionist in future centuries, it is pertinent to ask the question: Does Balthild deserve the reputation she achieved in the early modern period, and especially in the nineteenth century, as an icon for the abolition of slavery?

Freeing Captives and Slaves

The act of ransoming captives had a long history in Gaul as a conspicuously pious act. Bishops had a role as negotiators in the liberation of captives and sometimes ended up as patrons of those who were freed. In the turmoil of the fifth and sixth centuries some of these liberation acts were redressing legal wrongs within Gaul and involved the rescue of men of free status (women are rarely mentioned) who had been captured and for whom ransom (and possible repayment) was feasible. Bishops were on secure ground in such cases because they were restoring freedom to those who had a legal right to it and because they gained public gratitude. For this reason, ransoming captives was a virtue for which bishops were traditionally praised by their hagiographers and their actions were often framed as miracles.

It is less clear how often bishops were rescuing slaves who were not otherwise legally free. Freeing a slave with a master required compensation to the owner and thus this kind of rescue would be complicated and expensive. As in the previous century, in the seventh century we hear little of the lives of those born into servitude beyond what was legislated by kings and regulated in church councils. There were reasons for this. Slave labor was integral to the Merovingian economy and since slaves belonged to people, mostly landowners, but also the landowning church, slaves could not be freed without a great deal of trouble—the agreement of their master or mistress, compensation to owners or their heirs, and a potential loss of labor to the landowner. There may also have been a sense that too much emancipation among the local slave population would challenge the status quo and undermine the religious and secular views that had supported it for centuries.

When Gallic bishops assembled in council to consider the liberation of slaves, it was largely in the context of rescuing Christian slaves from Jewish owners, drawing for this ultimately on the precedent of the Theodosian Code, the collection of Roman imperial law compiled in the 430s that was most used in the west.[12] In some cases they deliberated on rates of compensation for the owner, for example, some sixth-century councils indicated that Christian slaves bought from Jewish households must be bought for a fair price, specified in the Council of Mâcon as 12 solidi. The Council of Clichy (626 or 627) convened during the reign of King Chlothar II (Clovis II's grandfather) specified that Christian slaves should not be sold to pagans or Jews, and Christian slave owners must sell their Christian slaves to other Christians.[13] Liberating Christian slaves was viewed as pious and was encouraged in church canons.[14]

It is in the seventh century that we begin to hear about individuals arriving in France as slaves from foreign shores in the context of trade. These slaves suffered a permanent displacement posing a challenge to be resolved on Neustrian soil. Their plight was not directly addressed in Salic Law. Salic Law forbade the capture and transportation of slaves abroad, imposing penalties on the guilty and subjecting them to an elaborate process of information discovery.[15] However, the scenario that the law envisaged, that Neustrian slaves—mainly agricultural and domestic workers—would be transported to places outside Neustria, or outside the territories of the Merovingian kingdoms, must have been rare. Still, the law enshrined a principle—that taking slaves out of the kingdom and overseas was problematic and certainly criminal when slaves were abducted from their owners to do so. However, the law did not address the legality of the importation of slaves into Neustria.

The crisis of traded slaves in the 650s and 660s can be traced in three major sources: The Life of Balthild, the Life of Eligius of Noyon, and the Council of Chalon-sur-Saône convened around the time of Balthild's marriage to Clovis II. Let's look at the council first.

The Council of Chalon-sur-Saône

Balthild and Clovis' marriage coincided with a time of reform in the kingdom. Sometime shortly before or shortly after their marriage in 650 Clovis and his palace mayor Aega convened the Council of Chalon-sur-Saône in the church of Saint Vincent. The precise date of the council is not known but based on the signatories it must have taken place between 647 and 653. It was well attended as the long list of signatories shows: six metropolitan bishops (and a delegate for a seventh), thirty-eight bishops, and other delegates of lower ranks.[16] The council meant business. The metropolitan bishop of Arles, who failed to turn up even though he was apparently present in the host city, was censured and removed from office, and two other bishops in the city of Digne were demoted. The council's avowed mission was to restore full observance of the canons of the church and, after affirming its orthodoxy by confirming the authority of the councils of Nicaea and Chalcedon, the assembled bishops addressed a long list of matters relating to the office and duties of bishops, the inalienability of church lands, and the problem of lay encroachment. Earlier canons were affirmed, including diocesan authority over oratories on private land, a prohibition on brandishing arms or using violence in or around the church precincts, and the importance of Sunday observance for farmers. In a mood of optimism, the assembled bishops also prayed that Clovis II would have a long life.

The council also addressed issues that related to slaves and captivity. It proclaimed two essential ideas. The first was that freeing Christian captives was as a pious act stating that "it is a merciful and religious piety for Christians to redeem souls from the bonds of captivity."[17] The second was that no one should ever sell a slave outside the limits or borders of Clovis' kingdom lest that trade result in Christians being placed in the bonds of captivity "or, what is worse, coming under the control of Jews." This line of thinking was not new. However, the emphatic tone of the canon was new. The presence of the king and the mayor of the palace among the assembled bishops made its pronouncements official royal policy. The prohibition of selling Christian slaves abroad was strengthened with Clovis' authority. The implication was that any infraction would incur not only the church's condemnation but also the king's justice. A new sense seems to be in the process of development, namely that a kingdom, in this case Neustria, can have an identity tied to the way it handles slaves. We see something similar in the Life of Balthild where her prohibition extends throughout the realm.

The council was an important event at the beginning of the young king's effective reign. Scholars have seen a progressive tendency in councils of the Merovingian era to ameliorate the conditions and legal constraints under which slaves lived.[18] However, concessions in such circumstances favored the status quo; we do not find councils debating slavery as a social system. To free local slaves *en masse* would require a social and economic revolution which was not something the church was interested in undertaking any more than were secular authorities, nor is it likely they believed in it. However, in the seventh century, under the influence of people like Eligius of Noyon, Clovis, and Balthild, there was a clear push to do something about a crisis of uprooted and dislocated Christians. Indeed, royal involvement may have started with Clovis' parents. We know that King Dagobert supported his treasurer, Eligius, with funds for the purpose of freeing slaves.[19] And although it is not recorded, it is possible Nantechild was also behind Dagobert's royal support for Eligius' activities. It was Balthild, however, who would be associated with the rescue of slaves in the eyes of posterity.

Balthild's Prohibition and Plan

The Council of Chalon-sur-Saône was a major event, heralding a new era of spiritual responsibility under the auspices of a young king. However, Balthild's policies as queen-regent a decade later was not a simple duplication of the council. Rather her policies addressed a specific problem: foreign slaves arriving in Neustrian ports. And, whereas the council articulated a general principal, Balthild undertook a concrete plan. Her hagiographer explained:

And this must be called to mind, because it pertains to the increase of her reward, that she forbade Christian men to become captives, and she issued precepts throughout each region [ordering] that absolutely no one ought to transfer a captive Christian in the kingdom of the Neustrians (*in regno Francorum*). And in addition, she paid the price and ordered many captives to be [redeemed] and she released them as free. Others of them, especially from her own race, men and also many girls (*puellae*), she sent into the monasteries as her own charges. However many she was able to attract, these she entrusted to the holy monasteries, and she ordered them to pray for her.[20]

This compact paragraph contains six elements in her policy that will be examined in the remainder of this chapter. Foremost is her prohibition of the trade in Christian slaves, echoing the Council of Chalon-sur-Saône. The second is a prohibition of slave transportation within or perhaps through Neustria. This differs in emphasis from the Council of Chalon-sur-Saône's prohibition against selling Neustrian slaves abroad.[21] The third is her purchase of their freedom, necessary because despite the prohibition, the slave trade was unregulated outside Neustria's borders and slave owners and traders would require compensation. The fourth element is the use of monasteries as a place of aftercare for freed slaves, both male and female. Fifth, we learn that those "of her own race," Anglo-Saxons such as herself, were her special target under this policy of monastic rehousing. And finally, these last would pray for her during her lifetime as queen, as a support for her endeavors.[22] It is useful to examine these points further.

We are told that Balthild "prohibited" the trade of slaves within the kingdom of Neustria (which is what 'regno Francorum' meant). This sounds like an official pronouncement, presumably in the name of her son. Her biographer does not provide clear information on how this royal prohibition was to be carried out or enforced. Nor do we learn what precisely the trade in slaves was like within Neustria in the 660s. From Audoin's biography of Eligius we get the sense that Neustria was more than a passive consumer in the slave market, and that slaves from outside Neustria, such as from the British Isles, Scandinavia, Saxony, or even the Mediterranean, were brought to Neustria, just as was Balthild herself, for the labor they could supply or else were traded onward. Whether they were free or unfree prior to captivity was largely immaterial once they were planted on foreign soil. The implication of Balthild's prohibition was that any trafficked

Christian must be purchased or released on touching Neustrian soil. However, she could not stop the tide of captive humanity that was brought to Neustria's ports—that was outside her control.

Balthild's concern to free Christian slaves fit the framework of piety articulated by the church council—Christian slaves must be rescued. However, whereas the council was concerned about Christian slaves sold abroad, Balthild was concerned with foreign slaves brought into Neustria. Her prohibition covered those who were like Balthild herself—captives who, regardless of rank or circumstance, were pressed into slavery and traded. This was a population for whom Balthild could do something: they were available for purchase, and as Christians they could be absorbed into monastic communities. They may not all have been Anglo-Saxons, but those who were will have had fewer language barriers than those who were not. Balthild's prohibition for Neustria could only address one half of the problem, however, since the trade was initiated elsewhere. For example, the first prohibition against selling countrymen abroad is not seen in Anglo-Saxon law until the early eighth century.[23]

Balthild and Eligius of Noyon

All sources point to a fruitful collaboration between Balthild and Eligius in responding to the crisis, but the problem of trafficked people predated Balthild's time. While Balthild's hagiographer is vague on some of the details and practicalities of Balthild's Neustrian policy, we get another view of the trade in foreign slaves from her contemporary, Bishop Audoin of Rouen. His account of Eligius' career, penned in the 680s, chronicled his friend's career from royal goldsmith to bishop of Noyon.[24] Audoin (sometimes known as Dado) relates that during his years at court, Eligius was active in ransoming slaves from foreign parts, and especially those from Anglo-Saxon England. We are told that while still in the secular life, before 641, Eligius' skills as a goldsmith were widely admired and he was well connected with travelers from foreign communities. Indeed, we are told that "his fame spread abroad so that Roman, Italian, or Gothic legates or those sent from any other province to make an alliance or on another mission to the palace of the king of the Franks, would not go first to the King but would repair first to Eligius asking him either for food or seeking healthful counsel." As a friend and guide to these outsiders, Eligius was well situated to facilitate their connections with people at the royal court, and to negotiate with them on a subject that was close to his heart—the ransoming of captives from overseas. Audoin continues:

> Religious men and monks also flocked to him and whatever he could collect, he gave to them in alms or gave for the ransom of captives, for he had this work much at heart. Wherever he understood that slaves were to be sold he hastened with mercy and soon ransomed the captive. The sum of his captives redeemed rose from twenty and thirty to fifty and finally a hundred souls in one flock when they were brought in a ship, of both sexes and from different nations. He freed all alike, Romans, Gauls, Britons and Moors, but particularly Saxons who were as numerous as sheep at that time, expelled from their own land and scattered everywhere.[25]

From this description we gain a view of a vigorous international scene in the Paris region, with people and ships coming and going and those caught up in the political fractures of their homelands finding themselves displaced and captive in northern France. The emphasis on numbers is interesting in that it is one of the few sources to give us a sense of how boatloads of slaves were transported from one place to another. This passage also helps us to understand Eligius' role in freeing slaves—he was the administrator, the factor whose place at the center of multiple networks allowed him to operate as intermediary. Yet, Eligius' personal piety is the purpose of Audoin's narrative, as ransoming slaves was considered a pious act. The religious context is emphasized when we learn that Eligius impoverished himself in order to ransom slaves and that he did so in order to further his own penitential aims:

> If it should happen that the number of people for sale outweighed his means, he gave more by stripping what he had on his own body from his belt and cloak to the food he needed and even his shoes so long as he could help the captives. And often it was pilgrims of Christ that he rescued. Oh, daily did he wish to be a debtor that his own debts might be forgiven? Daily did he not rip golden bracelets, jewelled purses and other gold and gems from himself so that he might succor the miserable?[26]

The comment about pilgrims caught up in the net of slavery was an enduring problem. And evidently the king was personally involved in resolving some cases—perhaps those cases of political exiles of whose position he needed to be aware—since we learn that "standing directly in the presence of the king, redeemed captives threw the denarius before him and he gave them charters of liberty." The payment of a denarius for a slave's freedom is found in Frankish law.[27] In the case of high-ranking captives any change in legal status would be important to the king and the realm and the payment would be documented. The liberated person would have a document proving their free status but there was more papyrus work involved: documentation generated for all parties by the royal chancery, the fee paid, and record-keeping.

But most interesting for understanding Balthild's policies with respect to slaves is the explanation given in Eligius' biography as to how slaves would be dealt with after they were liberated. The biography shows how Eligius followed through:

> To all of them he gave three choices: since they were now free, they could return to their own country and he would offer them what subsidy they required; if they wished to remain he would accommodate them willingly and include them not among his servants but as his brothers; and, if he could persuade them to embrace the venerable life of monks and take the cloister of a community, honoring those marked for the lord, he would supply clothing and whatever else was needed for their care.[28]

Here, we see the model for Balthild's own policy since her Life likewise states that she allowed some of the freed to go their own way and others to enter monastic life. It would make sense that Eligius and Balthild working together developed similar responses. Eligius was still a presence at court in the years when Balthild was in power; he died in 660 about three years into her regency. Indeed, we know that he was a friend to her and that he was one of the bishops she allowed to guide her. He stood as godfather to her eldest son. (Eligius' prophecy about Balthild's children is discussed in Chapter 6, pp. 122–39). He was also a signatory, and perhaps a prime mover, in the legislation against slave trading included in the provisions of the Council of Chalon-sur-Saône. It is likely, therefore, that Balthild's approach to redeemed slaves followed the pattern already outlined by Eligius: once freed, a captive could return home, remain in freedom in France and find employment, or join a monastery or convent. Balthild's concern for women, a category of slaves not singled out in church councils, may have made the option of entering a convent appealing to women who were displaced and dispossessed.

Like Balthild, Eligius showed a particular concern for Anglo-Saxon captives. We learn from Audoin that whereas slaves arrived at Neustrian ports from a variety of locations, in Eligius' time Anglo-Saxon slaves dominated the market being "as numerous as sheep at that time," and were thus the population in greatest need. Here we learn how political eruptions back home resulted in shiploads of refugees and captives crossing the channel. It is possible that Balthild had been caught up in just such an upheaval, but she must also not have been one of those people who could throw coins on the ground in front the king, gain a charter of liberty, and go back home. Her hagiographer insisted that she had been sold as a slave, and for a low price. For someone like Balthild being "bought" or "ransomed" made little difference. That she entered the domestic service of the person who purchased her fits with what must have been the conventional fate of those rescued from the ships since it was Audoin's point that Eligius was unusual in that his rescued slaves were "not among his servants but as his brothers." It seems that Neustrian households were taking advantage of a steady stream of unfortunate Anglo-Saxons to acquire cheap labor. Perhaps they benefitted from an enhanced reputation for piety by "ransoming" them. Eligius was not one of those who took advantage of them, Audoin seems to suggest. Nevertheless, the well-networked Eligius may have facilitated the transfer of those ransomed into jobs, as he could hardly abandon them. He encouraged those he could to enter the monastic life and he agreed to provide the necessary clothing to facilitate that transfer. Monasteries were always in need of labor. Is it too fanciful to imagine that it was Eligius (or one of his agents) who rescued Balthild, arranging for her transfer to Erchinoald's sympathetic household where she maintained some status as one rescued by Eligius and thereby, perhaps, shielded from a worse fate?

Eligius is an interesting presence in this Merovingian world with an anomalous career. He did not come from the top tier of society, yet he was a vigorous and accomplished man who made his name from his exceptional skill in metalwork. Unusually, we have a physical description of him: he had a rosy countenance and curly hair, we are told.[29] Finding patronage at the Frankish court, in his early years he constructed shrines in precious metals over the remains of the saints such as at Saint Martin's tomb in Tours, and at the shrine of Saint Denis outside Paris. Later, as bishop, he travelled widely to visit the monasteries and nunneries he had founded, and even some he had not, such as the famous Columbanian monastery of Luxeuil. He was a man who kept informed of things going on, including in Paris where he founded a nunnery of thirty nuns under the guidance of Abbess Aurora. He must have been about fifty-three years of age when he was ordained bishop of Noyon in 641 on the same day as his somewhat younger friend, and future biographer, Audoin of Rouen. Eligius had already lived a long secular career before he was appointed to high ecclesiastical office. Clovis and Balthild knew him only in his old age, but when he died in 660 at the age of about seventy-eight, he had outlived the young king.

Audoin situates his description of Eligius' slave-freeing activities in the years when he was still in the secular life; his pious activities presaging his worthiness to become a future bishop. Still, his biographer friend was at pains to point out that these activities extended over a long period of time: "Let me briefly comprehend how many multitudes of captives over successive periods of time he freed from the harsh yoke of dominion and how much alms he distributed to people of both sexes, diverse churches and monasteries, though no orator, however studious or eloquent, could tell the tale."[30] It would make sense that some of this activity was contemporaneous with Balthild's activity, and that Eligius advised her on this specific issue.

In order to carry out her policies, Balthild would have needed a team. Who were her helpers? As we have seen, there were allies such as Erchinoald, and her almoner Genesius. It was Eligius, who offered a developed network of helpers. Eligius had a broad—even international—team of laymen to help him with his efforts to rescue Christian slaves. Audoin names some of them. There was Bauderic, from Eligius' home province, who was part of his retinue and who provided honest help; another was the chamberlain Tituin, a Sueve; and there was Buchin, a pagan who had converted to Christianity and who later joined a monastery.[31] Additionally, Eligius had long-term connections with Anglo-Saxons—his pupil in metalwork, we are told, was a Saxon. In their early years, Clovis and Balthild may have been supporting this network financially as Dagobert had done before them, but during her regency Balthild was more directly involved, and eventually she would have inherited a network of facilitators when her mentor died as it is evident that she was able to carry on her own policies of slave liberation beyond Eligius' death.

One option available only to freed men was to enter clerical office. We learn from Audoin that Eligius helped three such, Andreas, Martin, and John, to enter the clergy and that countless others were in training.[32] The fact that these men were named may reflect how unusual this career path to the clerisy was. It had ever been so. In the sixth century, some promising slaves had been freed and ordained to the priesthood perhaps to offset an employment shortfall, but this was not encouraged, and such cases were the subject of waspish backlash in church councils. In a stratified society, the leap from servitude to priestly office was seen as presumptuous, and simply wrong on multiple levels. In the seventh century, we hear of such cases only rarely.

Housing Slaves in Monastic Communities

Balthild's most visible response to the crisis was to draft some slaves, men and girls, into monasteries "as her own charges."[33] We have seen that Eligius also sought to facilitate the transfer of freed slaves into the religious life, a work he may have done for women as well as for men. However, as the founder of a convent, what Balthild could provide at Chelles was a refuge suitable for female slaves in an environment sympathetic to Anglo-Saxon culture and under her protection.[34] Transferring slaves to monastic institutions is an interesting policy, and one can easily imagine that it was not without difficulties. One has to wonder who these slave girls were. Did they have a real choice in their fate? Male captives, especially warriors, might be ransomed as useful manpower. But what options were open to women? Once removed from the protection of their families, their choices may have been restricted to domestic labor, with all its attendant vulnerabilities, or else being taken into a convent where they could, even if only as servants, recreate a sense of community under the protection of the abbess and the queen. In later centuries, when marriage customs were different, a charitable act would have been to give the girls dowries. But, as we have noted, this was not the pattern of marriage in Neustria where it was the groom who endowed the bride. Low-born women would not have brought the family connections and landed property that Merovingian nobles (in contrast to kings) often sought out. Rescued women had far fewer options than men.

Convent life helped some women to be sure, but the influx of women also benefitted Balthild's reputation and her convent in direct ways. Populating convents could be slow business if left to normal channels. Drafting female slaves into her convent was an efficient way to jumpstart a major female community. A thriving, populous monastery made a bigger splash than one that remained small and grew slowly. Furthermore, a convent was a public statement of the value of chastity. Chelles provided Balthild a symbolic connection to the virtue of chastity while supporting the enterprise with resources she owed to her own fecundity.

A pressing issue on which the sources are frustratingly reticent is whether the rescued women entered the convent as servants or as nuns. What status did these rescued girls acquire within the convents they now joined? In this era, monasteries and convents owned slaves and employed slave labor, so for some girls their entry into a convent economy was a lateral move. One view expressed at the time was that the slaves of the church would work less and be happier than privately owned slaves; an aspirational, if probably naïve, sentiment.[35] Did these slave girls find their own level based on background, education, and experience? Or were they to hold a specific predetermined role within the convent? Monastic communities were hierarchical institutions that depended on manual labor. We get a glimpse into the way the abbess policed matters of status from the Life of Austrebertha of Pavilly, the convent founded by Philibert close to the monastery of Jumièges. After Austrebertha's death, a serving woman who wanted to enter the convent as a nun, but who had been denied this boon, approached the saint's tomb and refused to leave. The abbess found this disgraceful: "You were born a servant in this monastery, and you ought to do servile work as you would have to do outside. Do you dare to imagine that you can make yourself a lady by stealing the corpse of another nun?"[36] That night the abbess became ill and attributed it to her refusal of the girl's request; the girl was admitted as a nun. The author concluded with a salutary reminder that "in Christ there is neither bond nor free, but all are one and we are all enlisted under a single lord." It was a position that few were able to enforce literally. However, Balthild's rescued captives were not necessarily born to service. Rather, Balthild sent the rescued girls to the monasteries at her own charge, which could suggest one of three things: that she had paid for them to be released and then gifted them to the convent as labor; that she freed them and endowed them so that they were financially neutral in the monastic economy; or that she had endowed them on their entry to the convent making them eligible to be nuns alongside those who had entered the convent under different, perhaps more privileged, circumstances. One can imagine that the latter would be unpopular with resident nuns who had joined a royal convent for its prestige and security. If they entered the convent as freed slaves, they would have been a means of support to the aristocratic nuns allowing them the privilege of being among those who pray. The hagiographer, however, asserts that Balthild asked them to pray for her, which points to a role in which their prayers were valuable.

Balthild's policy may have worked in concert with Eligius' solution, but in finding solutions for displaced women Balthild may also have understood her role in light of a famous imperial model. The sixth-century Byzantine empress Theodora, a woman of low social origin, founded a refuge for women. This villa, named Metanoia ("Repentance"), was established for women whose poverty and circumstances had led them to a life of prostitution.[37] As places of repentance, monasteries could fill an analogous purpose, yet Balthild's succor of displaced, protectionless, slave women (the Frankish equivalent of Byzantine prostitution) does not draw on the language of guilt and repentance that was so central to the imperial enterprise. But, like Theodora, Balthild was responding to a pressing social crisis that could lead women into sexual servitude.

As would be the case in later centuries also, the entire enterprise of rescuing slaves was couched in the language of religion and salvation, but it was undoubtedly a social issue also. A twenty-first-century reader would like to think that a humanitarianism impulse lay behind Balthild's actions. That value is impossible to extract from the pious language used by the sources. We must also acknowledge that Balthild's efforts were limited to a particular population of slaves. It is highly unlikely that she freed her own slaves. But then the problem of traded slaves was quite different to that of laborers who were enslaved members of the general population. It was much easier to free a slave who suddenly became available on the market than to intervene in property issues at home. Furthermore, the plight of these displaced people (traded slaves, pilgrims, migrants, captives) was acutely visible and this impelled people to act. It was this particular category of trafficked slave that could "benefit" from the charity of the church and the support of Queen Balthild. While we must dispense with any notion approximating a full-blown abolitionist movement in Neustria in the seventh century in a modern sense, Balthild's focus on the slave trade in her policies was not unlike the focus of some early abolitionists in France in the early 1800s. Human suffering could spur public figures like Balthild and Eligius to action.

Slaves Who Pray

By the latter half of the seventh century, the idea that one could pay to have others to pray for you, was gaining traction. The idea that kings and kingdoms would benefit from prayers, was already well established.[38] Balthild asked those she had rescued to pray for her, presumably for her present safety and for the success of her endeavors. The Carolingian version of her Life added some new text which claimed that Balthild had asked for prayers for herself, for her dead husband, for the safety of her sons, and the peace of the realm.[39] By the Carolingian era the idea of including prayers for the dead was more common than in the seventh century, and the ninth-century nuns of Chelles were, of course, aware that in addition to their buried queen, one of Balthild's sons, Chlothar, also rested in their convent. In praying for both the living and for the dead, monasteries found a way to make themselves indispensable to royal patronage, and the landed aristocracy found a reservoir of real and supernatural power in which to invest family resources. But this was largely in the future.

What did former slaves add to the prayer economy in Balthild's time? A man or woman who was freed carried an obligation to their former master for their lifetime; it had been so since Roman times. While prayers for the dead could be valuable, so too was prayer for the living. Balthild's request sheds light on how royals viewed monastic establishments at this time—they were prayer-generators for present power. This prayer burden lay with all the nuns, but perhaps prayers of gratitude from those released from servitude added t added something more. From earthly slaves to 'slaves' of God, the rescued *puellae* represented a holy story of redemption in bodily form.

Further Social Reforms

The Council of Chalon-sur-Saône set the tone and agenda for the new reign. Its twenty canons were a mere digest of the topics that were discussed at that august meeting. Still, it is notable that this important council did not include some of the other social issues that Balthild addressed during her regency. For example, we learn from her hagiography, and not from the council, of the problem of infanticide and the need for providing respectful burial for the uncared-for dead.

Prohibition of Infanticide

Christian sources took note of infanticide, both prenatal and postnatal. Penitential manuals imposed heavy penalties on anyone who harmed a child and secular law sought to protect women of childbearing age. Women were commonly the targets of this legislation. Balthild's prohibition of infanticide, her biographer explains it, is unusual in that it blames infanticide on taxpayers (men). The culprits were "more eager to kill their offspring than to provide for them in order to avoid the royal exactions which were inflicted upon them by custom, and from which they incurred a very heavy loss of property." He praised Balthild's stance: "This the lady prohibited for her own salvation so that no one presumed to do it. Because of this deed, truly a great award awaits her."[40]

There is a lot one would like to know about the context for Balthild's prohibition of infanticide, and we are given very little to work with. Indeed, there is something sly about the way this information is presented to us. Infanticide was already prohibited under Frankish law and was regarded as a serious sin in church writings and penitential documents. Balthild's prohibition was, therefore, a restatement of existing law. So, was this a new royal edict the response to a current problem? Was this a prohibition that could even be enforced? The charge of infanticide (as opposed to failure to thrive) would be hard to prove in an era of high infant mortality, and there were options (not church-approved) for families who wished to limit the number of their children including contraceptive measures. Grinding poverty could certainly lead to infanticide. The option provided in imperial law for poverty-stricken parents to sell their children into slavery finds no place in Merovingian canons.[41] However, poverty was certainly recognized as a factor in infant mortality and could be used as a mitigating factor: the claim of poverty could reduce the penitential burden of a woman who killed her child, for example.[42] As in other societies, it is possible that female infants were especially vulnerable when times were hard.[43]

Was there really a correlation between taxes and the killing of babies? What was this tax, and who was being targeted? The author presents this declaration in the context of a customary tax, yet the fact that the prohibition was attached to Balthild's name suggests that this was something different—perhaps a newly imposed or newly increased tax. If so, we do not know if the tax was imposed universally. The loss of property suggests a taxation on land and goods. However, the immediate and drastic "solution" of infanticide suggests a poll tax. There is no mention of a special tax being levied at this time, but the sources are scant, and the poll tax was a common instrument, especially to finance special projects. We may be short on details, but resistance lies behind it. This may explain the hagiographer's curious framing of the problem and his curiously unsympathetic attitude to those so afflicted by the tax that they considered murdering their babies.

Surprisingly, Balthild's prohibition was cast not as an issue of poverty, but as tax-avoidance, and it finds its place in the same section of the biography that praises her prohibition of simony.[44] The connection between the two issues appears to be the abuse of money, viewed as a religious crime. The Carolingian version of Balthild's Life goes even further, accusing the tax-evading killers of "avarice," a more conventional spiritual crime.[45] The inference is that those who threatened infanticide were not the poor but rather those of means who were reluctant to pay the tax. In casting the issue in this way, the hagiographer sought to deflect from the queen any responsibility for the burden of royal exactions. Yet the work lauded the queen highly for her vast expenditures in support of religious institutions, almsgiving, and the rescue of foreign slaves. One criticism that could be levied at the royal household was the obvious lavishness of the court, but kings and queens were expected to live that lifestyle, and her hagiographer does not dwell on court life. Rather one wonders whether the resentment was focused on the way that resources were being used to support Balthild's projects—the founding and patronage of monasteries, and her slave-rescue project. Was the slave rescue initiative viewed in some quarters as a vanity project? One can imagine that to some it may have appeared that she helped her own people, foreigners, at the expense of Neustria's own. Balthild was all about projects. Expensive projects. These projects may have been done nominally in the name of her son, but her hagiographer was in no doubt that these were her projects. The threat of infanticide was laid at her door. With her own salvation at stake, we seem to hear, no one presumed to do it. But how would she, or we, know?

Burying the Uncared-for Dead

Beyond being a hygienic necessity, burial of the dead was traditionally viewed as an act of care, humanity, and piety. Care for the dead was also a Christian concern.[46] In the Merovingian period, burying and remembering the dead was largely the task of friends, family, and beneficiaries of the deceased. Respect for the dead was expected of all the rest.[47] As in most ancient societies, Merovingians buried their dead in cemeterial space outside of the space of the living. They did this to mitigate fears of both symbolic and real pollution. Clerics were generally slow to intervene in the burial of the ordinary dead, but they did show a concern to patrol their sacred space. Burial in hallowed ground was not permitted to all, according to the canons, and some of the dead fell outside of the usual provision for family burial, for example in cases of suicide or judicial execution. If the dead were not buried in a timely matter, things could get nasty quickly, and there was the additional danger of incurring the vengeful anger of the deceased: the unhappy dead were known to return as ghosts.[48] Seventh-century writings and practices show that the appropriate burial of the dead was beginning to attract more of the church's attention and that in a Christian society there was need to provide burial for those otherwise unprovided for. In times of violence, there was also an urgent need to deal with bodies left on the roadside and open to the elements.

Eligius identified burial of the dead as an urgent need requiring direct attention even before he became a bishop in 641. Audoin tells us that Eligius gained permission from the king (Chlothar II or Dagobert, we are not told) to bury executed criminals, and he appointed two men, Gallebodo and Vincent, to carry hoes with them when they traveled so they could bury corpses whenever they happened upon them. One time they almost buried a man alive![49] This urgent need to dispose of bodies sheds light on the cruelty of judicial punishment, the dangers of social alienation, and indigence. Eligius had to petition the king to undertake this work because the execution of criminals and the display of bodies as deterrence was ultimately under the authority of the king. Eligius would want to avoid conflict with those who were deputed to carry out royal justice. So when Balthild's hagiographer explained that Clovis II appointed Genesius to help the queen in her pious activities, and this included burial of the dead, we see Balthild providing support for an initiative that was already under some degree of royal oversight.[50] Once again, Balthild was supporting charitable work organized by Eligius, and perhaps continued by Genesius after Eligius' death in 660, but her support was crucial as it was an act of Christian piety that required royal support and royal permission. Others got the message. We learn in a contemporary Life of Anstrude of Laon that the abbess also counted burial of the dead among her many acts of community charity.[51]

While Balthild's support for the burial of corpses was largely overshadowed by her other projects, burial of the dead continued to be associated with Eligius's cult. In 1188 a charitable organization for the burial of the dead was formed after Saint Eligius appeared in a vision to two blacksmiths. The Confrérie des Charitables de Saint-Éloi still buries the dead eight hundred years later.[52]

Simony

The same ecclesiastical council that had judged the ransom of slaves a pious Christian act also addressed the impious practice of purchasing ecclesiastical office, simony: "Let no bishop, or priest, or abbot, or deacon acquire sacred orders by giving gifts. That he who does it should be entirely deprived of the dignity of that which he sought by gifts."[53] Whether it was sweetening a deal with gifts, or a more clear-cut negotiation in return for appointment to high office, simony was viewed as a persistent problem throughout the Merovingian era. High clerical office was synonymous with status and power in the seventh century and thus open to the influence of bribes, patronage, and other inducements. Simony was viewed as so dangerous and so contrary to the Christian enterprise that early councils in Gaul had decried the practice as a "heresy";[54] Audoin termed it a deadly virus (*mortiferum virus*) in the body of Christ. Both he and Eligius of Noyon had raised the alarm about this abuse at the Council of Chalon-sur-Saône; the council's published admonition of the practice, and the threat of removing simoniacs from office, was publicly supported by both bishops and the king.[55] However, as was often the case, the most strident voices against simony came from those who had benefitted from it. Both Eligius and Audoin were royal appointees even if they chose to view their preferment as "election," and they would have rejected the notion that they had paid for their office. The new injunction against simony was an attempt to keep clerical appointment within church control and to limit royal interference. The greatest danger came when vacant episcopal seats were contested.[56] In the seventh century, bishops and kings probably worked together to decide episcopal appointments and their decision tended to prevail over any grassroots attempt at community election. As queen-regent Balthild was embroiled in this process as much as anyone else. As episcopal appointments were political as much as they were religious, she probably viewed this as a legitimate arena of influence even if no bribery occurred. Knowing the extent to which Balthild was involved in religious politics, either her hagiographer was extraordinarily brazen in his representation of her position or he chose to take a very narrow, legalistic view of what simony specifically entailed. The murky events behind Balthild's political demise were deeply tied to the politics of episcopal appointments, especially her appointments of Sigobrand to Paris, Genesius to Lyon, and Leudegar to Autun.

Irish Monasteries and Benedictine Basilicas

By the mid-seventh century, kings and queens had to have a monastic policy, that is to say, they had to have a stance on how monasteries fit within the political and spiritual landscape of their kingdom. Balthild's regency was characterized by a particularly evolved monastic policy, and female monasticism was at the heart of it.[57]

Monasteries had been a part of the Christian landscape in the west from the late fourth century.[58] From the time of Queen Radegund in the second half of the sixth century, female monasteries became closely allied with royal power, providing a place of refuge for widowed queens, unmarried daughters of the nobility, and retired aristocrats. Nunneries relied on patrons and donors to provide a protective environment for their community because nunneries were expensive and their nuns were discouraged from any employment that brought them into close contact with men and the outside world generally. Some convents chose claustration (strict seclusion) for their nuns, but others sought support for costly enterprises such as care for the sick and education for young women.

In the late sixth century, the Irish missionary Columbanus had spurred a spiritual revival in northern France. In the seventh century, monasteries influenced by new ascetic ideals and missionary zeal were founded and supported on lands donated by kings, queens, and noble families. Traditionally, nunneries were founded within urban areas to benefit from the protection the city provided and to have access to the spiritual services of resident clergy. In the seventh century, however, new monastic foundations were increasingly located in rural areas to take advantage of the land grants and the agricultural revenue they generated. Nuns in rural monasteries were provided with protection by means of the double-monastery model in which monks and clerics were attached to convents but under the authority of an abbess. Male monasteries also moved to the countryside where they were given space to build much larger monastic complexes to accommodate the agricultural activities that supported them. By the mid-seventh century when Clovis II and Balthild were in power, monasteries were being founded in unprecedented numbers, and the patronage of the royal house was particularly valued because kings could grant vast tracts of land, wealth, and immunity from taxation. Clovis and Balthild were supporters of Columbanian monasticism, but they also supported monasteries that operated under other monastic rules and customs, including the Benedictine. In addition to direct support, kings granted lands to institutions founded by courtiers-turned-bishops and abbots. In so doing, kings and queens provided the means for political allies to become monastic patrons.

It comes as no surprise, therefore, that Balthild's hagiographer was keen to stress Balthild's own very active policy towards monastic communities in her realm. For kings and queens, however, rural monasteries were only one part of a bigger picture of religious control, since bishops and their cities were still, in late antiquity, centers of power, population, and political opinion. Balthild oversaw an intensified scrutiny of city churches and it was expected that the clerical staff and students attached to city churches should conduct their lives under the organizational principles of a monastic rule. Balthild was heavily involved in this process of reform, we are told, sending letters to the bishops and abbots concerned to ensure that the staff attached to the most important basilicas in the realm should live under a monastic rule (probably a mixture of the Benedictine and Columbanian rule).[59] This policy may have antagonized the bishops who were made to concede authority over these places and the revenues and gifts that they represented.[60] These great churches in the cities of Paris, Soissons, Sens, Orléans, and Tours were also burial places for the Merovingian royal family, with the royal necropolis at Saint-Denis newly joining their ranks. Balthild gave these establishments precious inducements in the form of taxation immunities and privileges so that they would comply with the reform she ordered and so that they could pray for the king and for the peace of the kingdom. Indeed, four documents recording privileges for basilicas and monasteries survive from Balthild's regency but there were likely more.[61]

Balthild's Monastic Foundations

Even before she became queen-regent for Chlothar III, Balthild would have known the importance of monasteries to political power. In his youth Clovis had been associated with Erchinoald in founding monasteries, including providing the lands on which Erchinoald founded the monastery of Lagny in 644, and then Péronne for the Irish monk, Fursey.[62] During his majority Clovis continued to provide patronage and privileges for monastic foundations.[63] Although Balthild was not a signatory to charters before her regency she may have been a partner with Clovis II in his monastic foundations. The Life of Philibert credits both Clovis and Balthild with providing the lands on which the saint founded the monastery of Jumièges. As regent Balthild continued to endow the monastery and later stories enshrined the image of the royal couple acting together for the benefit of Jumièges.[64] Once she became regent, Balthild achieved more direct power to establish and endow monasteries. She founded two important and long-lived monastic institutions: Corbie for monks, and Chelles for nuns. However, she was also generous to other monastic institutions in her orbit. Her hagiographer's description of this patronage informs us of the benefit that royal patronage could bring to a monastic institution, and conversely, what monastic support could bring to the reputation of a queen.

Royal support for monasteries and nunneries was valued especially for the extensive land grants they were able to give. Balthild's hagiographer opened his description of Balthild's monastic patronage by emphasizing her generosity in providing the very things that supported these institutions: "Who, then, is able to say how many and how great were the sources of income, the entire farms and the large forests she gave up by donating them to the establishments of religious men in order to construct cells or monasteries?" Revenues, agricultural lands, and forests—all were needed as financial resources for the future but also as a means first to build the monastic complexes in wood, then to finance stone churches with all the accoutrements popular at the time: columns and alcoves, stained glass, altars with liturgical vessels in silver and gold; walls and doorways furnished with heavy textile coverings, murals of geometric and imaged design, and "signs," perhaps to be interested as monograms and other religious symbols.[65] As the passage indicates, monasteries might start as "cells," essentially seed projects that, if successful, blossomed into larger institutions; Balthild was being credited here with investing in speculative enterprises, seeding the monastic future. Monasteries required help at different stages of their development. Land and property were needed at the outset: "To the religious man, lord Filibert, at Jumièges, in order to build that monastery, she conceded both a large forest from the fisc where this monastery of brothers is located, and many gifts and pastures from the royal fisc. Indeed, how many things, both a large villa and many talents of silver and gold, [did she concede] to Lord Laigobert for the monastery at Cobion?"[66] The word "talents" is used rather than contemporary currency (solidi and denarii) to convey a biblical framework of gifting. He continues:

> Likewise, to both Saint-Wandrille and Logium she conceded much property. Indeed, how many things, both many large entire villas and innumerable sums of money, did she give to Luxeuil and to the other monasteries in Burgundy? What [did she give] to the monastery at Jouarre, whence she summoned the holy virgins with the above-mentioned Lady Bertila to her monastery at Chelles? How many gifts of fields and how much money did she concede to that place? Likewise, she often gave large gifts to the monastery of Faremoutiers.[67]

Gifts of land were accompanied by gifts of money and other precious materials. In what was at least in part a symbolic homage to Saint Radegund, we are told that Balthild gifted her own belt as a pious donation to Corbion for, as her Life reminds the reader, "God loves the cheerful giver."[68] Appropriately enough, Balthild's gifts from the royal fisc went to support monastic foundations in the two kingdoms she controlled, Neustria and Burgundy. Her generosity extended also to existing urban churches: "Near the city of Paris she conferred many large villas to the basilicas of the saints and to the monasteries, and she enriched them with many gifts. What more is there? As we said, we are not able to relate everyone, not even with difficulty the half of them, and certainly all her good acts cannot be told by us."[69]

While some of the land and forests gifted to places like Jumièges may have been relatively undeveloped "wilderness," the farms and other valuable properties donated would have included the slave labor that made them a valuable source of revenue. In keeping with Balthild's image as a liberator of trafficked slaves, the land donations from the royal fisc mentioned in her biography do not specify the agricultural slaves that would have been transferred also. The hagiography is a paean to Balthild's virtue and generosity, not a land deed recording detailed transfer. However, we can see the pattern of slave transfer in the "testament" of Burgundofara for her foundation of Faremoutiers where she specified that the serfs were donated alongside the vineyards, woods, meadows, ponds, watercourses, and toll-rights.[70]

Important to her legacy, Balthild's founded the monastery of Corbie, east of the city of Amiens, sometime between 657 and 661. This monastery grew in importance in the Carolingian age when it built on its Merovingian beginnings to become a center for learning with a renowned library and scriptorium.[71] Her hagiographer recalled how she had done this—by transplanting monks from Luxueil to her new foundation. One of these monks, Theudofred, was made Corbie's first abbot. It was the method she used also at Chelles when she drew Bertila and other nuns from Jouarre. Transporting a core of monastics from an established monastery to a new one had the effect of accelerating the growth of the new establishment, rather in the manner of adding leaven to dough. Nuns and monks were an economic investment. Balthild's ability to draw on existing man-and-woman-power enabled her to establish a viable monastic institution quickly and efficiently. This was one way that a persuasive queen could have an immediate impact, signaling royal control over monastic religion in her kingdoms, drawing on the cachet of Luxueil for Corbie and on Jouarre for Chelles, and having both communities committed to prayer for the stability of the kingdom. The transplants to Corbie and Chelles ensured an enduring association with Columbanian monastic values. In the case of Corbie documentation has survived that illuminates how Balthild was able to support her own foundations with charters and ecclesiastical privileges that allowed them to flourish quickly.[72]

Founding the Convent at Chelles

Of all these projects, the convent at Chelles was her most personal project, both in terms of her direct involvement in its founding, and in this being the monastic space in which she spent her final years. Her hagiographer records that she built "a huge nunnery for women consecrated by God at Chelles, near Paris where she placed the religious handmaiden of God, the girl Bertila, in a position of the first mother. And in this place the venerable Lady Balthild in turn decided to dwell under the pure rule of religion and to rest in peace. And in truth she fulfilled this with a devoted will."[73]

Balthild's choice of the region in which Chelles was situated was a happy one. People had chosen to live in this area since Neolithic times, and from the Roman period it was a bustling community served by a road that connected to the Paris-Meaux thoroughfare; the community also had easy access to Paris via the rivers Marne and Seine.[74] Excavations close to the convent site indicate that there were heated baths with mosaics in operation at least until the seventh century.[75] And in many places on what would become the monastic site there is evidence of previous, Gallo-Roman occupation. Sometime in the early sixth century, the Merovingians had built a villa-palace estate to take advantage of the forest around (the forêt de Bondy), which made for excellent hunting. The exact site of this villa is not known, but its importance is well attested in written sources.[76] As a royal site, it saw some of the violence that clung like miasma around Frankish kings and queens. King Chilperic, from whom the Merovingian kings of the seventh century were descended, was assassinated there in 584 after returning from a hunt.[77] Gregory of Tours tells a particularly gruesome story about Fredegund's confrontation with Chilperic's son, Clovis, at Chelles that eventually led to the murder of Clovis and others.[78]

The royal villa was served by a church dedicated to Saint George that had been founded by Queen Chlothild in the early years of the sixth century. It was this church that Balthild renovated and enlarged, dedicating it to the Holy Cross, with an altar to Saint George on the right and an altar to Saint Stephen Protomartyr on the left. We know next to nothing about the fate of Chlothild's small community of virgins between its founding and Balthild's re-founding over a century later. Was it active? Was it important enough to attract nuns from overseas even before Balthild made that part of her mission?

We do not know the exact date of Balthild's founding of Chelles as a convent, but it is usually dated between 658 and 660 as it was during Balthild's regency that Bertilla was invited to move from Jouarre to head up the new convent as abbess. Theutlinda of Jouarre, who died in 660/61, was still abbess when Bertilla left Jouarre for Chelles, so the convent must have been founded before 661. The convent's connection with Anglo-Saxon England was early and planned, and there are Anglo-Saxon sources that confirm the connection between female monastic enterprises in England and in Francia.[79]

Bede is an important source of information on these monastic connections, explaining that many noble Anglo-Saxon women went to Francia for their education or to lead the monastic life there, specifying Chelles alongside Faremoutiers and Andelys as important destinations; some of these women from England even became abbesses of Frankish convents.[80] Bede's dating is wrong in one crucial case relating to Chelles, however. Bede informs us that Hereswith, mother of the East Anglian King Ealdwulf, retired to Chelles. The earliest she was likely to have made this journey to the continent is 662, which would accord well with continental sources about the date at which the convent of Chelles was in operation.[81] However, Bede also tells us that Hereswith's sister, Hild (latterly of Whitby) had herself considered moving to Chelles to join her sister. Bede states that Hild was thirty-three years old when she conceived this desire, and before she was given land in Yorkshire to set up her own community. This would have been in 647, three years before Balthild's marriage to Clovis, and a decade before Balthild founded the convent according to continental sources. If Bede was right about the dates, interesting possibilities are raised. It is possible that some form of convent was already there before Balthild "founded" it (the Life of Balthild, ch. 18, seems to suggest it was founded by Chlothild) but since Hereswith was purportedly already at Chelles (ca. 662) before Hild's expressed desire to join her (ca. 647), the dates simply do not align. If Hild had seriously contemplated joining Balthild's convent, it must have been at a later stage in her career, perhaps as a form of religious retirement to the continent that was so popular among Anglo-Saxon elites. Bede must have been mistaken about when Hild contemplated this move.

Although it is unclear if Chelles was a double monastery from its foundation, it was certainly so during Bertilla's tenure as abbess. Monks and priests assisted with the work and services under the authority of the abbess who, we are told "loved each of her sons and daughters like a mother, and all returned that love....Her sober and beneficent demeanor attracted many women and even men whose hearts were faithful."[82] It is likely that the community lived under a combination of monastic rules as guidance for the nuns. Balthild and her circle were champions of the reformed, enthusiastic monasticism that had been introduced into Francia by Columbanus and Irish ascetic influence would have been strong at Chelles. We can be sure that the rule of Benedict and the rule of Columbanus had some place in the convent's religious culture, and in all likelihood Caesarius of Arles' rule for nuns would have been used also as it was the rule used in Queen Radegund's convent of the Holy Cross in Poitiers, and provided guidance specifically for women. Recently a strong case has been made for the connection of another rule to the convent—Albrecht Diem has argued that the *regula cuiusdam ad virgines* (*A certain rule for virgins*) was written by the monastic author Jonas of Bobbio and that the meeting to which Jonas was commanded by Balthild, and which he recorded in his prologue to his Life of John of Réomé, may have been for the purpose of discussing Balthild's monastic enterprise.[83] As Diem shows, there are verbal convergences between the Life of the abbess Bertilla and the *regula cuiusdam ad virgines*, suggesting that this was a rule in known in the convent's orbit and possibly the rule that the nuns primarily followed. Balthild's life at Chelles is examined in Chapter 5 (pp. 88–121).

Church Councils and Reform in the 650s

We have seen that in the years around 650 the issue of trafficking attained a new level of visibility. The anti-trafficking pronouncement of the Council of Chalon-sur-Saône was an element in this. Council records in this period are highly reductive documents only hinting at the broader conversations that generated them. However, in addition to Chalon-sur-Saône there were other councils and synods that clustered around Balthild's lifetime. Indeed, they point to a level of productivity in ecclesiastical governance and royal involvement that was not to be repeated before the Carolingian age. Can we learn more about slave trading from these ecclesiastical documents?

There were two councils held in the presence of Balthild's second son, Childeric II: the Council of Bordeaux convened sometime between 662 and 675 which handled issues relating to Aquitaine, and the Council of Losne that largely dealt with bishops, convened between 673 and 675.[84] Another council held at Autun, focused on monasticism, took place sometime between 663 and 680, probably held during Balthild's retirement. Two further councils may have taken place at Rouen and at Nantes during Balthild's regency, but scholars do not agree on their date and authenticity. The likelihood of a Council of Rouen (between 650 and 655) and Nantes (between 658 and 666) being Merovingian councils rather than ninth-century fabrications must be considered briefly, not least because attempts have been made to connect them with Balthild because they include issues that occupied Balthild's circle.[85]

It is quite possible that a council was held in Rouen, Audoin's city, around the same time as the Council of Chalon-sur-Saône, or possibly a couple of years later; it repeats the earlier council's injunction against simony.[86] It might make sense that Audoin would bring an issue he was involved in legislating before the king to a later meeting in his own diocese. Additionally, the document also prohibits the veiling of widows, presumably those who did not enter a convent, an issue addressed also in the Council of Losne which is considered genuine.[87] Whether the Council of Rouen was genuine or not, it adds little to our knowledge of Balthild's circle.

However, a Council of Nantes, if it is genuine, could be important in that it contains an interesting canon that seeks to prohibit women from getting involved in public meetings and legal suits.[88] Odette Pontal suggests that this canon may find its context in Balthild's regency as it deemed women's involvement in public life to be problematic. Pontal also points to the canons on the abuse of purchase of office (simony) and burial of the dead as indications of a council that could have been held during Balthild's time. Unfortunately, the simony clause is all too common in church councils to help date it, and the canon dealing with burial of the dead does not address the specific issue of burial that occupied Eligius and Balthild but rather it relates to burial on church property.[89] Furthermore, there are other indications that make the text of this council suspect, including a canon on the visitation of the sick that does not align well with a mid-seventh-century date. Together with some other peculiarities, the likelihood that the text we have is a genuine Merovingian council of ca. 660 is weak.[90] This is a pity because a council militating against women being active in public affairs could provide an interesting commentary on contemporary perceptions of Balthild's regency. However, a ninth-century date provides an equally likely context for the anti-women in power sentiment, and arguably more so.

Gifts to Rome

In what first appears a tangential addendum to the chapter on Balthild's slave policy we learn that "she even often sent many generous gifts to Rome, to the basilicas of blessed Peter and Paul and to the Roman poor." Sending money and gifts to Rome was considered an act of royal piety and it is attested in other seventh-century sources. Later the practice was formalized within a taxation framework and became known as "Peter's pence." We do not know how formal Balthild's donations were, but in supporting the poor as well as the basilicas this payment was an extension of her almsgiving. The Carolingian version of Balthild's life added that these funds were also intended for the support of recluses, which may reflect a later expectation that Frankish kings should support monasticism in Rome, perhaps as a means of providing protection for travelers and pilgrims.

Francia's connections to Rome went beyond pious giving in the mid-seventh century. The primacy of the bishopric of Rome and the authority of Pope Martin I (pope 649–55) was much on peoples' minds in the wake of that pontiff's tumultuous papal tenure. Pope Martin had assumed the papal throne in 649 without waiting for the emperor's assent, and quickly convened a council in the Lateran palace to address the problem of the monothelete heresy (that asserted the primacy of Christ's divine will against his human will), which had arisen in the eastern Empire and that had garnered some imperial support.[91] In convening this council Pope Martin was acting against the emperor both in terms of his theological stance and in the act of convening the council unilaterally. Martin sought the support of the western kings and bishops for his position, sending letters to Clovis II and Eligius, and to Sigibert of Austrasia and Amandus of Maastricht. It is likely that Clovis II supported the pope since he convened the Council of Chalon-sur-Saône with a stated aim to affirm orthodoxy, but it seems Sigibert was opposed to a move that could damage Austrasia's relationship with Byzantium.[92] Eventually, Pope Martin was condemned and exiled to the Crimea where he died. It has been suggested that a traveler brought an eyewitness account of the pope to the Franks some years later and that this account forms the basis for a passage about Pope Martin in the Life of Saint Eligius.[93] In any event, the Franks were aware of papal politics and the struggle of Pope Martin in the cause of orthodoxy. Frankish support was requested and likely provided in Clovis II's reign. We are not told when Balthild's gifts to Rome started, but in providing financial resources to Rome we see Balthild engaged in yet another activity appropriate to a queen-regent.

Balthild's gifts to Rome are mentioned in the same chapter that recorded Balthild's anti-slave-trade policy and her housing of freed slaves at Chelles. Rome had a special connection for Anglo-Saxons. The Anglo-Saxon church promoted the story that their people had been converted to Christianity by Pope Gregory the Great. In the famous anecdote related by Bede and by a later Anglo-Saxon Life of Gregory, the pope saw beautiful slaves in the marketplace in Rome; when he asked whence they came he was told that they were Angli (Angles—or English) to which he responded, "Non Angli sed Angeli"—not English but Angels.[94] This encounter, so the story went, galvanized the pope's intention to send missionaries to the inhabitants of Britain to save their souls. We do not know how early this story was told—it is known to us only through eighth-century sources—but if some version of it circulated in the seventh century, it is easy to imagine that a story of papal succor would be a meaningful context for Eligius' and Balthild's work with Anglo-Saxon slaves.

Finding Balthild's Own Policies and Actions

Given how closely Balthild's religious policies mirrored those attributed to Eligius of Noyon, we may wonder how deeply her hagiographer drew on Eligius' career, and on Audoin's Life of Eligius, to construct his image of a pious queen. Was this a case of borrowed glory? I think this is unlikely. It makes sense that during her regency Balthild was in a position to support and promote conciliar decisions and reforms. The biographies of Eligius and Balthild in the 680s were close in date. Audoin's biography of Eligius provided an eyewitness account of some of the events it describes, including Audoin's own actions in some places, anonymized. However, the text as we now have it was somewhat worked over by later writers.[95] There may have been earlier biographies of Eligius that were reworked or replaced by the current text, but this cannot be currently ascertained. However, if we accept that much of the text is authentically Merovingian and authored by Audoin—and scholars generally agree that it is—then when did he complete it? It must have been written some years after Eligius' death as the work is furnished with a long list of miracles, but before Audoin's own death sometime in the early 680s. Audoin died not long after Balthild, so it is conceivable that Balthild's hagiographer made some use of the Life of Eligius. But it is equally possible that the author of the Life of Saint Eligius, aware of the Life of Saint Balthild which showcased her policies around slavery, sought to ensure Eligius' legacy was also preserved.

It would make sense that Eligius and Balthild worked together during her regency. Balthild's help would have been vital to the success of Eligius' projects during his final years. Audoin informs us that early on much of Eligius' slave-freeing activity was underwritten by money from King Dagobert.[96] It would make sense that Eligius would cultivate first Clovis and then Balthild for help in continuing his projects. In Balthild he found a person whose life experience inclined her greatly to support this activity, and even to extend it through her own resources, rescuing and rehousing Anglo-Saxon girls. It is from Balthild's biography that we learn how a desire to rescue slaves could be turned into a functional plan, and the crucial role that founding convents could play in this. In the name of her husband and then of her son, Balthild had the resources to make things happen. Our sources on Balthild and Eligius seem to reflect an active partnership of minds that saw the populating of monastic institutions as a solution for this particular social problem.[97] Ultimately, there was some irony in the fact that Balthild, who sent rescued slaves to Chelles, eventually ended up there herself.

5
Life and Death at the Convent of Chelles

Sometime in 663 or 664, Balthild's time as a regent for her son came to an end. Her regency had started in her early twenties, and she was probably now still under thirty years of age. The political jostling that characterized Merovingian government had turned violent, and although we cannot be clear what part Balthild played personally in this violence, by the time she entered the convent two bishops were dead: the bishop of Lyon had been assassinated (it is unclear whether on Balthild's orders) sometime before 664 and her protégé Genesius installed in his place, and the bishop of Paris, Sigobrand, "whose haughtiness among the Franks earned him mortal ruin," was also dead. Balthild's hagiographer was at pains to point out that Sigobrand was killed "against her will," which may mean that she wanted Sigobrand deposed without killing him, but it could also be that her hagiographer was covering for her.[1] All motivation in this remains obscure; however it appears that it was Sigobrand's murder that resulted in Balthild being escorted to the convent of Chelles by "certain noblemen" in a seventh-century version of house arrest.[2] Her hagiographer put a good face on this, explaining that this turn of events enabled Balthild to fulfill her longstanding and underlying desire to make a religious retreat to Chelles. However, a retreat to a convent effectively removed her from direct authority in the political sphere where it could be feared that she might influence her son. This confinement also removed the chance of a second marriage for her.

What did the abbess and nuns of Chelles feel on seeing their patroness approach their convent gates under guard? Once again, the hagiographer put a positive face on these events. The nuns, we are told, received her kindly, and she was "very lovingly received into the holy congregation by the holy maidens."[3] However, adjusting to this new turn of events must have been disruptive to the community, and the hagiographer does, in fact, give some indication of this.

First there was the fact that, initially at least, Balthild felt very aggrieved. This was something that even her hagiographer could not disguise. It seems that common opinion, perhaps even within the convent, held her culpable

Balthild of Francia: Anglo-Saxon Slave, Merovingian Queen, and Abolitionist Saint. Isabel Moreira,
Oxford University Press. © Oxford University Press 2024. DOI: 10.1093/oso/9780197518663.003.0005

in some respect for the disastrous events happening outside. We are told that she was angry at those she had "nurtured" and who had turned against her. Who were these people? Presumably those currently in power. As a political exile in the convent her arrival there would have immediately associated the community with her politics, and this may not have been the wish of the nuns and of the priests who supervised the convent's daily life. One might expect that some in her convent had political allegiances that differed from her own. If she was suspected of being implicated in the murder of a bishop, she would hardly find a comfortable place in a convent. Yet, this was a convent that she had founded and had visited often, and she had chosen the abbess herself.[4] Some of its inhabitants were rescued slaves who owed their safety to her personal generosity and foresight. Eventually, we are told, she forgave those who wrongly suspected her, and eventually peace returned.

A second challenge for Balthild and for her new home was that her convent now had to absorb a powerful figure, a queen in exile, into the rhythms of their small community. There was no doubt that in monastic life the nuns were under the charge of the abbess Bertilla. Bertilla was no novice. She had been a nun trained at Jouarre and was chosen by Balthild and her advisors to lead Balthild's new foundation. Setting up a new monastic foundation was a lot of work, and Bertilla must have been a capable organizer. Furthermore, Bertilla would have had many opportunities to get to know the queen as we are told that Balthild had been a frequent visitor to the convent. Yet here they were, two capable women, with political and well as religious power. Could they pull together? It seems that they did. Her hagiographer notes their closeness: "there was truly for them, as in the manner of the Apostles, *one heart and one soul* because they loved each other tenderly and most fully in Christ."[5] That, at least, was the ideal.

Entering the Convent

What was Balthild's position in the convent? If we want a picture of serene harmony and spiritual joy, we need look no further than the official biographies of the queen and her abbess. Balthild's hagiographer stressed the queen's personal humility and her obedience to Bertilla. Monastic communities were structured hierarchical and obedience a virtue; it was the requirement of every monastic rule. A clear command structure was essential to keeping things running smoothly. In convents, the abbess was the "mother" of her nuns: "all shall obey the mother after God,"[6] and "the mother should have as many souls as she has daughters under her guidance."[7] However, she was also the ultimate authority on all matters that arose within the community up to and including discipline, punishment, and excommunication.

Bertilla's relationship to Balthild is described in precisely that way in the Life of Balthild—Bertilla was a "mother" to the queen. Drawing heavily on the language and imagery of female monastic rules, the author of the Life of Bertilla, in turn, described the relationship between the two women in equally positive terms: "it was wonderful what delight and charity there was between them all their days" for "they shone like two of the brightest lights placed on a candlestick for the clear edification of many."[8] There is no reason to dismiss such assertions out of hand. Bertilla had been Balthild's choice as abbess, and they met regularly before Balthild entered the convent. Bertilla was from a noble Frankish family from the vicinity of Soissons, yet her hagiographer used a theological trope that connected her pointedly to Balthild: "she took no pride in the nobility of her stock. For sprung from free people at birth, she voluntarily consented to become a slave (*famulam*)."[9] While it is undoubtedly hazardous to take hagiographers at their word, it is appealing to imagine two capable women working together to rescue slaves and finding common ground in the metaphor that they were all slaves of God.

From the time of its founding, Balthild had a vision for her convent that it was Bertilla's task to carry out. Balthild wanted her convent to forge deep connections with Anglo-Saxon England, bringing men and women, including trafficked slave girls, to live at Chelles, and welcoming noble women from England into her convent. Bertilla was her ally in this, and indeed the activities lauded by the biographers of both women are described in strikingly similar terms. According to the Life of Bertilla, "As the holy woman's fame spread, even more men and women hastened to her, not only from neighboring provinces but even from across the seas, leaving parents and fatherland with love's strongest desire. And with pious affection, God's servant Bertilla received them all as a mother to her darling little ones."[10] We do not hear individual stories of Frankish women who came to join the monastery at Chelles during Balthild's time. However, from an early stage in its monastic history, the convent of Chelles seems to have offered a home to English royal women. We learn from Bede that Hild, daughter of King Oswy, contemplated going to Chelles to lead a monastic life there. Indeed, her sister Hereswith, mother of King Ealdwulf of the East Angles, joined the convent probably around 662 (see discussion in Chapter 4, pp. 55–87). Given how well Chelles was known in Anglo-Saxon sources, it may not be too much of a stretch to suppose that the noble siblings had been targeted by recruiters so that, inspired by accounts of Chelles, they viewed it as an amenable refuge for Anglo-Saxon nobles wanting to lead the ascetic life. Hereswith may have joined in 662, or perhaps shortly thereafter as news of Balthild's retirement to the convent spread and gave added impetus to noble women wanting to lead the ascetic life there. For women of the royal Kentish house, going to France meant going to Chelles. This continued into later centuries. King Aethelberht of Kent's great-great-granddaughter, Mildreth, went there for her education and reputedly had a bad time. Unsurprisingly, continental sources do not record the attempt by the abbess to roast Mildreth alive![11] In Balthild's time the convent must have rung with English voices, a suitable place for ex-pat nuns to learn the ascetic life, or to spend their final years in comfort in a place with better weather. We learn also that the learned nuns of Chelles were courted by Anglo-Saxon kings to return to English shores to found monasteries and convents there.[12] Balthild's influence on female monasticism in Anglo-Saxon England may have been greater than our sources show.[13]

We have already noted that there was some initial opposition to Balthild's presence in the convent. However, she lived at Chelles for more than fifteen years, so we must imagine that she settled in, and that life went forward in some satisfactory way. Bertilla appears to have managed the situation well, so that when Balthild eventually died, Bertilla led her community in promoting the queen as an icon of piety, and oversaw the beginnings of her cult. Within the convent, the authority of the abbess was absolute. Outside the convent, Balthild's relationship with her family, and her network of allies brought advantages: a degree of protection, financial resources, and an ability to recruit nuns from the highest echelons of society, even from abroad. The nuns of the convent also came to treasure their founding queen and first abbess as can be seen from the fact that from the time of Bertilla's death, both Balthild and Bertilla's remains were cared for by the nuns.

Once Balthild retired to Chelles we see little of her beyond what her hagiographer wrote. The final chapters convey little of her life there. Her activities seem rather generic—she was "incessantly in faithful prayer with tears" and she "often attended divine reading," which sounds as though she had other occupations at other times of the day. As noted in the previous chapter we do not know for certain which rule or combination of rules prevailed at Chelles during Balthild's lifetime, which is a pity as it would provide more information on daily life in the convent. The rules of Benedict and Columbanus were important in northern Gaul. However, female convents looked for specific advice on creating a meaningful spiritual life. The nuns were provided with priests to supply liturgical services (but perhaps only slightly later becoming a double monastery). However, female rule prevailed within. The queen and the aristocratic nuns were the convent's patrons, and the abbess was the supreme authority on daily life within its precincts.[14] The rule for nuns that we can be confident was known at Chelles, even if we do not know if the convent was fully guided by it, was Caesarius of Arles's rule for nuns. This was the rule used at Radegund's convent in Poitiers and Queen Radegund was an inspiration for royal recluses. However, whereas Caesarius' rule required that the nuns remain cloistered, confined to their convent right up to their death, the abbess, at least, was not expected to be cloistered at Chelles. Recently it has been argued that another rule, the anonymous *Regula cuiusdam ad virgines*, may have been used at Chelles. Albrecht Diem has shown convergences between the *Regula cuiusdam ad virgines* and the Life of Bertilla to make this case.[15] The Benedictine rule and the rule of Columbanus would also have exerted an influence on the convent's inhabitants. Taken together, all four rules, then, can offer insight into what life within Chelles might have looked like, at least in the ideal.

Balthild's hagiographer, who was able to gloss over fifteen or sixteen years of convent life in a few final chapters, painted a rosy picture of her life there. Balthild loved the nuns like daughters, we are told, a statement that placed Balthild somewhat higher than other nuns, even while she obeyed Bertilla as her spiritual mother. One point her hagiographer makes is that she visited the infirm. The context suggests that these were sick nuns within the convent, but it is possible that the nuns of Chelles were involved in care for those in the community also. The Life of Radegund may have encouraged the perception that care for the sick was a royal occupation, but from the start convents offered bodily as well as spiritual care.[16] (Eighteenth-century Chelles was renowned as a medical center; apothecary medicine was an important interest of the abbess Princess Louise Adélaïde.) The remainder of our information on Balthild's life in the convent relates to a severe bout of sickness she endured about a year prior to her death and a vision she received at the altar of Saint Mary.

We are told that Balthild did the most menial tasks for her fellow nuns, including serving the food in the kitchen, and cleaning the latrines. She did this all with a "cheerful heart." Job-sharing was dictated in most monastic rules, but there were also servants in the convent who did this work. Neither Caesarius' rule for nuns, nor the *Regula cuiusdam ad virgines* mention nuns cleaning the latrines. The latrine-cleaning duties are a dead giveaway that we are dealing with a pious trope. Latrine-cleaning was precisely the exceptional work that Queen Radegund reportedly undertook, and rather like kissing lepers (which Radegund reportedly did, but which Balthild did not), was a way for her hagiographer to dwell on her humility. Having lifted her from servitude to become a queen, God evidently remanded her to a convent to take up menial duties again. Did this ring true even to the pious readers of her hagiography? Was it at all likely that Balthild willingly debased herself and became a nun like any other after having started life in menial service and been raised from the dirt? Did she, in fact, become a nun at all?

Was Balthild a Nun?

Not all inhabitants of convents were nuns, any more than all inhabitants of monasteries were monks. There were, of course, the obvious disparities of social rank and seniority that governed such institutions, but monasteries and convents also served other purposes. Some, like Luxeuil, served as prisons for the Merovingian equivalent of white-collar criminals and political exiles.[17] Some of these individuals would have buckled down and integrated into the religious life. But there were others who were biding their time and plotting their escape. The most famous example of this was the enforced remand of the political enemies Ebroin and Leudegar. Their escape from Luxeuil to re-enter the political fray was accomplished even though Ebroin had been forcibly tonsured as a deterrent to re-entry into political life. Balthild's opinion about her own fate, and her acceptance of her situation, may have changed over the many years she spent in the convent. Perhaps she, too, hoped that a political reversal would bring her back to power. Her sons visited her at Chelles, and thus she kept up with the political events of the day. She may even have visited them at court. But they did not invite her to resume the power she had once held.

Convents were generally more dependent than male establishments on a continuing stream of noble and royal patronage. Balthild urged the abbess to "constantly visit the king and queen and the palace nobles in befitting honor with gifts."[18] The practical advantages of Balthild's urging are expressed by the hagiographer. Visits to the court would help maintain the patronage connections that supported the continued prosperity of the convent. However, the visits by Balthild, Bertilla, or some other agent, were also a way to keep Balthild's presence in the public eye.

Was Balthild a nun in her convent? This is a difficult question to answer because her hagiographer wanted to emphasize her humility and service and ended his narrative by claiming that she was a "true nun" in the convent. Yet he does not pick up the theme of penance that had been such an important aspect of Radegund's reclusive life a century earlier. As a supporter of the Columbanian monastic movement, which greatly emphasized penitential practices, this was a significant omission but perhaps understandable. A penitent in royal garb might have carried the implication that Balthild's political life, and that of her allies, were somehow in the wrong. Furthermore, as a penitent nun, Balthild would have had an extraordinarily hard life within the community—a double debasement, as it were, because she would have lost secular status and also endured exclusion rituals that would have been hardly bearable.[19] Furthermore, as a cloistered nun, her ability to maintain contact with her sons and former allies would have been non-existent. Balthild's life was not really like Radegund's at all. The sixth-century Radegund's penitential exercises befitted a saintly founder who had removed herself voluntarily from her husband to pioneer a new way of life for herself and her nuns. Radegund had adopted a rule for nuns that imposed a highly restricted life of claustration, a refuge from an unwanted husband who had been forced on her. By contrast, Balthild was a widow who did not choose to enter the convent when she did. While Chelles probably did not have the degree of confinement that Radegund's convent had adopted, if Balthild had taken monastic vows immediately this would have removed her from her family for the remainder of her life. Seventh-century monastic rules such as the rule of Columbanus and the *Regula cuiusdam ad virgines*, which were often layered with the older rule of Saint Benedict, enforced harsh forms of physical discipline and punishment for offenders, including use of the whip. If Chelles operated under a mixed rule, as convents generally did in the Merovingian era, the constraints on life within its walls would have been harsh indeed. In such a context, Balthild's urging Bertilla that she regularly visit to Paris for the convent's benefit was in clear contravention of the spirit, if not of the letter, of some rules.

There were good reasons why Balthild may have kept her secular dress in the convent. The monastic habit was a symbol of conversion to the monastic life. Once clothed in the monastic garb, an individual could not leave the convent and re-enter secular life without excommunication. For this reason, those who entered the convent of their own volition, or because they had been placed there by their family, maintained the clothes in which they entered for one year (or three years if the convent was not strictly cloistered) before they changed into monastic clothing.[20] There would always have been women in convents in secular dress of sober color, whether they were young women being educated there, or widows. The difference between Balthild and these other women, postulants, was that their position resolved in time whereas as foundress and political recluse Balthild could maintain a liminal position indefinitely. This I believe she did until her final illness.

A final reason for not rushing to become a nun was that a nun was required to hand over to the convent all privately owned property. Balthild no longer had access to the royal fisc, but her *morgengabe* would have consisted of properties and revenue streams that she may not have been immediately able or willing to surrender to the convent, especially if she hoped to resume secular life. The harshest rule of any monastic community was the curse of eternal damnation that would attend anyone who maintained private property beyond the time when they assumed the monastic garb.[21] Avoiding taking the monastic habit allowed Balthild to retain her options. Yet her hagiographer tells us that Balthild came to fully adopt her new life: "As a true nun she happily completed her blessed life under complete religious practice."[22] In view of her hagiographer's insistence that Balthild became a nun, is it fair to question this essential part of her biography? Archaeological evidence suggests that it is.

The material remains of Balthild's burial and later cult include exceptionally well-preserved textiles, hair, and hair bindings.[23] Although not enough is known of the physical appearance of nuns in seventh-century Neustria, we do know that long hair was a sign of free status for women, and that the authority of Merovingian kings to rule included their ability to display long hair. The Merovingian kings were "long-haired kings," and their wives, for different reasons, would have been long-haired queens. Within the cloister, nuns may have had their hair shorn; Gertrude of Nivelles' mother Itta cut her daughter's hair with shears into the shape of a tonsure before placing her in charge of nuns.[24] Shorn hair was also a sign of penitence. Even if not shorn, nuns "accepted the veil," covering their hair, as any respectable married woman would. A protracted wearing of veils, and concerns about hygiene, may also have encouraged short hair. In Balthild's case, however, her long hair was preserved as a relic, and thus portions of her hair and hair-bindings can help us reconstruct an image of Balthild's time at Chelles. First, the bindings and thick stub of hair that survived as a holy relic of the saint indicates that Balthild had very long, luxuriant strawberry-blond hair. Although much of her hair was gifted away as pious relics over the centuries, the length of the bindings that once held her hair suggest that it was very long.[25] Encased in its bindings, Balthild could have worn her hair up or down. The familiar images from elite female burials reveal the popularity of long tresses, cheerfully bound with colored tapes and falling on either side of the head to the abdomen. However, the bindings of her long hair could equally have been used to style her hair above her head with the cloth of the bindings adding reinforcement and height to the positioning of a veil. Indeed, Caesarius' rule for nuns tried to regulate the height of the nuns' hair, which suggests that such styles were common.[26] Either way, a long veil could easily cover the hair. However, in Balthild's case, a curious discovery suggests that she did not hide her hair from view. When archaeologists analyzed her remains in 1983 they observed that the remains of her hair were dyed blonde to cover the gray beneath. This discovery seems to tell a significantly different story about the queen's appearance in the convent from the image of a "true nun." First, it suggests that her hair would have been visible to others. This would certainly have made her appear different to the nuns since visible hair was viewed as attractive to men and thus unseemly in a nun. It also suggests that she wanted to preserve a youthful appearance that would have been associated with vigor and power. Perhaps this was important if she visited the court, or when she received noble visitors. It also suggests that her blond hair was an important identifier—a look that communicated her continuing identity as a former queen. Whatever one makes of the claims that she was a beautiful woman (a consistent observation), her dyed hair suggests that she considered her hair to be part of her image. If Balthild had worn her long hair as a nun, she could be criticized for holding to a standard different to the others in her community. It seems more likely that Balthild maintained her royal image as a reminder of, or insistence on, her queenly status, and that in urging Bertilla to keep up connections with the court, she was intent on maintaining a recognizable presence there. It is possible that Balthild hoped for many years after her forced retirement for yet another reversal of fortune that would see her restored to court life, with her long hair intact.

Meanwhile... Outside the Convent Walls

In the immediate aftermath of the events that brought Balthild to Chelles there must have been a great deal of interest in political events within the convent. Her son, Chlothar, had been king under her regency from the age of about seven to the age of thirteen or fourteen, with Ebroin as mayor of the palace. In 673, at the age of about twenty-three, Chlothar died of a fever. Like his father, Chlothar had died in his early twenties. It is not recorded if he had married, or sired issue. Balthild had been in the convent almost a decade when her son died, but her hagiographer tells us next to nothing about this momentous event, although from other sources we know that Chlothar's body was brought to Chelles and interred there, probably in the church of the Holy Cross.[27] On Chlothar's death his brother Theuderic briefly became king of Neustria under the protection of Ebroin, but the Frankish nobles quickly deposed him, having the king tonsured so that he could no longer rule, and they invited his brother Childeric, who had been king of Austrasia from a young age, to succeed him as Childeric II, king of Neustria and Austrasia.

How well did Balthild know this son who had been sent to his distant kingdom at a tender age (probably between age seven or nine) and forced into a strategic marriage to his first cousin Bilichild?[28] On his ascent to the throne of the combined kingdoms in 673 Childeric, and his Austrasian entourage headed by the mayor Wulfoald, managed to become so unpopular that he, his wife Bilichild, and their unborn child, were assassinated only two years later at the infamous Easter court at Autun in 675. Again, the hagiographer is silent on Balthild's loss and the terrible death of her son, her pregnant daughter-in-law, and her unborn grandchild. Her other grandsons, Dagobert and Chilperic II (Daniel), are not mentioned. On Childeric's death Balthild's third son, Theuderic III, was now restored, ruling the combined kingdoms of Neustria and Austrasia until 691. From the time of her widowhood to her death, Balthild never knew a time when one of her sons was not a king of Neustria and/or Austrasia. However, as was recognized at the time, and presumably by Balthild also, her sons ruled in little more than name as successive mayors of the palace jostled for power: in Neustria, first Ebroin and then Leudesius (son of her old protector Erchinoald), Wulfoald in Austrasia, and then Waratto and Berchar over both kingdoms. With the "do-nothing" kings, *les rois fainéants*, and the ambitions of a succession of ministers, the center of power oscillated between Neustria and Austrasia, always contested, aided by murder and death on the battlefield.

The son Balthild must have known best was her eldest son, Chlothar, for whom she was regent and whose burial at Chelles in 673 she must have overseen. Her second son, Childeric, who became king of Neustria in addition to Austrasia in 673, was not well thought of by those who wrote history. Childeric was considered "too light and frivolous" and blamed by the continuator of Fredegar's *Chronicle* for his own fate: "The scandal and contempt that he aroused stirred up sedition among the Frankish people."[29] His savage humiliation of a Frankish noble named Bodilo was the catalyst for the insurrection against him: "He ordered, illegally, that a noble Frank named Bodilo, should be bound to the stake a thrashed; and this infuriated the Franks who saw it." He and his wife were killed in the forest of Livry according to Fredegar. The slain couple were interred in Paris in the church of Saint Vincent and the Holy Cross. Perhaps the bone relic of Saint Vincent found in the relic treasure of Chelles, provided a connection for the queen with her son.[30] Her youngest son, Theuderic, who had been king shortly before being tonsured and removed from power, now returned as king. He married a woman named Chrodechild, and they had sons: Clovis III and Childebert III, and possibly Chlothar IV, although the sources are unclear and the latter may have been a grandchild. Theuderic III ruled with mayors, first Ebroin, who had taken him along into battle against the Austrasians at a very young age, and then, after Ebroin was murdered, by Waratto, "an illustrious man" with a "noble and vigorous wife" named Anseflidis.[31] On Waratto's death, the Franks installed a man named Berchar as the next mayor, "small in stature, of only modest intellect," who also fought with Theuderic at his side against the Austrasians, only to be murdered at the instigation of his mother-in-law, that same vigorous Anseflidis! When Theuderic died, in about 691, he had reigned nineteen years according to the author of the *Liber historiae Francorum* or seventeen years according to Fredegar's continuator, outliving his mother by over a decade.[32] At the age of thirty-seven, he was by far the longest-lived of Balthild's sons.

Like Other Holy Queens

In the final chapters of his work, Balthild's hagiographer shaped the queen's legacy to align with those of other holy queens of Merovingian France: Chlothild, Ultrogotha, and Radegund. The hagiographer knew the virtuous attributes of each of these sixth-century queens but, as he noted, Balthild was a recent queen whose record was known and so, he stated confidently, "we do not think her to be inferior in merits of those earlier [queens]; rather we know her to have outdone them in holy striving."[33]

The three queens whose lives formed the basis for comparison with Balthild's were all connected in some way with Chelles. Chlothild had a direct connection to Chelles, having built a church dedicated to Saint George there. Chlothild was viewed as the founding queen of the Merovingian dynasty having famously converted her husband Clovis I from paganism to Christianity. Once widowed, she was also credited with having built many churches and congregations. Indeed, Chlothild's contribution to Chelles is acknowledged in the Life of Balthild where it is stated that it was Chlothild's church that Balthild had enlarged and improved, dedicating it to the Holy Cross, with an altar to Saint George on the right side of the basilica, and an altar to Saint Stephen on the left.[34] The Life also stated that Chlothild was the first to build a small convent associated with the church.[35] At first sight this seems to contradict the hagiographer's claim that Balthild founded the convent of Chelles, but it is possible that consecrated women lived in Chelles before Balthild's initiative, and that Balthild was building on, or reviving, a cell of consecrated women who were already in place at that site. Curiously, Chelles is not mentioned at all in the Carolingian Life of Chlothild which is otherwise informative on the churches and monastic communities, which by the Carolingian era, at least, were associated with Chlothild.[36]

Unfortunately, no biographic Life of Queen Ultrogotha, King Childebert's queen, survives. King Childebert's kingdom was centered on Paris and during his reign Ultrogotha was associated with her husband in the foundation of the Church of the Holy Cross and Saint Vincent in Paris (later, Saint-Germain-des-Prés) in 558, and with the acquisition of the spectacular relic of Saint Vincent's tunic it was built to house. Although Childebert's military activities and conquests extended the king's reach to southern Gaul—the royal couple founded a hostel for the sick (*xenodochium*) in Lyon, and they collaborated with Bishop Aurelianus in founding a monastery in Arles—Paris was their royal base.[37] After Childebert's death in 558, her brother-in-law

Chlothar had sent Ultrogotha into exile with her two daughters, Chrodoswintha and Chrodoberga. We do not know where they went or what kind of exile they endured, but a convent would be a natural place for a royal exile. Ultrogotha was eventually freed and was buried next to her husband in Paris in the church they had founded. But her daughters reputedly became nuns. Was their forced exile to Chelles (close enough to be supervised but far enough away to be out of sight)? If there was indeed a small community of pious women at Chelles before Balthild founded the convent, as Queen Chlothild's daughter-in-law it might make sense that Ultrogotha and her daughters ended up there. Perhaps Chelles had served as a detention center for royal woman before Balthild's own exile. Since Ultrogotha is one of the saintly queens to whom Balthild was explicitly compared (and the convent of Chelles reportedly had a relic of Saint Vincent) the connection of Childebert's family with Chelles may have prompted the comparison. Unfortunately, this can only be speculation.

For Balthild's hagiographer, perhaps even more than for the queen herself, the model for queenly retirement par excellence was Queen Radegund. The profound importance of Radegund's example as a holy queen is readily found in Balthild's biography. Radegund's adoption of a female rule for her convent in Poitiers, and her acquisition of holy relics for her convent, were both royal activities that Balthild could emulate.

Of the saintly queens listed by her biographer, Balthild was the only one who was not of royal birth. Radegund was a Thuringian princess who had been captured by king Chlothar I, who killed her parents and her brother, and then married her. The hagiographer's consistent use of the Life of Radegund for his Life of Balthild shows his perception of an affinity between the two queens. Both were captured and both ended up as convent founders who lived their lives in the convent under the authority of an abbess they had appointed. If we knew more about how Radegund actually lived her life in her convent of the Holy Cross, we might know more of Balthild's life in the cloister, and how a Merovingian convent could incorporate the presence of a queen. Radegund and her abbess Agnes had famously received courtly notes, poems, letters, and gifts of food from the poet Venantius Fortunatus. If the picture of convent life described by its detractors in the proceedings that followed the revolt at Radegund's convent after her death is any indication, then we might imagine a level of comfort at Chelles in which high-status ladies could continue to indulge aristocratic pastimes like playing backgammon and maintaining correspondence with friends and family. However, such genteel pursuits were not in the spirit of Columbanian monasticism, or the *Regula cuiusdam ad virgines*, and it would have been quite shocking in the life of a simple nun.

Returning to the earlier question of Balthild's status within the convent, it is important that the comment that she had lived there as a nun is found in the final chapter of her biography: "After the many good things which she did before her evangelical perfection, she gave herself over to voluntary holy obedience and as a true nun she happily completed her blessed life under complete religious practice."[38] No timeframe is given for this consecration. Indeed, this sentence is constructed with great care. It indicates that she lived as a true nun only after some activities that resulted in her evangelical perfection. This could have referenced her move from secular life to the religious life, but it might also be a clue to different stages in her convent life. In view of Balthild's hair dye, and her continuing relevance in the political life through her sons, it may be that Balthild indeed became a "true nun" (*vera monacha*) only when she knew she was seriously sick and might die. A year before her death Balthild had a health episode so severe that death seemed close. Was it the terrible episode presaging her decline that inclined her to take such a drastic step that would finally remove her from any viable return to court and the relationships she prized? If so, her vision at the altar showing her escort to heaven, an event placed by her biographer between her colic and her death, helped to explain to her contemporaries her decision to fully join the community at last.

Relic Collecting at Chelles

Acquiring relics for basilicas and monasteries was a powerful yet fraught business. Clovis II was accused of being inspired by the devil when he took an arm relic of Saint Denis.[39] Balthild's hagiographer wanted his readers to know that she was in no way inferior to the queens who had gone before.[40] Yet there was one way in which Balthild could not fully compete with her holy model, Saint Radegund. This was in the very important business of high-status relic acquisitions. Radegund had most famously acquired the most prestigious relic of all—a fragment relic of the True Cross—for which she had been compared to Helena, the mother of the emperor Constantine.[41] Yet we know of no high-profile relic acquisitions specifically made by queen Balthild during her time in the convent, although the collection early on included relics of her close associates Saint Genesius and Saint Eligius. Unlike Radegund who had maintained contact with her distant family relations in Byzantium and had made a direct appeal to the imperial couple, Justin and Sophia, for a relic of the True Cross, Balthild's lack of international network once in the convent, and perhaps her lack of royal birth, may have precluded high-profile, global avenues of relic patronage for her convent. Over the centuries, the relic collection of Chelles became substantial as can be seen in the relic list of 1544 which numbered one hundred and seventy-eight items including a piece of the True Cross.[42] It would be interesting to know when each of these relics entered the convent's collection over the intervening nine-hundred-year period. Still, some of the relics were closely bound to the people that surrounded Balthild in her lifetime.

One way that relics can be identified is by their labels. When the contents of the "Florus" reliquary in Chelles was exposed in 1983, approximately one hundred and fifty labels were discovered. These authentication labels had been written at various points in time; some may have labeled relics when they entered the collection, others were copies of relic tags that had faded or disintegrated over the centuries. Most exciting was the presence of about thirty labels that could be identified by their script ("script b") as having been written at Chelles in the second half of the eighth century. Jean-Pierre Laporte tentatively suggested that these labels may have been labels for relics that came into the collection under Abbess Gisela, benefitting from Charlemagne's geographically wide connections and documented interest in relics.[43]

In time, the convent came to acquire many impressive relics. The inquiry of 1544 documented a vast array assembled over the centuries, including relics of the True Cross, various rocks from significant sites relating to Jesus' life on earth (one with Jesus' blood still on it), the Virgin's milk, clothing, and possessions of the apostles including Saint Andrew, who was, and is, the patron of the parish church of the Ville de Chelles, and of Saint George who was the patron of the church that Queen Chlothild had built at Chelles and which Balthild had replaced with the church of the Holy Cross. There were relics of saints associated with France such as a relic of Saint Denis, and relics of Martin of Tours, Hilary of Poitiers, and Radegund of Poitiers. Relics of Balthild's contemporaries found their way into the collection, including relics of the important bishops of her day: Leudegar of Autun, Audoin of Rouen, Eligius of Noyon, and Genesius of Paris. What is evident from the list is that with a few exceptions this was a very localized collection: it is a very French list. This may hint at the weakness of Balthild as a patroness of the convent. The relics cluster suspiciously around the collections of other relic-collecting saints. For example, Saint Radegund had famously acquired a relic of Saint Andrew and Saint Mammas of Caesarea in her quest to obtain the relic of the True Cross: relics of both these saints found their way into the Chelles collection. Balthild may have used her influence in this regard. Moreover, some relics could have been sourced locally. In the Paris region alone Chelles could have come by its relics related to Saint Vincent (the Parisian church of Saint Vincent, founded by King Childebert and Queen Ultrogotha held the saint's tunic; Chelles claimed to have a bone relic) and Saint Denis. The relics of Balthild's contemporaries may have been available through her influence, although she was not always successful. There is a whiff of desperation in Audoin's account that Balthild sought to have the body of her mentor Eligius of Noyon brought to Chelles, but since this would have been poaching from Noyon her attempt was unsuccessful (at least in the short term).[44] Having a small relic collection was a limiting factor for a monastic community. The modest nature of the relic collection at Chelles might explain Abbess Hegilvid's desire to exhume Balthild's body in 833: she needed relics to exchange with other communities to build her own collection, and plug into the prayer consortia that were being formed at this time. Hegilvid's strategy was successful. After the elevation of 833, pieces of Balthild's body and burial matter were distributed to allied monasteries such as Corbie and Jouarre. Throughout the remainder of the life of the convent of Chelles, Balthild's body, and to a lesser extent Bertilla's, were given out as the prize relics of the convent.

Sickness, Health, and Diet

The final year of Balthild's life saw her endure sickness, pain, and decline. An episode of colic of the viscera was so severe it was feared she would die. We cannot diagnose her condition from the Latin description or determine whether this was the same condition that killed her, but the Carolingian Life points to its being intestinal.[45] The intervention of medical doctors (note the plural), however, extended her life a little. This "most evil" affliction may have been an early symptom of her impending decline and death.

Medical care was certainly available at Chelles. Although hagiographers may have downplayed instances of medical intervention to highlight spiritual healing, it is clear from the sources that people availed themselves of medical advice and care when they could. Unfortunately, we are given few details about the nature of that care. If we examine medical writings of the early Middle Ages, we discover the enduring influence of ancient medical authorities such as Hippocrates and Galen, and more recent ones such as Oribasius who died around 403. However, for a sophisticated court and convent, Byzantine dietetics may also have played a role in health care.[46]

Anthimus' *On the Observance of Foods* is a good example of a work that combined knowledge about food and diet with physical health and well-being.[47] The work, in the form we have it, was written as a letter to the Frankish king Theuderic (d. 534) by a self-described "count and legate" named Anthimus who, exiled from Byzantium, was sent to the Frankish court by King Theodoric the Ostrogoth (d. 526). The advice given can be simply understood—for example, the advice that cooked foods are easier on the digestion than raw, and that some foods should be avoided. The work might be classified as a type of preventative holistic medicine, but its strictures also converged with monastic sensibilities in that it advocated dietary simplicity and restraint. We learn that the Franks were attached to a very particular remedy for stomach ailments—raw pork. Anthimus admits that this was new to him, and he wondered who had introduced the Franks to it. His own advice was to eat bacon boiled rather than roasted. But he believed that for the Franks, at least, eating raw bacon was efficacious, reporting that "if they have any difficulties with their bowels or intestines, it cures them."[48] With her terrible intestinal colic, this could have been a remedy prescribed to Balthild. Meat was permitted by most early monastic rules for those who were sick and needed additional sustenance.

Monastic diet was regulated by the rule. At Chelles, the nuns lived under the authority of the abbess who was herself guided by a miscellany of ancient writings that most likely included the Benedictine rule, the rule of Columbanus, Caesarius' rule for nuns, and possibly the *Regula cuiusdam ad virgines*. These rules regulated food consumption as a guard against gluttony and excess. The Benedictine rule advocated a simple diet, largely vegetarian, often pescatarian, but also amenable to the diet of any region in which a monastery was established, including meat consumption if that was appropriate. The nuns in a convent with connections and resources could have eaten well. The rule of Columbanus advocated that food be poor, *cibus sit vilis*, and specified "vegetables, beans, flour mixed with water, together with the small bread of a loaf, lest the stomach be burdened and the mind confused."[49] The *Regula cuiusdam ad virgines* expected nuns to eat two dishes of vegetables and a flour pastry a day and a measure of beer and wine if the abbess permitted it.[50] The Benedictine rule held appeal for a convent with high-ranking inmates—it allowed for a high-table arrangement whereby the abbess and her guests could eat apart from the other nuns. Bertilla and Balthild could have eaten more privately, and thus differently, from the nuns, and furthermore, the abbess and Balthild may have entertained guests, thus requiring a supply of specialty foods. The royal palace at Chelles could provide food for the royal circle when they visited the town, often to hunt, and some entertainment of guests was provided for even under the guidance of the stricter monastic rules.

The convent was well positioned on the river Marne both for local fishing and for the transportation of food from Paris. The distance of Chelles from central Paris as the crow flies is approximately eleven miles (eighteen kilometers). The still-viable Roman road system meant that the inhabitants of the town had good access to Paris, and a horseman or good carriage could travel between the city and the town in a matter of hours. Even conservatively, an oxcart bringing supplies could make it by the same day or the next day if moving on a stone road.[51] The river Marne flows into the Seine, providing yet another means of travel and transportation. Accessibility was one good reason that early kings used the forests thereabouts for hunting, and the influx of a new monastic population would have benefitted also from access to food and supplies that were available locally, and that came from elsewhere. For example, wine would have been available to the nuns as it was permitted by most monastic rules and was necessary for liturgical services.

Balthild Envisions her Death

Before her death, Balthild reported to a select few that she had experienced a vision at the altar of the convent's church. Her hagiographer wrote:

> It was as if a ladder was raised up, standing before the altar of St. Mary, with its top reaching heaven, and with the angels of God accompanying

her, the Lady Balthild ascended it. From this revelation it was clearly understood that her lofty merits, patience, and humility would quickly lead her as one to be exalted to the height of the Eternal King and to the crown of her reward.[52]

This simple vision, we are told by her hagiographer, was interpreted by Balthild herself as a sign that her death was close and that she must make her final journey to that heavenly place where she had stored up her best treasure. The crown of salvation neatly replaced the honor she had held in the world, although it is not thought that crowns were worn as a unique royal sign in the seventh century. The stairway or ladder (*scala*) was a conventional spiritual symbol with biblical resonances and a direct connection to the ladder image in the Benedictine rule (Fig. 5.1).

She kept the vision secret, we are told, and hid the gravity of her illness. Bertilla and the other nuns tried to cheer her, but she knew from the vision that her end was not far off. Bertilla, too, was sick at this time, and so Balthild, we are told, did not want to add to the abbess's suffering by revealing the gravity of her own condition. She was sufficiently successful in her secrecy it seems that when it came her death seemed sudden. The hagiographer tells another story about this time. Balthild had a goddaughter "whom she wished to go with her" and the child died suddenly before Balthild herself. Later sources state that the little godchild's name was Radegund, a fitting name for the godchild of a queen who drew so much inspiration from this earlier foreign queen and saint. Nuns were forbidden to become godmothers to children once they entered the convent, another indication that Balthild's position was not that of a nun.[53] What can we make of this story? To a modern reader it sounds as if Balthild had willed the young girl to die so that she would not have to enter heaven alone. However, this comment may rely on a common seventh-century trope; Columbanus' disciple and biographer, Jonas, described such boons granted to some nuns at Faremoutiers. Nuns did not want to die alone.

Balthild's deathbed was described touchingly. Making the sign of the cross, she turned her eyes and hands to heaven and her soul "was loosed from the chain of her body." At the moment of her death "a splendour from most high glistened most brightly in the little room. And without a doubt this holy soul was gloriously received by a chorus of angels, and her very faithful friend, the late Lord Bishop Genesius, came out to meet her, as her great reward demanded."[54] There is no way to verify these poignant details. Did she see her old friend Genesius in her last hours? Or was the point of

LIFE AND DEATH AT THE CONVENT OF CHELLES 107

Fig. 5.1 Balthild's vision of a ladder. Prefatory image to Étienne Binet, *La vie excellente de sainte Bathilde* (1624). The image is based on a block cut by Alexius Lindt (1517), print by Leonhard Beck (British Museum #1920,0430.7). However, in this image we see how the convent looked in the seventeenth century when Binet's work was dedicated to Abbess Marie de Lorraine. Balthild is shown praying in front of the altar where she sees a vision of a ladder and her soul being carried to heaven.

the story to make a direct connection between her reward in heaven and the alms she had given to the poor through her almoner's hands? Whatever virtues and sins might be attributed to her in life, the queen's generosity to the poor and to the nuns of Chelles meant her salvation was not too hard to imagine. It was also meaningful to the community that the convent's foundress had received a supernatural sign that legitimized the daily life of the nuns as an effective path to salvation.

The hagiographer comments that the vision became well known. The ladder in Balthild's vision became the convent's emblem; it was etched into the milestones on roads around the convent guiding travelers to Chelles in later centuries. An example of such a milestone is held in the collection of the Alfred Bonno Museum in Chelles. The vision was depicted in numerous publications on her life in the seventeenth and eighteenth centuries. From later evidence we know that the celestial ladder was on the convent's seal in the eighteenth century, appearing alongside the royal fleur-de-lys.[55]

Death, Lamentation, and Burial

Balthild died in 680. Prayers and psalms should have accompanied Balthild's final hours. If all went well, she would have time for penitential reflection. She would make her confession to a priest, be reconciled, and receive communion. We know that priests were present at her death, but to the nuns' dismay they themselves were not all informed of the queen's impending demise. However, the nuns would have prepared Balthild's body for burial. The body would be washed. That was woman's work. Then the body would be placed on a bier for transportation. Even though Balthild's burial was within the monastic precincts, there would have been a short procession with psalms and a vigil at which the nuns could say their farewells. Balthild was then interred in her sarcophagus.[56] Given her high status we might expect that a bishop, most likely the bishop of Paris but possibly the bishop of Meaux, would have presided over it the funeral service.[57] Then prayers would ask that her soul be cleansed of any trace of sin so that she could evade the gates of hell.

Dead saints are always lamented in Merovingian sources. Intense grief followed on Balthild's death we are told so that "it was as if this gem which everyone wanted had been snatched from them." The nuns prayed that Balthild's soul would be "guided to Saint Mary in the chorus and company of the saints."[58] "Then, as was fitting for her, they buried her with great honor and much reverence," the short sentence cloaking the great attention we know to have been given to the queen's burial. While some of the items that accompanied Balthild's bones may have been placed there subsequently when her tomb was moved in 833, given the lapse of one hundred and fifty years it is more likely that, with the exception of the Chasuble, many of the items associated with her were deposited at the time of her burial.

Abbess Bertilla's first important business was to promote the liturgical commemoration of the saint: "Then the Lady Abbess Bertilla, taking care because of the eagerness of her piety, requested the holy priests that her holy memory should be preserved constantly throughout many churches in holy sacrifices. And throughout many places deservedly her [memory] is still steadfastly celebrated."[59] Bertilla's plan was successful. Balthild's name was included in liturgical prayers early on.[60] Her feast day is January 30. Healing miracles were attributed to her intervention. Yet more miracles were recorded when Balthild's corpse was moved to the new and improved abbey church of Notre Dame in 833. Abbess Hegilvid's elevation of Balthild's corpse in 833 generated a new source of relics—items removed from Balthild's burial to give out as gifts to other monasteries. Corbie had some of Balthild's hair as a relic by 840. Such gifts solidified the connections between monastic foundations, and relic exchanges were part of the busy exchanges between institutions. Each new relic provided gave the community an opportunity to ask for God's guidance, and each relic gained provided an opportunity for liturgical celebration. When Corbie received Balthild's hair, the relic would have been viewed as a proxy for the saint herself, as if she had come to live among them. At Chelles, in addition to Balthild's feast day on January 30, the community celebrated March 7 as the date on which Balthild's body was installed in the new church with its own festival of remembrance. A surviving account of the 833 translation of Balthild's body was written sometime after the middle of the ninth century providing some precise details of the event.[61]

We do not have a witness account of Balthild's funeral and burial in 680. However, having accepted the body of Balthild's son Chlothar III in 673, the community had a model for what was due to a royal burial prior to Balthild's death. Both Balthild and her son were buried in the convent's church of the Holy Cross (formerly Saint George) which already had a mortuary function with a necropolis outside.[62]

While no contemporary written account of her burial survives, further information can be deduced from archaeological sources. The record of the translation of her body from the church of the Holy Cross to the new church of Notre Dame in 833 preserves some precious details. Furthermore, recent excavations at the site of Balthild's church, and the presence of burial items and textiles associated with her, together with the investigation of the package of "dust" removed from Balthild's tomb in 833, provides clues as to the funerary environment and activity that accompanied Balthild as she was consigned to her grave.

Balthild was initially placed in a sarcophagus in a crypt beneath the church of Holy Cross which she had built over the original church dedicated to Saint George. We know from the 833 translation record that Balthild had been laid to rest in a sarcophagus, and that this was located on the ground. A crypt burial would fit this description, and indeed excavations of the Holy Cross church have supported evidence of a crypt. This would be entirely in keeping with what we know of other privileged church burials in the Merovingian period.

The tomb was also accessible from the first. The hagiographer records the miraculous cure of a demon-possessed boy who was brought to her tomb and was flung by the demon to the pavement (*pavimentum*) in front of her tomb.[63] The sarcophagus would have been made of stone or of plaster. It is possible that her sarcophagus was made of stone like that of Theodechild and her brother Agilbert that survive in the crypt at Jouarre. (The presence of plaster in the "dust" package could point to a sealing substance, as Laporte thought.) However, given the proximity of Chelles to Paris with access to a river route, and in view of the remains of plaster sarcophagi found at Chelles, Balthild's sarcophagus may have been a molded plaster sarcophagus of the type so well attested for this period and made at various workshops around Paris.[64] It could have been decorated with roundels and stylized flowers, as in the fragments of plaster sarcophagi excavated at Chelles, or with geometrical designs or crosses as found at other sites in the region.[65] A sturdy burial container would befit the queen, and in the Paris region stone and plaster could be easily obtained; a sealed burial container could also preserve a body so that it appeared remarkably preserved when opened.

The "dust" collected from her tomb in 833 contained leaves and herbs that may have been used to deodorize and decorate her body. A single grape seed was preserved, a stray find in the "dust," perhaps left by a funeral attendee or grave preparer, or dragged in with clothing or the leaves. Vines were tended in this area.

Exhumation and Expectations

We are not accustomed to hearing about the unearthing of relatively recent burials today unless for forensic analysis. However, in the case of a holy royal burial, the possibility that the body would be exhumed in the future could have been anticipated and therefore planned for. Such a consideration would encourage the careful arrangement of the body, its clothing, and its other contents. A holy body in its coffin was on its way to becoming a relic, so the nuns who buried Balthild, and later Bertilla, prepared their bodies for the afterlife as relics as well as for the afterlife of the soul.

We know of a couple of important exhumations of female saints that took place contemporaneously with Balthild's burial and that can provide some insight into the thoughts and expectations that exhuming holy bodies inspired in the seventh century. Like Balthild, the exhumed nuns were Anglo-Saxons. In around 673, the tomb of the Ethelburga, daughter of the king of East Anglia, Anna, who was a nun at the Frankish convent of Faremoutiers, was opened. This took place seven years after her death but miraculously, her body was found to be incorrupt: it was washed, clothed, and moved to its new location in Saint Stephen's church.[66] We know this story from Bede, an indication that stories of Anglo-Saxon nuns who died in France made their way back to England. Because this occurred at Faremoutiers, a convent that Balthild had patronized as queen, such an important and miraculous event would also have been known also at Chelles.

We learn even more details about the exhumation of female bodies from the case of Aethelthryth, another daughter of King Anna of the East Angles and half-sister to Ethelburga. The Anglo-Saxon queen-abbess, Aethelthryth (Etheldreda or Audrey in the medieval tradition), died in Ely in 689, a year before Balthild's death. Aethelthryth's body was exhumed sixteen years later in 695. Bede's source for the queen-abbess's life was probably an account from Ely, but he also explained that he had verified some of the more remarkable details of her heroic virginity from Bishop Wilfrid of York. Bede's account of the virgin queen-abbess's life and burial provides a useful comparison to Balthild's and, indeed, it bears some resemblance to it.

Aethelthryth was able to retain her virginity through a brief marriage to Tondbert of the South Gyrwe, and then through twelve years of marriage to the Northumbrian King Ecgfrith.[67] Eventually she was permitted to enter the religious life, first at Coldingham where she lived as a nun for a year becoming its abbess, but then returning to her homeland in East Anglia to found a convent in Ely where she lived in great piety as abbess until her death. Her death was attributed to a tumor on her neck or jaw which she considered a punishment for having worn precious jewels in her youth. The story is so clearly reminiscent of the story of Balthild's necklace told in

Audoin's Life of Eligius that it confirms the movement of stories back and forth across the Channel.

Initially, Aethelthryth had been buried in a wooden coffin but after sixteen years her sister Seaxburh, who had succeeded her as abbess, decided to exhume her body to move it to the church. Seaxburh was able to source a white marble sarcophagus from some distance away. When Etheldreda's wooden coffin was opened her body looked intact—as if she had died that very day—and an incision performed by a physician to lance a tumor under her jaw was discovered, in death, to have healed into a faint scar. The physician, whose name was Cynifrid, attended the exhumation and was able to verify this remarkable observation. Bede tells us that the nuns came prepared to wash the body and that the linens found buried with her had remained fresh. (In her lifetime she never wore linen, we are told, but only wool.) After it was inspected and cleaned, Aethelthryth's body was transferred to a more prestigious white marble sarcophagus into which she fit precisely.

The account of Aethelthryth's life from which Bede drew, and the details of her exhumation, may have arisen from an early Life of the saint followed by a translation account when the body was exhumed (as in Balthild's case), or the work may have been written as a direct response to her exhumation as an aid to propagating her cult. The East Anglian nuns who trickled into Chelles after 695 will have known of this famous case; perhaps they even brought a copy of the Ely account with them. But given the fact that Aethelthryth was Ethelburga's sister, the story could also have been known from communication with Faremoutiers. In short, the stories of the remarkable exhumation of the two sisters were circulating, alerting Bertilla to a similar future for Balthild's tomb if her efforts were successful and the queen came to be venerated as a saint. Exhumations raised expectations as well as bodies.

A Holy Packet

Much of the magnificent burial display that Bertilla and the nuns provided for their dead queen and foundress survived in the form of a parcel of relics that were cared for and protected by the community of Chelles for centuries. These relics comprised textiles, small objects, and most importantly for modern science Balthild's bones and hair, and the bones of the abbess.

In the ancient world, slaves were bodies, to be used, disciplined, and disposed of. Although the medieval cult of saints has left tangible remains of many treasured saints, lovingly conserved and visited by their devotees, there is some poignancy in the fact that modern scientific advances have enabled us to inspect Balthild yet one more time as a body, subjected to scrutiny, her bodily remains exposed.

Although only a small percentage of her skeleton survived to be examined in 1983–85, the investigation of Balthild's human remains revealed some basic information about her physical person. It was possible to determine that her height was almost 5′2″ (1.58 m), an average height for a woman in the seventh century. There was no sign of disease in her bones, although much of her skeletal bone has been lost. Her skull had been placed in a head-reliquary and other portions given out as gifts, so that all that remained of her cranium in 1983 was two small fragments of bone—not enough to do facial reconstruction. Bones that were sent as relics to other monasteries did not always survive the depredations of time or the French Revolution; much of her body has long since vanished into the anonymity occasioned by lost records and lost labels. Jean-Pierre Laporte provides a useful list of the known relics of Balthild that were gifted away over the centuries.[68] For example, a portion of her jawbone with two teeth still attached was gifted to Corbie in 1647 and ended up in the parish church after the Revolution. Laporte reports that in 1914 British soldiers tried to open the relic chest with an explosive device—the curé of the parish church sought to repair the damage with glue, but stuck two teeth on the jaw that were not Balthild's![69] In 1655 a piece of her temporal bone was sent to Jumièges; after the French Revolution it was held by the diocese of Rouen until it ended up at the abbey of Saint Wandrille where it remains to this day.[70] Further relics of Balthild and Bertilla were gifted to Pope Pius IX in 1853 and presumably survive. Lost bones are lost opportunities. Since 1983 there have been scientific advances that could determine the geographical region in which Balthild spent her youth through isotopic analysis of her teeth, and whether she had suffered malnutrition in her youth or anemia, all of which might give insight into the contested issue of her origins and social status prior to marriage. From what remained of the Chelles cache of relics, the team in 1983 determined that Balthild had blood type A, and that she appeared healthy. The archaeologist termed her body "gracile," or slight.[71] Her hair was strawberry-blond, dyed to hide the gray, and abundant in that it required long ribbons to bind it.

The 1983 examination of the relics and the archaeological investigation that occasioned it was only the last in a very long series of inspections of the bones and artifacts associated with Balthild and Bertilla and of their close associates, Genesius, Eligius, and Audoin. Through the centuries the relics of the two women were repeatedly exposed, scrutinized, removed, packaged, re-housed, venerated, poked, plundered, hidden, fragmented, reassembled, and displayed. The long history of the relics and their medieval and modern caretakers is carefully reconstructed by Jean-Pierre Laporte in *Le Trésor des Saints de Chelles* (1988). Whether for piety or curiosity, or both, Balthild, together with her abbess Bertilla, have been made to exist and circulate above ground in a kind of aerial immortality that has lasted for centuries. This state of existence had its start with the first major inspection of Balthild's tomb on February 26, 833, when Abbess Hegilvid (or, Helvide) obtained permission from her son-in-law Emperor Louis the Pious, to open up Balthild's coffin and move the body to the new church, Notre Dame, built by the abbess Gisela.[72]

The events of 833 were full of wonder. On opening the tomb, the assembled nuns found the queen's body intact, incorrupt, as if she were only sleeping.[73] This was one hundred and fifty-three years after Balthild's death. Jean-Pierre Laporte suggests that this may not have been purely wishful thinking as burial in a stone sarcophagus in a church may have preserved the body sufficiently well that her features could have been recognizable, and the textiles would still have been in good condition at this date.[74] Body-preservation was a technique practiced by the Merovingians. Among the contents gathered in 833 available to be analyzed in 1983 was dust formed from the remnants of textiles, vegetation, plaster (from the coffin sides), and body magma.[75] An intact body was expected. The bishop of Paris, Erchenrad, arrived eighteen days after the tomb opening and the formal process of translating the body to its new resting place was undertaken on March 17. Miracles were recorded in the *Translatio*, a text that recorded the 833 elevation, and it was also recorded that Balthild's goddaughter's body (Radegund) was moved at that time into the tomb that Balthild's body vacated. Items from Balthild's tomb were soon distributed. Hegilvid, already known to have gifted relics of other saints in the 830s, and was probably the first to do so, and by 840 some of Balthild's hair was at Jouarre.[76] A relic of hair was easily gifted while the body continued its slow path to full decomposition. Hair and clothing, so easy to detach, continued to be given out as gifts. At some point bones joined them, although the first record of this is in the seventeenth century when a piece of her jawbone along with a slipper were sent as gifts to Corbie in 1647.[77]

At some early juncture, Bertilla's body was also elevated and kept as a relic at the convent. Her cult was lower-key than Balthild's, being a local, community saint. The Life of Bertilla was duly written, and her feast day was celebrated on November 5. However, there is no written record of when her body was elevated, although Laporte's suggestion that it was done on May 26, when another feast for Bertilla was celebrated in the convent, seems likely. Bertilla's lesser profile as a saint meant that more of her body was kept at Chelles and thus available for examination by Laporte and his team. At under 5' (1.5 m), Bertilla was shorter than Balthild. Like the queen, Bertilla was interred with splendid textiles.

Clothing in the Grave

The clothing in which Balthild and Bertilla were buried, and which form the extraordinary textile collection held by the Alfred Bonno Museum in Chelles, were valued as relics early on. One wonders what the Carolingian nuns thought of the bright silk garments uncovered in the tombs. When the nuns opened Balthild's tomb they would have seen the enormous, fringed shawl that wrapped her, and when they opened Bertilla's tomb they would have seen the dress of striped purplish-brown and yellow silk; the sleeve of this gown was the only part of the ensemble that could be reconstructed in 1983. By the Carolingian era, most Christians and certainly nuns would have been given a simple burial. However, kings were still buried in splendor, as was the case with Charlemagne. As a royal burial the precious items in Balthild's grave may have been understood in that way. Abbess Bertilla's clothing, when it was first seen, may have raised more eyebrows, as it would have looked worldly to an audience used to seeing religious buried in sober shrouds. However, sumptuous burial was the Merovingian way for the seventh-century elite, even if there was a move away from this in the second half of the seventh century. We see parallels with the sumptuous burials of religious figures elsewhere, such as the burial of the hermit-bishop Cuthbert of Lindisfarne and, closer to home, Theudechild of Jouarre; both were similarly enveloped in fine fabrics.[78] The voluminous tunic (a "grande robe") and a floor-length fringed cloak or shawl (Fig. 5.2) were attributed to Balthild by the 1983 team. At a height of 8' 10" (2.7 m) the fringed cloak,

Fig. 5.2 Fringed shawl after restoration. Alfred-Bonno Museum, Ville de Chelles. Laporte, *Le Trésor des Saints de Chelles*, Plate III.

originally yellow and pink edged with braid, would have fully enveloped the queen and may have been used to cover her head also.

The most remarkable item to be preserved was the "chasuble of Chelles," the linen tunic with its silk-thread embroidered necklace (Fig. 5.3). The chasuble owes its good condition to two possible factors: that it was laid over the body of the queen with sufficient material between it and her body so that no damage was done by body fluids; or second, and more likely, the item was kept outside of the burial from the first and kept as a relic. The linen "chasuble" sometimes termed an "apron" in medieval sources, no longer has its back panel, but the garment was long and would have reached her ankles. As the most spectacular item in the collection, with its complex and multi-hued embroidered necklace, this item has been extensively studied. There is a consensus (further deliberations can be found in Laporte's work) that the item is consistent with the late seventh-century date. The embroidery—with its alternating colors, representation of multiple strands, and medallions—represents a necklace aesthetic found elsewhere in this era in royal and imperial contexts, such as in the mosaic portrait of Empress Theodora in the church of San Vitale in Ravenna and the pectoral cross with the votive crown and cross given to the monastery of Monza by King Agilulf of the Lombards in the early seventh century. Laporte suggests that the embroidered necklace was a replacement for a real necklace once owned by Balthild that she had gifted to the church. He points to a story told in the Life of Eligius, Balthild's mentor, that relates how the deceased bishop had appeared to a courtier in a vision with a message for Balthild that the necklace should be relinquished. If there is any truth to this story,

LIFE AND DEATH AT THE CONVENT OF CHELLES 117

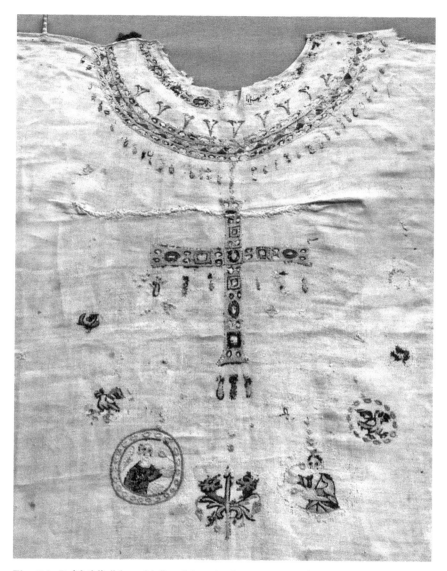

Fig. 5.3 Balthild's "chasuble" or "chemise." 117 × 84 cm (3.8 × 2.75 feet). Linen with silk embroidery. Alfred-Bonno Museum, Ville de Chelles. Photograph: © Genevra Kornbluth, Kornbluth Photography.

Balthild's decision to have it represented on her clothing shows some attachment to it. Still, as noted above, it is possible that even in the convent Balthild wore emblems of her royal status, especially when there were visitors, including her royal sons.[79] One wonders where she sourced the beautiful necklace on which the embroidery was based—was it a gift from her husband? A diplomatic offering? Had the jeweler-bishop Eligius himself made it as a copy of earlier necklaces? Had Balthild been the first to own it? Could she, for example, have inherited it from Nantechild? It is interesting to observe that the most immediate known parallels to Balthild's necklace were sixth and early seventh century, and thus fifty to one hundred years earlier than when she wore it.

Other items formed part of the burial. The multi-colored ribbons with animal and geometric designs were the kind of elaborate braiding that could be attached and detached from clothing. Laporte suggests they could have been part of a belt. Similar embroidered ribbons were deposited in Saint Cuthbert's grave. The burial items in Cuthbert's grave and Balthild's are a kind of pair. A very small gold pin in the form of a snake likely eluded detection when the clothing was removed from the coffin; it conforms to known pin types from the time, not least a very similar example found in the Staffordshire hoard.

The bones, dust, and textiles that comprised the relics were enclosed in precious reliquaries and were bundled at some point into parcels. Laporte's study traces the history of these packages over the centuries and makes a strong argument that the major items historically attributed to Balthild (the chasuble, the cloak, ribbons, and gold pin) were attributed correctly, and that the stripey silk dress belonged to Bertilla's burial. Conversely, the very fine embroidered shoes sometimes thought to have belonged to Balthild in the Middle Ages are more likely to have been ceremonial shoes worn by a bishop. Laporte suggested they could have belonged to Eligius and/or Genesius.[80] Altogether, what the relics indicate is that both Balthild and Bertilla were provided with richly furnished burials that included secular clothing and precious objects.

The Making of a Saint

Was Balthild viewed as a saint immediately after her death? This was certainly the line taken by her hagiographer who wrote that Balthild "reigns in glory with Christ."[81] In his work Balthild was given the honorifics that were customary for queens in the Merovingian age: she was termed Lady (*domna*), and a venerable and great woman.[82] It was also common in the Merovingian era to term holy people as saints; such titles bestowed informally before the papal saint-making processes introduced more specific conditions from the late eleventh century. Writing very soon after her death her hagiographer claimed that "she received the crown of great reward," and that she "enjoys what she had longed for: an immense and everlasting joy."[83] Healing miracles happened at her tomb soon after: suppliants were relieved of fever, demon possession, and toothache. One case of miraculous healing was described in greater detail as it was connected to one of the convent's benefactors. A bishop Leudegandus from Provence came to Chelles seeking relief for his son who was possessed by a vicious demon and after being deposited on the floor in front of the tomb, the boy was healed. Miracles at the tomb were considered proof of Balthild's intercessory power and a sign that she was a saint in heaven.[84]

Nevertheless, despite Bertilla's early efforts, the cult of Saint Balthild appears to have developed slowly and locally at first. Her hagiographer records that after Balthild's death Bertilla asked the bishops to remember Balthild in the mass. As Robert Folz expressed so well, at some point commemorative services *for* Balthild turned into a cult *of* Balthild, and the day of her death (January 30) became her cult's feast day.[85] The earliest evidence for this was a *Missa domnae Bathildis* at Corbie in 822 recorded in the ninth-century statutes of Adalard.[86] This was fully eleven years before Balthild's exhumation and her move to the new church which, together with two newly recorded miracles, consolidated her position as a saint. This late development of her cult may have been reflected in the modest tomb in which she was initially buried, and into which her goddaughter Radegund was placed after Balthild vacated it.[87]

Balthild's entry into the church's cycle of saint veneration took time. Her feast day was not included in martyrologies before the ninth century (Wandalbert, Usuard, Saint-Wandrille's Jerome martyrology) perhaps coinciding with the growing impetus of the cult under the influence of Louis the Pious and his mother-in-law Hegilvid.[88] Balthild's solicitude for the peace of the kingdoms of France, described in her Life, must have appealed to medieval kings and queens and formed part of the language of her commemoration throughout the centuries.

Even as her cult began to flourish from the ninth century, it remained fairly local to the extended Paris region and to those monastic institutions with which she was strongly associated either as founder or as patron. In particular, the monasteries of Corbie and Jumièges preserved Balthild's memory in their liturgical customs, often with embellishments drawn from the hagiographic Life. At Chelles and at Jumièges, excerpts from the Life of

Balthild drew not on the oldest Life but on the Carolingian "B" version, which emphasized Balthild's royal birth. Only at Corbie, where the earliest office was known and where the commemoration of Balthild fell into abeyance between the ninth and late twelfth century was the Merovingian "A" version of Balthild's vita maintained when the office dedicated to Balthild was reprised.[89] However, as far as Chelles was concerned, Balthild emerged from her tomb as a queen of royal blood with the "B" Life, and the liturgical commemoration dependent on it, effectively shaping a claim for Balthild's royal status from her birth. Her royal identity, together with the liturgical prayers for the peace of her kingdom drawn from her Life, meant that she embodied the ideal of a medieval royal saint. Her life as a slave was evoked primarily as a lesson about the rewards of chastity.

The Viking Invasions

In the ninth century, Vikings attacked monasteries in northern France including Chelles, whose position on the river Marne, a tributary of the Seine, allowed easy access. The nuns were able to hide and protect their relics and treasures. Jean-Pierre Laporte makes a convincing suggestion in supposing that it was probably at this time that the nuns exhumed the bones of Bertilla, the child Radegund, and others, so that they could move them away from the marauding armies. By this time the relics would likely have included some of Genesius and Eligius also.

From the ninth century onward, with their royal founder recast as royal from birth, the nuns of Chelles burnished Balthild's cultic identity as a queen. This was to be a very effective strategy, although the fortunes of the convent waxed and waned for the remainder of its history. There were calamities for the community such as a great fire in 1226. Possessing the remains of Balthild and Bertilla as prized relics among their constantly accumulating collection, the nuns directed their energies to preserving and honoring the bones of their founder. Indeed, the survival of the relics of Balthild and Bertilla are testimony to the extraordinary care provided by generations of nuns of Chelles. Over the centuries they were examined, documented, pulled apart into smaller relics, and given away as pious gifts, venerated, repackaged, rehoused in reliquaries, and in the modern era they were hidden from revolutionaries in 1790, and protected from marauding armies at various points in their history. In the twentieth century they were valiantly protected by the townsfolk of the Ville de Chelles and their priest (see Chapter 7, pp. 140–75). Their complicated history through the Middle Ages, through the French Revolution, and to the point when they were housed in the museum has been reconstructed with great care in Jean-Pierre Laporte's publications on the relics of Chelles. We will meet them again in the remaining chapters of this book.

6
Mother, Mutilator—and Murderer?

Most Merovingian saints whose names survived the centuries as religious patrons slid quietly into the dry bones and ghostly apparitions that fed and sustained a medieval cult. But Balthild is rather different. Even within the first few years after her death, her reputation was strange and conflicted. Over time, stories about her arose that had their roots in the half-truths and fictions that circled around her reputation as a mother and as a murderer. In Merovingian and Carolingian Francia she was a mother and a saint: a mother of sons, and nuns, and her people; a saint of royal status and founder of the important medieval convent of Chelles, and the monastery of Corbie. In Anglo-Saxon England, however, she acquired an altogether different reputation. In the eighth-century hagiography of Wilfrid of Ripon and York, penned by Stephen of Ripon (Eddius Stephanus), she was accused of the murder of nine bishops. By the thirteenth and fourteenth centuries she emerged as the principal actor behind a ghoulish medieval romance about the mutilation of her sons. It was not until the early modern era and into the nineteenth century that her political career as queen-regent of France emerged again into the light, serving as a muse for a Bourbon princess and later as an abolitionist queen. Balthild's modern reputation as an abolitionist is examined in the final chapter of this volume. In this chapter, we will encounter the oscillations of her strange and colorful reputation as a medieval saint.

A Woman of Contradictions

Early medieval sources are not subtle in imagining or ascribing inner motivations of women. Most commonly queens appear as actors in stories to explain unwanted reversals in the fortunes of men. Women were worthy of attention when they were saints or sinners, mothers or murderers. And that is where they are generally left in the sources. Balthild was described as all of these things: as saint, sinner, mother, and murderer. She is somewhat

Balthild of Francia: Anglo-Saxon Slave, Merovingian Queen, and Abolitionist Saint. Isabel Moreira,
Oxford University Press. © Oxford University Press 2024. DOI: 10.1093/oso/9780197518663.003.0006

exceptional, therefore, in attracting the attention of both supporters and detractors. However, when placed in the company of other powerful women who attracted polarized opinion, like the Byzantine empress Theodora, or Queen Brunhild in the sixth century, we can see how Balthild, as a powerful women, could attract entirely opposing judgments from observers.

Although we know Balthild largely through a hagiography, we should not be seduced by her hagiographer into thinking that Balthild was indeed a "saint," or viewed universally as a positive influence in her lifetime. We have seen how her political career was supported by factions held in check, and just as she was, at one point, viewed as indispensable for the security of the realm, so eventually its security required that she become dispensable. On the positive side of the equation, Balthild was a mother of future kings and thereby a protector of the dynasty. On the negative side of the equation, she was an operator in the cutthroat politics of the day, which included episcopal expulsions and murders. Balthild's reputation, therefore, was always more complicated than any single source suggests. Was she guilty of all, or any, of the accusations against her? That is not a question that can be answered confidently with the sources at our disposal. However, we may want to bear in mind the comment made by Stephen about Saint Wilfrid, a divisive figure in his time: "lightning strikes the peaks first."[1]

Dynastic Mothering

Before we delve into the later medieval stories of Balthild's mothering, it is worth giving some thought to how contemporary sources viewed her, as a mother to her children, as a mother of a royal dynasty, and as a symbolic mother to those who were effectively adopted by her through monastic rescue. How much can we know of Balthild the mother?

The most salient fact about Balthild was that she bore three healthy sons who survived into adulthood. It is rare to be told of children who died in infancy. Gregory of Tours is an unusual example in chronicling the early death of King Clovis I's and Chlothild's daughter who died immediately after her baptism. We are not informed of any such in Balthild's case. Miscarriages and stillbirths were, and are, sadly common, yet they are hardly ever mentioned in the chronicles unless there was a direct political consequence.[2] Nor are we told whether Clovis and Balthild had daughters. A daughter was always of less interest to chroniclers than a son unless she lived to make a dynastic alliance. A monastic source like the Life of Balthild would probably mention a daughter if she had entered the convent of Chelles with her mother, but we do not hear of this. Balthild had a goddaughter named Radegund in the convent with her, but she was too young to be Balthild's own daughter. It may be that Balthild was exceptionally fortunate in having three sons in a few short years, especially as it took three sons to ultimately secure the dynastic line.

One might expect that the hagiographic Life, the most positive source on Balthild's life, would display Balthild's motherly qualities. Yet her hagiographer is remarkably terse on the point, remarking merely on the birth of her sons, and stating that he wrote in the reign of her third son: "the royal offspring reigning now is hers."[3] This reticence may have arisen from a desire to focus on her saintliness. Yet there were some strong models in the Christian tradition for holy mothers of sons. Monica, the mother of Augustine, was one example; the mother of the Maccabees was another. There were some mother-daughter models, such as Jerome's description of Paula and Eustochium, but Balthild's hagiographer did not avail himself of these models. Rather, as we have seen, the models used for Balthild were earlier queens—the Merovingian queens Chlothild, Radegund, Ultrogotha, Helena the mother of Constantine, and the Old Testament queen, Esther.

One reason to distance Balthild from the reputation of her sons may have been the political frictions around the succession and especially the still recent scandal of the murder of her second son, Childeric II, at Autun in 675. The shocking events that deprived Balthild of her son, daughter-in-law, and unborn grandchild are entirely absent from her Life. The hagiographer wrote when Theuderic III was king. With Chlothar III dead without royal issue, and Childeric assassinated, it may not have been easy for her hagiographer to dwell on the characters of recently dead and, frankly, unpopular kings.

Yet we are not entirely dependent on Balthild's hagiographer for information about her sons. Her eldest, Chlothar III, had succeeded his father as king and it was during his youth that Balthild had been regent. It was as regent for Chlothar that Balthild had made pious donations to monasteries and churches, reformed the clergy, and worked to change the slave trade within Neustria. When Chlothar pushed for independence with the connivance of his counselors, and Balthild was forced to retire to Chelles, their relationship did not end. The royal court must have come to Chelles periodically; with a favored royal villa and the convent adjacent, there was ample opportunity for maintaining a mother-son relationship. One can imagine that he drew both comfort, support, and political mentorship from his mother. When Chlothar died in his twenties with no sons to succeed him, he was buried in the convent of Chelles, undoubtedly at his mother's request.

With Childeric secured as king in Austrasia, there was an expectation in some quarters that her son Theuderic would be king of Neustria next, but the question of who the new king should be was answered temporarily by Childeric's coup, supported by the mayor Ebroin, that was intended to unite Austrasia, Neustria, and Burgundy under Childeric's sole rule. What was Balthild's relationship with her second son? Childeric had been sent from her care at a young age to rule in Austrasia. We can wonder how close she was to this son who became king of Neustria by ousting his brother? We are left no documents to help us unravel their relationship, but his life ended horribly. His murder just five years before her own death meant that this was relatively fresh news at the time her hagiographer was writing. Theuderic III's reign was still in its early stages.

Whereas her official hagiographer did not dwell on her motherly relationship with her sons, Balthild and her sons were interesting figures to other hagiographers of the era. The reigns of the three brothers appear in stories as contextualizing elements in a group of Merovingian hagiographies, suggesting that the identity of the young princes, and the succession issue, was familiar enough to serve as a ready identifier for audiences. For example, the Life of Lantbert of Lyon informs us that the saint came to court during the reign of Chlothar and his brothers who in turn became kings of the Franks; they are named as Chlothar, Childeric, and Theuderic.[4] In the Life of Ansbert of Fontanelle, later bishop of Rouen, we are told that the saint's birth took place during the reign of Chlothar, son of Clovis II and Queen Balthild, and of their other two sons, Childeric and Theuderic.[5] Ansbert of Rouen was said to have been confessor to King Theuderic, and so in some of the stories Balthild's last reigning son, Theuderic, featured in some of the stories alongside the holy bishop. We learn, for example, that Theuderic did not expect to become a king but that Ansbert predicted that one day he would.[6] Just as Chlothar's royal birth was prophesied by Eligius, Theuderic's reign was also prophesied by a holy man. Clearly, Balthild, Clovis II, and their three royal sons were a recognizable point of reference for later audiences. However, it is in Audoin's Life of Eligius of Noyon that we see the fullest picture of Balthild in a maternal role.

Audoin is an important contemporary witness to Balthild's time on power and he relates a few stories that inch closer to portraying Balthild as an expressive woman. It is worth remembering that although their deaths were twenty years apart, the biographies of both Balthild and Eligius were written around the same time, in the 680s; the authors may have been writing somewhat in sight of each other. Audoin mentions that the three realms were united at the time he wrote, which means that he was writing in 679 or later. Balthild died in 680, so it is possible that she was still alive when he was writing some portions of the work. Audoin also died in the early 680s. He knew the queen and her close connection to Eligius. While he mentioned that Eligius was a counselor to three kings—to Chlothar II, Dagobert, and then Clovis II—it is Eligius' relationship to Balthild that is the most personal royal connection he describes.

In Audoin's work, Eligius is a dynastic prophet. We are told that he foretold King Dagobert's death, and that of his royal brother Charibert II (in Aquitaine), and the birth of the little Chlothar, Balthild's firstborn. (Foretelling royal births and deaths was evidently not as dangerous an activity as it would later become!) We learn that a pregnant Balthild was afraid that she might have a daughter rather than a son and that the kingdom might be imperiled because of it. Eligius predicted that she would have a son.[7] This reassuring message was followed sometime later by another prophecy, at a time when Clovis and Balthild had two more sons and were "peaceful and happy." This later vision portended the death of Balthild's husband and that of all her sons—deaths that we can only hope he did not confide to the queen! Of course, Eligius's hagiographer, Audoin, had the advantage of significant hindsight in fashioning Eligius' prophecies as the boys were still youngsters in 660 when Eligius died, a reminder that it is Audoin writing in the 680s who is our source for these stories set in the 650s.

The importance of the birth of Balthild's first son for the security of the realm can be gauged by the fact that, unusually, we have two accounts of the boy's baptism and naming. In the anonymous Acts of Aunemund, the bishop whose martyrdom was laid at Balthild's door in a later hostile source, is said to have baptized the baby, raising him from the sacred font as a godson.[8] Audoin credited Eligius with the same role at the boy's baptismal ceremony: Chlothar was Eligius' godson, a *filiosus*. While it is possible that the boy had two godfathers, and both men were involved in the ceremony, it is not possible for both men to have baptized him. But, according to Audoin, it was Eligius who gave the baby his name, which may or may not be a way of claiming Eligius' role in the child's baptism.[9]

Is there anything to be made of the choice of Chlothar's name? Was it viewed as auspicious in some way? By the seventh century, Merovingian kings were using name repetition for their sons.[10] Chlothar was a Merovingian name carried by two kings before him. Chlothar I was one of Clovis I's sons, and he lived long enough to become sole king of the realm before his death in 561: he represented unity of the three kingdoms. Religious people knew him also as the husband of the saintly Radegund, a queen who had been captured in the aftermath of the defeat of the Thuringians and who had retired to the religious life in Poitiers. His grumbling acceptance of his wife's defection and his generous donations to religious foundations offset his reputation for multiple marriages and for marrying two women who were sisters. Even a century on, this Chlothar would have been known through Gregory of Tours' Histories, and the two Lives of Radegund. More likely, the frame of reference would have been closer to home—to Clovis II's own grandfather, Chlothar II, who had been a great man, combining dynastic and religious aims in the creation of a royal center at Clichy, close to the royal burial site at Saint Denis. Chlothar II was also the first king to inherit a combined kingdom of Neustria, Austrasia, and Burgundy rather than fight for it: he, too, was a symbol of the unity of the three kingdoms. More to the point, Eligius had personally known the second Chlothar. King Chlothar had favored him as an artisan, and at Chlothar's court Eligius had been part of the circle of friends around the king's son Dagobert, for whom, in time, he also served as royal jeweler and beautifier of holy monuments sacred to the dynasty. The choice of name was perhaps meaningful, but hardly remarkable, and there is no reason to think that it would have been a problematic choice for the royal couple. They went on to name their other two sons Childeric and Theuderic. If Childeric was named for a former king, it could only have been Childeric I, pagan father of the dynastic founder Clovis I, an unusual choice. However, Childeric I's wife Basina was a Thuringian so the name of Balthild's second son may have made a connection with the eastern regions of Austrasia, to which the young Childeric was eventually sent as king. Her third son, Theuderic, could have been named for an earlier Theuderic who had ruled Austrasia and Burgundy. The three names of Balthild's sons, therefore, referenced earlier kings with connections to Neustria, Austrasia, and Burgundy, respectively, signaling a desire for regnal unity.

Balthild and her sons make another appearance in the Life of Eligius as mourners at the bishop's funeral, alongside nobles and soldiers in attendance.[11] Eligius' biographer wanted to show the great esteem in which Eligius was held by members of the royal house, and so he provided an extended narrative of the final obsequies. First, he tells us that Balthild wept, wanting Eligius' body to be taken to the convent of Chelles for burial. This was not to be. Indeed, the body could not be moved, a sure sign that it was not Eligius' posthumous wish to be buried among the nuns. In her extreme grief Balthild uncovered his face, kissing it, drowning his hands, breast, and cheeks in a sea of tears.[12] It was then that a miracle happened: blood started to come out of the corpse's nose. This was mopped up quickly with linen cloths and so provided Balthild with the much-desired relic for her convent. She then set about fasting and mourning for three days, weeping, with her sons. It was winter, but she followed on foot behind the bier that bore her dead friend. Later, Eligius appeared in a vision to an unnamed person in the royal household with a message for her: that she should not regret removing her insignia ornamented in gold and gems.[13] (Had he fashioned them himself?) Balthild's response on learning of this message was to divest herself of her jewels. She kept nothing except her gold bracelets, we are told. Every other part of her dress she gave in alms. And she ordered that a gold cover be made for Eligius' tomb. Later still, Balthild and her counsellors decided to move the body, and it was she who provided the embroidered vestments that he was reburied in. All was placed under a seal.[14]

Through Audoin's eyes we encounter a version of Balthild not readily visible in her hagiography. Here, Balthild is an emotional woman, anxious about the birth of a child, and later weeping, huddling with her young sons at a funeral, feeling the loss of a supporter and friend and comforter—someone who had given her acceptance and respect and guidance, and who had been a mentor in her desire to free imported slaves. Was the story about her jewels and royal insignia misplaced in the narrative? It seems better placed as a story relating to her eventual renunciation of royal power. That the royal jewels were associated with Eligius would make sense if he had designed and fashioned them. Balthild's care for Eligius' dead body, supplying the decorated vestments, was a womanly function around burial; her care for his tomb, covering it with gold, was queenly. Balthild and her sons made their appearance in just a few paragraphs of the very long Life of Eligius, but it is only here that we encounter an image of Balthild as a soft mothering figure: as a grieving widow with her young sons, lamenting the loss of a protective friend.

Murderer of Nine Bishops

Writers favorable to Balthild likened her to earlier royal saints. But in the eighth century we are presented with an entirely negative reference to Balthild in which she is likened to the quintessentially evil and immoral biblical queen, Jezebel. In his account of the deeds of the long-lived bishop, Wilfrid of York, Stephan claimed that Balthild was a Jezebel who had murdered nine bishops. Even accounting for some medieval love of exaggeration, this was a bit much. And as an accusation it was also clearly wrong. The story is interesting, however, because it does point to some issues that resonate with Balthild's record as a queen of Neustria at a time when bishops were political actors among whom she had both supporters and detractors. Bishops were essential to Balthild's survival as a queen-regent and, as we have seen, some were also personal supporters. Balthild's close connection with bishops and their ambitions was real.

So how did an Anglo-Saxon source come to such a negative view of the queen? Was it a case of mistaken identity, or a whiff of the partisan politics of the past? First, let us look at the accusation. Stephen tells us a story in which a young Wilfrid had a lucky escape. Wilfrid had been living on the continent for some time, having taken a trip to Rome where he received the pope's blessing. He then stayed on in Lyon for three years where he was ordained by his friend, mentor, and symbolic father, the Merovingian bishop of Lyon, who Stephen wrongly thought was named Dalfinus. The perilous event took place in the late-650s at a time when Balthild was ruling as queen-regent:

> But God had something better in view for our race. For at that time there was an evil-hearted queen named Baldhild who persecuted the church of God. Even as of old the wicked Queen Jezebel slew the prophets of God, so she, though sparing the priests and deacons, gave command to slay nine bishops, one of whom was this Bishop Dalfinus, whom the dukes with evil intent summoned to their presence. But he made his way with undaunted heart to the place of trial, knowing what lay before him. Saint Wilfrid the servant of God went with him, and though the bishop wished

to prevent him, joyfully replied, "Nothing could be better for us than that father and son should die together and be with Christ." So the holy bishop won a martyr's crown; but when Saint Wilfrid, despoiled and ready for the prize of martyrdom, was standing by fearlessly, the dukes asked, "Who is that handsome young man who is preparing for death?" "A foreigner from the English race from Britain" they were told. Thereupon they said, "Spare him and do not touch him."[15]

Some blatant inaccuracies in this story have long been known. The bishop of Lyon at this time was Aunemund (the same Aunemund who had baptized Balthild's son, Chlothar), and indeed Aunemund was murdered on his way to face trial. The identity of Dalfinus is not clear. Dalfinus could have been another name for Aunemund, but it has also been suggested that he was Aunemund's brother who, unnamed in the source, was the city's count. City counts in this era were royal appointments with responsibility for collecting taxes and they had a judicial role that they shared with the city's bishop.[16] This was certainly a powerful family with two brothers holding the two most important offices in the city of Lyon. In Stephen's story, the offer made by "Dalfinus" was that Wilfrid should become his heir by marrying his niece. This niece, then, could have been a daughter of his brother the count. Provided with a choice between a secular career and a religious one, Wilfrid chose the latter. Sometime around 658, when Balthild was queen-regent, the bishop of Lyon, Aunemund, was indeed murdered, as was his brother before him, so the question is—was Balthild implicated in this? And how did Stephen make the leap from the murder of one bishop to nine?

Wicked queens were the manufactured nemeses of would-be saints, as saints were also of wicked queens. Wilfrid encountered not a few during his career, according to Stephen who liked the trope. So, in finding a simple answer to the murder of bishop Aunemund, the queen in question was Balthild. However, it should be noted that in the Merovingian text the king is explicitly named alongside Balthild as having Aunemund' brother decapitated.[17] It is possible, then, that Stephen misremembered what he had heard from Wilfrid, or from the oral tradition around Wilfrid after his death, or what Fredegar's *Chronicle* had stated about an earlier queen, Brunhild, namely that she was charged with killing ten Frankish kings.[18] Finally, the C version of the Life of Wilfrid gave the name of "Brunechild" as the wicked queen in his story, also termed a "Jezebel" in sources, suggesting that a slip of some magnitude was made somewhere along the way.[19] In short, as a source for Balthild's politics and actions, Stephan simply cannot be viewed as a reliable source.

In fact, we do not have to rely on Stephen for details about Aunemund's murder since the Merovingian biography of Aunemund records his violent death. Summoned to trial for treason by the king (this would have been the young Chlothar with Balthild as regent), Aunemund was traveling north with a military escort when, close to the city of Chalon, the party pitched their tents. Aunemund evidently slept in his own tent where he was murdered during the night by two men who had been "sent" for this purpose. The two men accomplished the task with swords, creating a bloody mess that was found the next morning when the armed escort came to Aunemund's tent and uncovered his face.[20] We are not informed who sent the assassins, but Aunemund's hagiographer implicated certain nobles with the desire to kill the bishop; Ebroin's agency is suspected. The biographer's reticence to name the person who sent the killers could have been an attempt to hide the queen's agency. However, Wilfrid was not present at this event and it seems that that Stephen's garbled story was an attempt to show his hero's willingness to submit to martyrdom alongside his mentor.[21] As for the story of Balthild's role in Aunemund's murder, the installation of her favorite, Genesius, as the next bishop of Lyon and her role in the death of Aunemund's brother may have supplied sufficient cause for suspecting her of having a direct role in the murder of Aunemund. Aunemund is thus one bishop whose murder may tentatively be set at Balthild's door.

But one bishop is not nine bishops. And the murder of bishops was not uncommon in these years of intense factionalism among the aristocracy from whom the episcopal cadre was largely, although not exclusively, drawn. Paul Fouracre points out that Balthild's anti-simony policy (examined in Chapter 4, pp. 75–76) may have been a means by which Balthild could replace existing bishops with her own appointees.[22] Balthild's forcible removal from court coincided with the murder of Bishop Sigobrand of Paris, her appointee; another of her appointees, Leudegar of Autun, was also later deposed, tortured, and murdered, which shows that Balthild's circle of bishops were closely associated with her person and that such appointments were viewed largely politically. In the political purge that led to Balthild's removal from power, the queen may have been lucky to escape with her life. Her role as the mother of kings likely saved her.

As for the accusation that she was a Jezebel, this was simply par for the course. A wicked queen and a sexual seductress may have played to ideas about her former servile status, but it was also a way to cast doubt on the legitimacy of her sons and the dynasty.

"Mère sans merci": Balthild, Medieval Romance, and Hamstrung Justice

We have seen that Balthild, first through her husband, and then her eldest son, was a generous monastic patron. Among the monastic houses greatly favored by the royal couple was the monastery of Jumièges (dép. Seine-Maritime) in Normandy.[23] Stories arose over the centuries connecting the lives of the royal couple and their sons with the institution, and with its founder Saint Philibert. At their heart, these stories served to recall the generous donations of Balthild and Clovis to the monastery. One medieval story about Balthild and her sons had a lasting impact on French culture; a legend immortalized in poetry and in art. This was the story of the hamstrung princes. The Merovingian core of the medieval legend is simply told. Philibert, the founder of Jumièges, had grown up at Dagobert's court at the time that Eligius and Audoin were also there and, like them, he decided to pursue a religious career. After some years at the monastery of Rebais where he served as abbot, he was aided in his desire to establish a monastery by a magnificent donation by Clovis and Balthild. The Life of Philibert recorded the generosity that enabled the monastery of Jumièges to be built.[24] Like Balthild, Philibert's career was buffeted by the power struggles that beset the kingdom. During Ebroin's time in power he fled to Poitiers where the bishop, Ansoald, helped him found the island monastery of Noirmoutier off the Atlantic coast. Eventually Philibert was returned to favor and he founded first Pavilly, a nunnery, and at the end of his life, the abbey of Montivilliers close to the Seine estuary. Pavilly, the nunnery, was built close to Jumièges, effectively making them a double house. Indeed, the male and female communities were so close that a charming legend arose to emphasize their connection. It was said that the nuns used to launder the linens for use at Jumièges, and that these cloths were taken to the monastic church by a donkey who was so familiar with the route that he walked there and back unaided. One day the donkey was killed by a wolf. The abbess of Pavilly, Austrebertha, came across the bloody scene and admonished the wolf who thereafter took on the burden of the creature he had killed, carrying the linens back and forth between the monastery and nunnery.[25]

It is worth a short digression on the medieval history of the monastery of Jumièges to set the scene for the medieval legend about Balthild and her sons.

Located on the lower Seine, close to where the river flows into the sea, Jumièges, occupied a prime site surrounded on three sides by the winding river. The site bore the name Gemmeticum, which was considered aptly descriptive of its gem-like qualities. Geographically close to the monastery of Fontenelle (later St. Wandrille), it was founded as part of the reformed monasticism associated with Columbanus. Balthild was a supporter of this reformed monastic movement. The monastery grew and prospered so that it was soon reported to house nine hundred monks and fifteen hundred servants (*famuli*). Unfortunately, it was an easy target for Viking raiding in the ninth century. It was not until after the raids had subsided that the monastery was rebuilt in the tenth and eleventh centuries in an imposing, massive Norman architectural style. The monastery dominated the landscape until Jumièges was again destroyed during the French Revolution. Relieved of some of its burdensome stone weight for other building projects, by the nineteenth century the ruins had become romantic. Its remains became a historic site.

The medieval story of Balthild, Clovis, and their sons appears to have been inspired by the tombs of two young men at Jumièges. The original occupants of the tomb must have been long forgotten for them to come to be attached to a seventh-century legend. The style of the carved figures is clearly twelfth century (Fig. 6.1). With their coiffed hair and their robes decorated with fleurs-de-lys, they are the product of a much later age. Attempts to assign the tombs to the Carolingian exiles Tassilo of Bavaria and his son Theodon is questionable.[26] But the two men placed alongside each other in death suggested a story. Somehow, the story and the sculptures came together to form a legend that was to have a surprisingly long life in French culture even into the modern era.

The medieval story is known as the legend of *Les énervés de Jumièges*—the hamstrung boys of Jumièges. The story was preserved in multiple later medieval manuscripts in Latin and medieval French, and eventually in print.[27] The story in its bare bones is as follows: Clovis II married Baltechildis (alternatively named Baltet, Bautheuch, and Bautheur in the French versions).[28] They married and had sons. Then one day, Clovis decided to go to the Holy Land to visit the Holy Sepulchre. While he was away, he left his

Fig. 6.1 A color sketch of the tomb of the two princes made in 1828 by Espérance Langlois, daughter of Eustache-Hyacinthe Langlois who wrote a history of the monastery of Jumièges. Archives départementales de la Seine-Maritime (6Fi02/76).

kingdom in the care of his queen and his elder sons. Sometime thereafter, tired of sharing power with their mother, the sons mounted an armed rebellion. Many nobles joined their cause. Balthild sent word to Clovis of the rebellion. He returned immediately, and easily quashed the insurrection. The nobles who had rebelled were executed. But what was to be done about the two sons? What should their punishment be? The king and queen recoiled at the thought of killing them, and so did the king's counselors. So Balthild, as their mother, was given the responsibility of punishing them. Balthild prayed and received a vision that aided her in finding a solution. The two young men were brought into the presence of Clovis and the court. A white-hot rod was used to "boil away the nerves in their hams", so that they were hamstrung. It was Balthild, too, (divinely inspired) who came up with the idea that they should then be placed on a barge, and left to float down the river Seine, so that wherever they landed would become the place of their exile. God would determine their fate because the barge had no rudder or means to navigate the river, although it was loaded with supplies and a manservant to tend to them. The barge floated for many days until it reached the area around Rouen at a time when, by divine inspiration, Philibert, the abbot of the monastery of Jumièges decided to take a walk by the river. He spied the vessel with its unusual cargo and ordered that it be brought to dry land. The boys decided to remain at the monastery and become monks so that they could live out their lives as penitents. When the king and queen were informed of this fact, they were delighted, and they hurried to the monastery where they witnessed the boys taking the habit. The royal couple endowed the monastery with great riches—indeed, according to one version, with a quarter of the royal fisc.

Except insofar as it sought to explain the royal couple's great generosity to the monastery, the legend was entirely without historical basis. No Merovingian king went to the Holy Land in the seventh century! Clovis died at about the age of twenty-four, so his sons could not be old enough to mount a rebellion against their father and mother. Indeed, it is entirely medieval as can be seen in Clovis' anachronous crusading desire, the queen's royal origins, and the mature ages of their sons. However, the memory that Balthild had been a regent of Francia lived on.

The progressive elaboration of the legend can be traced in the successive French versions of the story. The oldest of these is the *Vie de sainte Baltet roine*, a prose story of the thirteenth century in which a princess from a (continental) Saxon royal line was abducted by malefactors "mescreans" from her home (Sessoigne) and sold to Erchinoald.[29] In this version she was able to be royal, a slave, a model of humility, and a mother to five children.

Her story also appears in a fourteenth-century collection of miracles of the Virgin Mary. Her story is miracle thirty-four, the "Miracle de sainte Bautheuch" in the *Miracles de Nostre Dame, per personages*.[30] In this version, Clovis II decided it was time to get married, but he could not find a suitable bride. It was suggested to him by his counselors that he marry a virtuous princess, Bautheuch, from Soissongne in Frisia, who lived in Erchinoald's household. After six months of marriage, Clovis declares that he wants to go on pilgrimage to the Holy Land. (It is not explained how he fathered two sons so quickly!) The sons rebelled against their mother's powers of regency and she was left to effectively handle their punishment after the rebellion was quashed.

In *Ciperis de Vignevaux*, a fourteenth-century work, King Dagobert arranges the marriage of Balthild to his brother (here, Clovis), but his nephew Ciperis (Childeric) contests Clovis' right to the crown. Balthild mediates and builds Corbie where the monks will pray for Ciperis' soul. As Jacques Merceron explains, the context for this story is a dramatization of the prohibition of royal succession through the female line enshrined (or so it was thought) in Salic Law.[31] Balthild saves the male succession. In yet another version of the same era, but developed further in the late sixteenth century, *Theseus de Cologne*, Balthild and her brother Theseus are the children of Alidone and her husband Floridas, king of Köln. In this version Saint Denis was matchmaker and the marriage is pitched as a dynastic alliance intended to bring peace to the realm. Drama is added by the attempt by a would-be usurper, Duc Lambert d'Anjou, to abduct Balthild with the intent of marrying her.[32]

Whereas the Latin versions of the story remained in manuscript form, the medieval French versions eventually found their way into print. The story also made its way into epic literature. Pierre de Ronsard included the story in his *Franciade*, published in 1572, where Balthild (unnamed in the text) was the "mère sans merci," who ordered her sons' legs to be boiled.[33] In the nineteenth century, the story of the hamstrung princes became its own cultural phenomenon, operating as a cultural point of reference for Balthild that largely paralleled knowledge of Balthild as a saint. Balthild's public reputation in the nineteenth century is the subject of the final chapter. By the time the legend of the hamstrung princes flourished in the nineteenth century, Balthild's image had been refashioned multiple times. By the nineteenth century, Balthild was no longer mother and murderer: she was a saint, a queen, and an abolitionist.

An important source for nineteenth-century readers interested in the medieval tradition of the hamstrung princes was the book by Eustache-Hyacinthe Langlois (1777–1837) published posthumously in 1838, *Essai sur les Énervés de Jumièges et sur quelques décorations singulières des Églises de cette abbaye; suivi du miracle de Sainte Bautheuch, publiée pour la premiere fois*. A Normandy native, and author of an important book on the choir stalls of Rouen cathedral, Langlois's interest in the Middle Ages had drawn him to the fable of Jumièges. After his death, his editor and friend Edouard Frère drew together Langlois' 1824 essay (now furnished with notes by Deville) with two texts of the medieval legend taken from manuscripts in the royal library: the *Vie de saincte Baultheur* copied by Floquet, and the *Miracle de Nostre Dame et sainte Bautheuch* copied by Jubinal from a fourteenth-century manuscript.[34] Langlois' essay also included (pp. 34–45) extracts from a fifteenth-century French text that appears to have been a direct translation of the Latin text in a manuscript in the Rouen library. Frère stated that he undertook the volume in fulfillment of a promise made to Langlois who, he felt sure, would have done the work himself had he had lived. The volume's frontispiece contained an engraving of the tomb covers at Jumièges made by Langlois, who was a skilled illustrator. In the illustration, the left-hand figure was headless because the head had not yet been located. Today, the stone head has been returned to its body and the two figures are fairly intact (Fig. 6.2. above). Some of the paint was still visible on the tomb in the nineteenth century and this informed the color sketch of the tomb made by Langlois' daughter, Espérance Langlois, in 1828 (Fig. 6.2.), preserved in the collection of the department archives of Seine-Maritime.[35] Furnished with a kind of "Merovingian noir" story, the purported tomb of the Merovingian princes provided nineteenth-century visitors to Jumièges with a gruesome tourist attraction while they snatched souvenirs from the already dilapidated site.[36]

The medieval story of the two hamstrung princes, now attached in local fable to the recumbent sculptures at the ruined monastery, was catapulted from a local interest story to a national cultural phenomenon when the story was chosen as the subject of a painting by Évariste Vital Luminais. His painting gripped Parisian society when it was exhibited at the salon in 1880.[37] Described as the "Augustin Thierry of painting" Luminais was

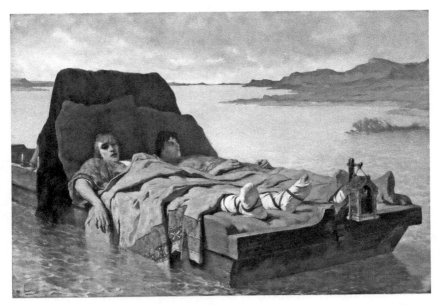

Fig. 6.2 Évariste Vital Luminais, "Les Énervées de Jumièges." Now in the Gallery of New South Wales, Australia with the title "The Sons of Clovis II. 1880." Accession number 712. A copy of this painting with minor modifications was made by Luminais, now in the Musée des Beaux Arts, Rouen.

already well known for his painting of historical subjects; this painting, however, mesmerized audiences.[38] The boys, with their pained faces, lay recumbent on their wooden barge in a gothic image of medieval savagery. The painting was eventually purchased by the Art Gallery of New South Wales in Australia, and it hangs there still.[39] Over his career, Luminais painted alternate versions of the famous painting, differing in some details from the version displayed at the salon. After his death it was acquired by the city of Rouen and today hangs in the city's museum.[40]

The improbable story of the painting continues because it has gone on to become an iconic image in French culture today. The memes began almost immediately. A cartoon in the May 1, 1880, issue of *Charivari* showed two old men on a raft floating on the Seine with a copy of a newspaper, with the caption, "The unhappy ones try to suppress their suffering by reading *Civilisation*."[41] In time the subject was rendered in different media, such as stained glass, knitting, and felting. Re-enactments of the perilous journey have been made by young men with the precaution of life jackets. And in

1986 film director Claude Duty made a short film (eighteen minutes) in which the young men are seen floating helplessly down the Seine. In Duty's film there is a baffling subplot in which a woman in a transparent shift gets very wet taking a knife to the youths on the barge and is then killed by a stalker.[42] The popularity of the story together with Luminais' paintings of the horribly mutilated boys on the barge, sustains a continuing identification of Balthild with the mother-mutilator image of medieval legend.

7
Abolitionist Icon

In 1848 the sculptor Victor Thérasse presented his white marble statue of Queen Balthild to the salon in Paris and received the final installment of his fee. The statue had been commissioned to stand alongside other marble figures of the most "illustrious women and queens" of France as part of a beautification program for the Luxembourg Gardens in Paris initiated during the reign of King Louis-Philippe (1830–48). Of the twenty illustrious women represented in the garden, three were from late antiquity: Genovefa (Geneviève), the fifth-century savior of Paris from the Huns, buried somewhere on the hill of the Panthéon and visible from one part of the gardens; Chlothild (Chlothilde), wife of King Clovis, first Christian king of France, who reputedly converted her husband to the Christian religion; and our own Balthild (Bathilde), the seventh-century Anglo-Saxon slave girl who became queen, regent, and saint of France. However, whereas the iconic contributions to French society had been long established for Genovefa (savior of Paris) and for Chlothild (Christianizer), Queen Balthild joined this estimable marble company in a new guise: abolitionist.

Clutching her marble book, Balthild was presented to the public as modern, as an icon of progressive thinking, and as a figure newly relevant in the political life of nineteenth-century France. For centuries the convent community of the abbey of Chelles (often termed the royal abbey of Chelles) had nurtured a particular image of the saint: that of royal founder. Royal patronage had secured the convent's survival (if not always its comfort) across the centuries, and the high nobility had consistently patronized the community, often supplying it with its abbesses. Indeed, a great-great-aunt of King Louis-Philippe, Louise-Adélaïde d'Orléans, had been a celebrated abbess of Chelles. This was reason enough, perhaps, to include Balthild among the illustrious women of France. But even before the July monarchy collapsed in 1848, Balthild had signified something more to the sculptor Thérasse than just another saintly queen. Visitors to the salon of 1848 encountered Balthild not simply as an emblem of royal continuity (now problematic as the monarchy had just fallen), but as a figurehead for the

Balthild of Francia: Anglo-Saxon Slave, Merovingian Queen, and Abolitionist Saint. Isabel Moreira,
Oxford University Press. © Oxford University Press 2024. DOI: 10.1093/oso/9780197518663.003.0007

abolition of slavery: On the book held by Balthild in Thérasse's statue, an abolitionist sentiment was added: *Abolitio servitutis* (Abolition of slavery).[1] A reference both to Balthild's historical reputation as a freer of slaves and France's claim that on its soil all slaves were free, the motto fixed the statue to a distinct moment in time when France was on the brink of declaring itself an abolitionist state.

The sculptor Victor Thérasse is an elusive figure; his personal research before taking on the commission was precisely two days. One wonders who he talked to and what he read that led him to foreground Balthild as an abolitionist. But what his commission makes clear is that by the late 1840s, despite the dissolution of the convent of Chelles during the French Revolution, the figure of Balthild had been assured a place in the French public imagination, and that through Thérasse she was poised to represent the cause of abolition in France.

Before we look in greater detail at the context of Thérasse's commission, it is useful to see how Balthild's reputation had emerged from quirky medieval myth into the modern age.

Chelles "la Noble"

Clément Torchet, a nineteenth-century historian of Chelles, recorded a folk saying: "Faremoutiers la Sainte, Jouarre la Riche et Chelles la Noble."[2] "Noble Chelles" was an apt description of a convent that drew consistently on the patronage and family members of the highest French nobility to secure its prosperity.

In pre-Revolutionary France, Balthild was "Balthild of Chelles." The Benedictine convent was institutionally robust, it attracted a steady stream of well-born novices, and with its proximity to Paris and its important royal history it was Balthild's legacy in founding the prestigious convent that made Balthild an important saint. From the sixteenth through the eighteenth centuries, we hear of the abbesses traveling back and forth between Chelles and Paris, just as Balthild had encouraged Bertilla to do, to seek patronage and favor. The convent of Chelles was included alongside the other major monastic houses in the great *Monasticon Gallicanum* project of Dom Michel Germain, a monk of Saint-Germain-des-Prés (see Fig. 7.1). Two engravings of the convent of Chelles, representing views from different sides of the convent (from the road, and from the fields) in 1688, provide

Fig. 7.1 Seventeenth-century view of the Royal Abbey of Chelles, in Dom Germain, *Monasticon Gallicanum*. Matériaux du Monasticon Gallicanum de Dom Germain. BnF. Latin 11820.

our best evidence for what the convent had become in the seventeenth century before ambitious renovations were undertaken in the eighteenth century: it was a formidable monastic complex with formal gardens whose hedged walkways and orchards were protected from the road by a solid wall.[3] The bones of the monastic structures lay in the traditional needs of a monastic community: the church, dormitories, cloister, refectory, infirmary, and cemetery—and at Chelles, an apothecary. However, there was also a substantial main building housing various rooms including "parloirs," of generous proportions and with large windows, and a "Logis abbatial," which gives a sense of an elegant and private second floor corridor (in this case, enclosed) from which to admire the view of the river and the forests beyond. Clerics attached to the convent were housed in their own space in the parish church of Saint George with sleeping quarters in one corner of the complex. In addition to the gardens and arable land needed to supply the community's food needs, there were more elegant spaces for the nuns and visitors to enjoy. The nuns had opportunities to relax, exercise, and promenade in the fashionable spaces of the orangery and grottos, and they could stretch their legs in a star-shaped quadrant that contained hedged "allées de charmes" added by Madame le Begue in 1676.

Balthild in Print

Balthild's story and cult become more accessible in the print era. Abbess Marie de Lorraine (1583–1627) commissioned Étienne Binet (1569–1639) to compose a biography of Balthild in French.[4] Binet was a Jesuit and a prolific author. His works included theological treatises (he wrote one on how to shorten one's time in purgatory, for example) but writing biographies of early medieval saints was a passion. Alongside his ecstatic biography of Balthild, he also wrote biographies of Saint Brigit of Sweden and Saint Aldegund of Maubeuge. Binet's dedicatory letter is a masterclass in religious flattery; Marie de Lorraine's virtues were imagined to hold a mirror to the saint's own. Binet's biography takes the Carolingian Latin Life as its starting point, embellishing it with many reflections on the saint, and weaving into it copious material from the Life of Eligius of Noyon. Binet was able to expand the relatively short Latin account into three hundred and thirty-one pages brimming with happy thoughts about Balthild as a "Saxon rose among the fleur-de-lys of France" and interspersed with sermon-like reflections on the queen's six virtues and other lists of this kind.[5] Centered on the B version of the Balthild's Life that was most favored in the convent, Balthild's royal status was at the forefront of his work, but it also included an account of the 833 translation of her relics and of the miracles recorded at that time. Binet's work provided the nuns of Chelles with an inspiring account of their foundress in modern French together with flattering ruminations on the convent of Chelles as an earthly paradise. The frontispiece shows how the convent imagined their founding saint at this time. Dressed in the habit of a Benedictine nun, with her thick ermine cloak, staff, and baroque crown cast down on the floor before the altar, Balthild looks up to see a vision of two angels ascending a ladder to a third angel who is holding a scroll; the caption instructs readers that to serve God is to reign.[6] Charmingly, a door opens into the sun-filled courtyard beyond where we get a glimpse of the convent as it was in the early seventeenth century.[7]

Forty years later, in 1664, a three-page abridgment of Balthild's Life in French was produced by Arnaud D'Andilly in a handsome volume entitled *Vies de plusieurs saints illustres de divers siècles*. Although he claimed his account was a translation from the Latin Life, D'Andilly's digest was full of inaccuracies, including his unequivocal claim that Balthild descended from the royal house of Saxony.[8] Yet his short text was influential with French readers. In particular, he summarized Balthild's policy towards slave trafficking in such a way that he attributed to her the "abolition" of trade in Christian slaves.[9] This change in terminology from "prohibited" in the Latin to "abolished" in French was to resonate with subsequent, politically inclined readers, as we shall see below.

The Last Abbesses of Chelles

Marie de Lorraine's commission of a French-language biography of the abbey's founding saint was only one way that abbesses promoted the Balthild's cult. They also cared for the treasured relics, maintained liturgical veneration, provided services for the local community and encouraged ties with their convent's benefactors. The early modern era saw long-lived and formidable abbesses who used their aristocratic status and connections to the court both to obtain their positions and to provide the best services for the convent's needs.[10] The influence and social status of an abbess in the seventeenth and eighteenth centuries could be considerable. At Chelles, the post was viewed as a benefice to be sought from the king as a royal favor. The abbess Catherine de Scoraille de Rousille-Fontages who held her post 1680–88, was granted her position through the influence of her sister Marie-Angélique de Scoraille de Rousille-Fontages, Louis XIV's mistress; the reward of the latter was to be made a *duchesse*. The quality of the abbess, however, depended on what she chose to make of her appointment, and where she stood on the spectrum between a mere inclination for the religious life and the most dedicated piety. There was much that could be obtained from such connections to benefit and elevate the spiritual life of the nuns. A good example of this can be seen when Abbess Madeleine de La Porte de la Meilleraye (1626–71) realized that more confessors were needed for the convent. Madeleine de la Porte was sister to the Marquis de la Meilleraye, niece of Cardinal Richelieu, and cousin by marriage to Cardinal Mazarin. She was able to use her connection with Cardinal Richelieu to strongarm the reluctant Congregation of Saint-Maur to provide monks for that purpose.

Madeleine de la Porte was an important abbess in other ways. This was an era not only of relics and their miracles but also of convent-generated hysteria. The abbess oversaw the opening of Balthild's tomb (the "reconnaissance" of 1631); the saint's relics were then used to cure six nuns who exhibited curious behavior that included writhing with "contortions and convulsions," levitating, and making predictions, all of which symptoms the doctors were unable to treat.[11] It was Madeleine de La Porte who commissioned an imposing silver reliquary for Balthild's remains and who saw the relics deposited there on Balthild's feast day in 1635 under the supervision of Jacques Charton, "grand pénitencier" of Paris. It was she who in 1647 sent a portion of Balthild's jawbone with two teeth attached to Corbie, and later sent a part of her skull to Jumièges, as part of the ongoing relic exchanges between the religious houses that observed Balthild's cult. In 1665 Bertilla's relics also found a new home in a silver reliquary chest.[12] Madeleine de La Porte's successor abbesses, Guyonne Marguerite de Cossé de Brissac de Rousille (abbess 1671–80; 1699–1707), Catherine de Scoraille de Rousille-Fontages (abbess 1680–88), and Agnès de Villars (abbess 1707–19), continued the energetic relic exchanges with other foundations, collecting and rehousing the convent's relics including those of Saint Burgundofara and Saint Eligius.

The abbess who made the biggest splash was undoubtedly Princess Louise-Adélaïde d'Orléans (abbess 1719–34, Fig. 7.2). A princess of royal

Fig. 7.2 Pierre Gobert's portrait of Louise Adélaïde d'Orléans, abbess of Chelles. Her name in religion was "Soeur Bathilde," Sister Balthild. Image courtesy of Wikimedia commons.

blood born at Versailles, her father was King Louis XIV's nephew, Duc Philippe II d'Orléans who was regent for the young king Louis XV; and her mother was Françoise Marie de Bourbon, legitimized daughter of Louis XIV and his mistress Madame de Montespan. Louise-Adélaïde was thus a member of the extended royal family. She was presented in later fictionalized accounts as a figure of scandal, however Louise-Adélaïde appears to have been personally pious if somewhat erratic. She had spent some of her childhood at the convent of Chelles to receive an education as a "pensionnaire" together with her sister Charlotte Aglaé and some other young noble girls. In young adulthood she returned to court where it was expected she would marry into the aristocracy of Europe as her sisters had done. She turned down good offers. One account relates that at the age of eighteen she had wanted to marry a royal page, but her choice was not considered suitable. A year later, on March 31, 1717, she entered the convent of Chelles and took the veil. In 1719 the presiding abbess, Agnès de Villars, was pushed into retirement and Louise-Adélaïde was appointed abbess of Chelles at the age of 21.[13]

Louise-Adélaïde's induction into her new office was a grand affair, presided over by the Cardinal de Noailles, attended by one hundred and fifty bishops, thirty abbesses, forty monks from Saint-Maur, and a rich array of the high nobility. A feast was provided for six hundred attendees.[14] There was nothing small or retiring about the new abbess, and she put considerable energy and resources to the improvement of the convent. She made an immediate splash by taking "Soeur Sainte-Bathilde" as her name in religion. Sister Sainte-Bathilde arrived at the convent educated, cultured, with a love of fine things, with new ideas, and an interest in projects for the improvement of the convent. She loved music. She was responsible for reforming the chant at the convent and she had the convent's bells replaced with new ones that were more melodic. She was also a practical woman. She addressed a lack of reliable drinking water by commissioning a subterranean hydraulic system to provide a water supply not only to the convent but also to the town. She supported a school run by the Sisters of Nevers and installed a physician to preside over a new infirmary, with one of the nuns in charge of the pharmacy. Her improvements included a new dormitory for the convent, a spruced-up refectory, and a refurbished cloister. She was a patroness on a grand scale. But it was also recorded that she refused to use a magnificent dais gifted to her by her father because it would set her up high above her nuns when she dined. When she died, it was her theological works that were considered notable, among them a treatise on the rule of Benedict.[15] According to her *Confession*, there was a time following her father's death when she had relaxed her constraints and went a little wild (from the age of twenty-five to thirty-three) before committing again to a more penitential lifestyle.[16] She was accused of not setting a good example to the nuns, of not following the Benedictine rule. In February 1731 she left Chelles to take up a penitential life at the priory of Traînel in Paris (her successor as abbess was appointed to deputize her responsibilities in the meantime). The princess and the nuns of Traînel wanted a relic of Balthild and so in August of that year Balthild's coffin was opened again and the Traînel community obtained a portion of Balthild's femur. Louise-Adélaïde continued to visit Chelles on occasion and had a close friendship with Anne de Clermont, who was the acting abbess. She stayed at Traînel until her death from smallpox in 1734, thus closing one of the more colorful chapters in the life of the convent of Chelles. Anne de Clermont was present at her deathbed and pleaded unsuccessfully on behalf of the community that Louise-Adélaïde's body be returned to the convent for burial. They may not have had her body, but this did not stop the community from hosting a lavish funeral service at the convent at a cost 25,000 livres.[17]

The abbess who succeeded Louise-Adélaïde was Anne de Clermont-Gessan de Chaste who governed the convent for fifty-five years (1735–89) from a time when the convent was at the height of its influence to the eve of the French Revolution. She died in the early months of disruption and violence that marked the opening months of the Revolution, but well before "the Terror" that saw the execution of so many of the families that had had connections with the abbey. As Abbé Clement Torchet narrated in his history of the abbey, the early decades of her abbacy saw prosperity, new construction, and environmental challenges. Early in her tenure as abbess, in 1738, lightning struck the church that housed the silver relic-chests of Balthild and Bertilla and they were damaged by fire; the following year another storm did great damage to the convent roof. In 1739 the abbess and convent sponsored the construction of a stone bridge, replacing the wooden bridge of the sixteenth century and in later years did further work to improve access. In 1741–42 an epidemic struck the town and convent with seventy-seven deaths recorded in the monastery and parish between September and May; another epidemic of a non-specific "military fever" caused deaths in the town; the convent, as always, provided medical care. During the Seven Years War, the convent contributed many of its silver vessels to the cause, putting considerable pressure on their financial resources.

It was during Anne de Clermont's long tenure as abbess that a young historian, a nun, or novice (or perhaps a boarder, "pensionnaire"), penned a history of the abbey from the convent's beginnings up to 1782. The work was written in a regular but improving hand with occasional marginal notations. It drew carefully on original sources and histories available in the 1780s but it also recorded information otherwise lost to history, such as the date when the ceremony of the blessing of the bread loaves ("pain de Sainte-Bathilde") was instituted to raise funds.[18] In the final years of her tenure as abbess, Anne de Clermont witnessed the terrible general distress of the French population caused by floods, crop failure, and extreme hunger that spurred revolt. On her death she was buried in the crypt of Chelles alongside her abbess predecessors, but it was a final act of normality. As Torchet recorded, in 1834 her family reclaimed her body from her tomb that had been vandalized and stripped of lead in the intervening years.[19]

The final abbess of the convent, the fifty-eighth by Torchet's reckoning, was Madeleine-Elisabeth-Delphine de Sabran. She was fifty-five years of age and her brief tenure saw public religious cult activities outlawed in France, confiscations of religious property, the closing of the convent in 1789, and the suppression of the religious orders on February 13, 1790. Torchet noted the calamity—here was an end of twelve hundred years of history, "de grandeur et de vertus."[20] He provides the text of the declaration of goods held by the convent, dated February 25, 1790, signed by the abbess. It includes properties, debts, annual expenses, and furnishings. The list includes seventeen horses, livestock (twenty-seven cows, three hundred and sixty sheep, etc.), tapestries, two feather beds, and the kitchen utensils of the abbey among other things. The church had six paintings depicting the life of Balthild. Unfortunately, these paintings are not described and did not survive, however, if the engraving of 1635 (with the coat of arms of Abbess Madeleine De La Porte) with seven scenes provides a clue to what were viewed as the principal episodes: (i) Balthild being sold for a low price, (ii) her marriage to Clovis, (iii) her freeing of captives, (iv) her construction of Chelles, (v) her taking the habit, (vi) her menial tasks in the convent, and (vii) her vision of the celestial ladder.[21]

On dissolving the convent, the state pensioned off the nuns. The abbess received 2,000 livres, the professed nuns received 750 livres apiece, and the lay nuns received 350 livres.[22] At the time of dissolution, thirty-one members of the abbey community were receiving pensions from the state. Madame de Sabran died on January 19, 1820, in Narbonne where she had relocated after the dissolution. In 1829 her remains were moved to the chapel of Sainte-Anne in Apt. The portion of Balthild's skull relic that she had taken with her from the convent was never recovered.

As for the grand *Abbaye de Chelles*, during the Revolution it became the property of the state and was sold in June 1798, and then demolished. In 1861 a town hall (*Mairie*) was built over it on three sides of the cloister. When the abbatial church of Notre Dame was razed, its graves were disturbed; the few that survived into the nineteenth century were reinterred. Clément Torchet included some of the epitaphs in his history of the abbey.

Today, little remains of a convent that had flourished for over a millennium and that had conserved the precious relics of its saints. However, in addition to the famous relics of Balthild and Bertilla that were secreted into the reliquary of Florus in the Église Saint-André during the Revolution, a few devotional items from the convent were rescued and are today preserved in the parish church of Saint André: two crucifixes (one fourteenth century, the other sixteenth century), statues of the virgin and child (one fourteenth century, the other fifteenth century) a sixteenth-century bas-relief panel of Notre-Dame-de-Lorette.; a stone pietà; a seventeenth-century polychrome wooden statue of Saint Roch; and a series of white stone statues— a seventeenth-century image of Queen Balthild in Benedictine habit and crowned; Saint Peter with a lyre and two keys; and various other statues to Saint Martha, Saint John the Baptist, Saint Vincent, Saint Andrew, Saint Genesius, and Saint Eligius.[23]

Plans to situate a new Hôtel de Ville over the site of the convent led to rescue excavations in 1987 that sought to establish the chronology of the abbey's development, especially changes made from the thirteenth century onward.[24] Earlier buildings had been destroyed, first by the Vikings, then by fire in 1226, requiring substantial reconstruction. Nothing structural remains of the earlier buildings except what can be determined through excavation. For example, the exact plan of the convent's habitations in the Merovingian period cannot be established. However, recent excavations have discovered traces of the original church of Saint George founded by Queen Chlothild that was enlarged in Balthild's time and dedicated to the Holy Cross.[25] Fragments of stone and plaster indicate that the church was used for burials, and it also served as a parish church early on. (The rebuilt church continued as a church and graveyard for the priests who served the convent.) Gisela (Charlemagne's sister) built her church of Notre Dame to the east of Balthild's church and moved Balthild's remains there. Excavations have revealed evidence of buildings and habitation that sprang up to the southwest of the new church in the Carolingian period, but the Merovingian conventual buildings are currently lost to recovery. As the convent prospered over the centuries, new buildings would extend down to the south. The discovery of Merovingian graves and sarcophagus slabs in 1987 (now in the Museum's collection) helped locate the position of the ancient burial grounds of the convent around Balthild's church and in Gisela's church.

Through the Middle Ages, the convent had become a dominant institution in the life of the small town of Chelles. The former monastic complex is now mostly covered by the new Hôtel de Ville and the gardens to the south (Parc de Chelles and Parc du Souvenir Émile Fouchard). The former abbey church of Notre Dame is located partially under a parking lot and partly under the current Alfred-Bonno Museum at the corner of rue Louis Eterlet and the Rue Adolphe Besson. Only a few stretches of wall and cloister arches remain visible today enclosing the tranquil "Jardin du Cloître" that was opened on September 15, 2007, by the mayor of Chelles, M. Jean-Paul Planchou. In the floor of the hallway leading to the cloister, a glass panel covers an ancient grave. Up the hill (called immemorially "la-Montagne"), the parish church of Saint-André (situated since at least the eleventh century over Merovingian burial grounds), displays the reliquaries associated with the convent that were moved there for safety during the French Revolution. However, Balthild's relics and Bertilla's relics and their reliquary boxes have been housed in the Alfred-Bonno Museum since 1985 for reasons of security given their historical importance.[26] The collection of artifacts at the museum includes the textiles associated with the burial of Balthild and Bertilla, eighteenth-century paintings of abbesses, and a scaled model of the abbey as it appeared in the seventeenth century.

Balthild the Abolitionist

Although the nuns and abbesses of the *ancien regime* gave considerable thought to the education and welfare of the poor and to providing amenities that improved the prosperity of the town of Chelles, there was nothing in the last abbesses' lives that connected them directly with Balthild's concern for slaves. Care for the physical and spiritual welfare of the poor was certainly a major activity of the nuns, but every worldly benefit the convent accrued came from aristocratic patronage; the convent had fully earned its soubriquet "Chelles le Noble." However, Balthild's experience of slavery was not forgotten entirely. We have seen that the episode in which she was bought for a mean price featured as one of the engraved vignettes published in the time of abbess Madeleine De La Porte, and if the paintings of the life of Balthild that had adorned the convent walls bore any resemblance to this engraved panel, then the nuns would have had an image of Balthild being sold as a slave in front of their eyes daily.

The earliest French publications on the *Vie de Sainte Bathilde* recalled that she had worked to end the slave trade for Christians and specified that this activity as a boon to France. "She made a prohibition in France so that one could no longer sell any slave that was Christian to foreigners" wrote Étienne Binet in 1624.[27] This was an accurate representation of the information given in the Merovingian Life in that it specified the limitations under which Balthild's anti-slavery activities operated. Balthild had not "prohibited" slavery in a global sense. Rather, she made it an offense to enslave Christian men and women in France and to sell them abroad. She also rescued captive Christians. Binet makes the point that Balthild freed the majority of these but that she also tried to convince others to become the "slaves" of Christ by committing to the religious life. It was the *conseiller d'État* Robert Arnaud D'Andilly (1589–1674) who, forty years later, couched her policy in more national terms: "France is indebted to this blessed queen for the fact that there are no longer Christian slaves. For it was she who abolished the abuse (unworthy of the sanctity of Christianity) of a disgraceful traffic of those who were rescued by the blood of Jesus Christ and reborn through baptism."[28] With a view only to a definition of slavery that was ancient and geographically confined to France, Arnaud D'Andilly's French synopsis of Balthild's Life considered slavery a scourge that had been eliminated many centuries before.[29] More significant is D'Andilly's introduction of the word "abolish" into his description of Balthild's prohibition: "car ce fut elle qui abolit cet abus." Up to this point translators of Balthild's Life had reported that she "prohibited" slavery, drawing on the Latin text. However, the use of the word "abolish" here is a clue to new forms of discourse around the issue of slavery in the 1660s. It also helps to explain how Balthild's story came to have a new, more contemporary political relevance.

Balthild's prohibition of the Christian slave trade in France, and the new terminology of abolition, provided substance for the naïve historical claim that after her time, and as a result of her efforts, there was no longer slavery in France. (In fact, in political discourse about slavery in France King Louis X (1289–1316) was also invoked for having freed the serfs in 1315). The specific claim—that there was no slavery in France—was a potent means of differentiating France and the French from their activities in the colonies. It was a claim that was also occasionally upheld. For example, it is recorded that in 1571 African slaves arriving in France were liberated. Étienne Binet and Arnaud D'Andilly were writing glowingly about Balthild's prohibition of slavery at a time when foreign slaves who arrived in France had their claims to free status upheld. Yet, France's colonial interests and plantations continued to bring slavery to the forefront of politics. In 1685 King Louis XIV (with his minister Colbert) issued letters patent known as the Code Noir and this was the beginning of many reassessments and modifications of France's stance on slavery.[30] The Code Noir regulated the status of slaves in the colonies and its amendments sought to regulate the status of slaves when they arrived in France, usually when they accompanied their plantation owners as domestics. So while France congratulated itself on having no slaves in France, in reality France's colonial history resulted in a slave population in France that did not always find freedom when they stepped onto French soil. Furthermore, some protections available under the *ancien regime* were rolled back by Napoleon I's first Empire.

Religion was also factor in the Code Noir. From the beginning it was specified that slaves in French territories were to be instructed in the Roman Catholic religion and baptized. However, baptism did not make them free. It merely provided them with some protections and obligations associated with their observance of the religion. For D'Andilly Christian slavery had been an abuse because he thought it was unworthy of the "sanctity of Christianity" to traffic those who had been rescued by the blood of Christ. But twenty years later Christianity was no longer so offended.

For as long as Balthild was viewed primarily as the royal patron of aristocratic nuns, the irony of France being a slave-holding country while the nuns venerated an "abolitionist" saint was not confronted at Chelles. Balthild's example was not evoked in calls for social or political change. Yet after the convent had been destroyed and the nuns dispersed, and the cause of abolition rose to national importance, Balthild's policies with respect to slavery emerged again.

Abolitionism in the 1840s

When France abolished slavery in 1848 it was one of the last of the European colonial powers to do so. However, by the time it happened the appeal of at least a notion of abolition was strong in France. We have seen that in the seventeenth century, Arnaud D'Andilly presented Balthild's anti-slave trade position as a boon to the nation of France. Yet, as was the case in the rest of Europe, the process by which French colonial slavery was finally abolished extended into the first half of the nineteenth century. Abolitionist societies and their publications were key to the progress of this endeavor. The later years of the *ancien régime* saw the founding of the anti-slavery society, the *Société des amis des Noirs*, founded in 1788. As was the case for all the future major abolitionist societies centered in Paris, the newly formed *Société* was deeply indebted to the support and financial backing of the British abolitionist movement. During the French revolutionary era, and in response to the Haitian slave revolt at Saint-Domingue in 1791, the Convention abolished slavery in 1794. But the directive was never enacted. Napoleon I revoked the abolition in 1802, although he made a last ditch appeal for support by reinstating some abolitionist provisions in 1815 during the "One hundred days." Under the restoration Bourbon kings Louis XVIII (ruled 1814–15; 1815–24) and Charles X (ruled 1824–30) sanctions against slave trafficking intensified, as they did also under King Louis-Philippe from 1830, but these measures were half-hearted and largely ineffectual. Abolitionists were cast as radicals in the reigns of the two Bourbon kings, and by the time Louis-Philippe came to power, the pro-colonial, anti-abolition lobby had grown in influence. Furthermore, as the French abolitionist movement was backed by the mentorship and financial aid of the British abolitionists, those opposed to abolition could always point to British support as foreign interference in French affairs. The founding of the *Société de la morale chrétienne* in 1821 with its political and socially influential membership, provided abolitionists with an important platform.[31] However, taking planters' interests into consideration, the Society was limited in membership and advocated only a gradual schedule of emancipation. Furthermore, the society's membership was so strongly tied with liberal opposition politics that its aims suffered somewhat from being so directly associated with one political party. Interestingly, Louis-Philippe was a member of the *Société de la morale chrétienne* before his rise to royal office in 1830. However, during Louis-Philippe's reign the influence of the planter lobby together with internal dissention and the king's own increasingly autocratic approach to rule meant that his reign did not see slave emancipation. Nevertheless, his reign saw important advances in the cause of abolition that were contemporaneous with the choice of Balthild as a statue for the Luxembourg gardens.

The year 1834 saw the founding of the *Société française pour l'abolition de l'esclavage* which put further pressure on the government, and these years of the July Monarchy saw the final push for abolition in the government, the press, and the social sphere. Yet, slavery was not outlawed under Louis-Philippe. Instead, in 1840 his government established a commission (death to progress!) to investigate the issue of slavery and abolition. The commission was a stalling tactic and the anti-abolition lobby continued to be vocal in printed media funded by colonial planters. Yet, as Lawrence Jennings notes, by the 1840s emancipation had come to be seen as "accepted fact" with Paris the center of strong abolitionist sentiment.[32] Still, slavery was not finally abolished until April 27, 1848, by the provisional government of the second Republic that had ousted Louis-Philippe only two months before.

King Louis-Philippe's Project

It is generally accepted that the twenty female figures in the Luxembourg Gardens were chosen by King Louis-Philippe as part of his royal program of beautification of the gardens. As we will see, there were good reasons for Louis-Philippe to want Balthild to be numbered among the queens. But was the king behind Balthild's newest guise as an abolitionist? Was he even aware of it? It seems unlikely on both counts. King Louis-Philippe commissioned the statue for family reasons, as we shall see. But it seems unlikely that the king who resisted abolition politically was behind the message of abolition that statue was made to convey. It is especially unlikely given Balthild's placement in front of the building that housed the assembly of peers (later known as the senate) since that would have been viewed as a provocative political statement had the July monarchy survived.

The Luxembourg palace and gardens renovation project was a substantial multi-year project comprising a rehaul of some of the principal rooms of the senate house (historically known as the Medici palace), and the gardens. Indeed, it was the expansion of the palace's footprint to accommodate more room for legislative debate that necessitated a readjustment of the garden plan. The man in charge of reconfiguring both palace and gardens was the palace architect, the "architect of the senate," Henri-Alphonse de Gisors.[33] De Gisors published his account of the project in 1847.[34] By the time he published his account the statues had been commissioned but not all had been installed. Thérasse's statue was listed among the those not yet in place. The short description of the statue's subject makes no mention of abolition. In the bigger scheme of things, any individual statue in the garden was a small matter to De Gisors and he gave scant attention to the queens of the garden beyond his abbreviated descriptions. For De Gisors, at least, the statues of the queens appear to have been viewed as public decoration more valued as a solution to the reconfigured space than to their collective meaning or artistic potential. There is no indication in his account that he contributed to the political message inscribed on Balthild's statue by Thérasse.

While Queen Balthild did not have the public stature of Queen Clothilde or Saint Geneviève, Balthild was a natural choice for King Louis-Philippe's project primarily because she was a family saint for the Orléans family. Louis-Philippe was a direct descendant of the Duc Philippe d'Orléans, brother of Louis XIV and founder of the cadet branch of the Bourbon monarchy. Louise-Adélaïde, the larger-than-life abbess of Chelles who bore the name in religion of Soeur Sainte-Bathilde was Louis-Philippe's great-great-aunt, and female members of his family carried versions of her name: his mother, for example, was named Louise Marie-Adélaïde. Bathilde was also a family name—it was the name of Louis-Philippe's aunt (Philippe Égalité's sister) who died in 1822 and who was buried at the royal chapel at Dreux, outside Paris.

Balthild may also have resonated with Louis-Philippe because in his youth he had been an anglophile and Balthild was an Anglo-French figure. Louis-Philippe lived in exile in England (in Twickenham) in the 1790s and again 1815–17. Indeed, early on a marriage had been proposed between himself and George III's daughter Elizabeth, but nothing came of this and he married instead Maria Amalia of Naples and Sicily. During his time as king, Louis-Philippe visited England, and hosted Victoria and Albert in Normandy twice, establishing an "entente cordiale" between the two nations. The archives show that his agents bought English, Scottish, and Irish art, especially paintings, for his residences. Yet politically, as king, he was a reluctant ally of England. His principal supporters were not friendly to British interests. Finally, in the wake of the 1848 uprising, Louis-Philippe fled again to exile in England where he lived out the remainder of his life, dying in 1850, although finally and fittingly he was buried with his family at Dreux.

Balthild could be seen as a symbol of Anglo-French affinity, especially in her connection to an abolitionist movement that was viewed in some circles as tantamount to an Anglo-French enterprise. Yet Balthild was also viewed by Parisians as a local saint. She was an honorary Parisian by virtue of her queenship centered on Paris, her connection to the convent of Chelles that always maintained its Parisian presence, and by the connection of her cult with the house of Orléans for over two centuries.

We cannot be sure if Louis-Philippe thought of all these factors, but the connection seemed evident to those planning royal public monuments in these years. Indeed, the commission to add Balthild to the Luxembourg Gardens came soon after another royal project, the embellishment of the Orléanist (now royal) chapel at Dreux. The chapel's windows were to include an image Saint Balthild. So Thérasse's commission was not the only representation of the queen being produced in royal art at this time.

Plans for the lavish ornamentation of the royal chapel at Dreux, the necropolis for the Orléans family, show that Balthild's cult was already associated with the king.[35] Shortly before Thérasse received his commission, the celebrated painter Jean-Auguste-Dominique Ingres had been commissioned by order of the king to produce eight oil paintings to serve as cartoons for the stained-glass windows to be installed in the newly refurbished chapel. This refurbishment had become a priority after the death of Louis-Philippe's eldest son Ferdinand-Philippe who had died tragically young at the age of thirty-one in a carriage accident. The subjects for Ingres' talents were: Saint Denis, Saint Rémy (Remigius), Saint Germain (Germanus), Sainte Chlothilde, Sainte Geneviève (Genovefa), Sainte Radegonde (Radegund), Sainte Isabelle de France, and Sainte Bathilde (Balthild). In July 1846 the director of the royal museums suggested to the Intendant General that he fix the price at 7,000 francs for Ingres' work, to be taken from the funds of 1844.[36]

The commission for the royal chapel at Dreux is interesting because of the identity of the five female saints: three of them were also subjects in the Luxembourg Gardens collection. However, Balthild's presence in the royal chapel was that of a royal saint and Orléanist family cult figure, not as a regent queen or as an abolitionist. This can be seen plainly in the image that Ingres produced, now housed in the Louvre. In Ingres' painting Balthild is shown in romantic style, swathed in beautifully colored garments, eyes downcast, with thigh-length plaits bound with ribbons, holding in her hands a long belt, untied and in readiness to be gifted. Her body is held in a sinuous pose, gracefully svelte, in a romantic feminine pose. Her head is ornamented with a gold crown and a gold nimbus. Ingres drew directly from the traditional religious accoutrements of the saint: the staff with which Balthild had reputedly caused a spring to miraculously appear, and the belt which was given as a gift to the monastic community of Corbion. As a painter of historical subjects, the highest art form of the period, Ingres sought to recreate Balthild's historical costume, rejecting the centuries-old image of her as a Benedictine nun. In Ingres' image she is presented as a queen, but one whose curves, notwithstanding her torso body-armor, suggest something of the exotic; like his famed obelisks, Balthild had been sold for her body and her beauty. A preliminary nude sketch of Balthild made by Ingres for his painting still exists, further underscoring the influence of the erotic in his casting of the feminine form.

As a royal choice, then, there were good reasons for Balthild's presence both at Dreux as a family saint, and in the Gardens as queen-regent. The king had wanted to project the notion that his reign was a model of good government but also to recall the importance of his own family to the well-being of France as a political "liberator." However, as noted above, while he had shown some support for the cause of gradual abolition in his younger days, now as king he was not quick to move. A commentator Guillaume de Félice noted in 1847 that "the king is opposed to emancipation, not for any love of slavery, if I am well-informed, but because he has adopted the maxim of not touching things that time can resolve."[37] With Louis-Philippe dragging his feet on abolition, who was really behind the abolitionist Balthild with its uncompromising motto? There are strong arguments to suppose that it was the sculptor Victor Thérasse, perhaps with others in his circle, who decided to portray Balthild in this way.

Victor Thérasse Undertakes a Commission

The sculptor commissioned to provide a statue of Queen Balthild for the Luxembourg Gardens was Victor Thérasse. Thérasse is a hard man to trace beyond the occasional notice his work received in the press. He was born in Paris on March 25, 1796, to Pierre-Thomas Thérasse who had worked for the "département de la guerre" and Marie-Françoise Perdriel. He died in obscurity a few weeks shy of his sixty-eighth birthday near Auteuil in the 16e arrondissement of Paris, February 4, 1864.[38]

In 1813 Thérasse entered the École des Beaux-Arts in Paris where he trained under François Frédéric Lemot and Pierre Charles Bridan. He was an accomplished sculptor of historical subjects who enjoyed modest success exhibiting his work at the salon where, in 1834, he took second prize for his bust of Abraham Duquesne. This was the highpoint of his recognition. His known works range from 1831 to 1857 when the newly reconstituted Academy of Beaux-Arts was under royal direction. At the time of Thérasse's commission this was King Louis-Philippe (1830–48). Many of Thérasse's commissions were sculptures and busts destined for public buildings and spaces such as Versailles and the Louvre, and the Luxembourg Gardens. The July monarchy (1830–48) saw a number of public beautification programs in and around Paris and sculptors were employed to contribute to large-scale projects. Along with many other artists, Thérasse was not always successful in having his work accepted for the Salon, and on one occasion this caused so much heated feeling among his neighbors that the jury was called out for their decision, publicly and intemperately, by a very vocal, very local short-lived publication.[39] Before he worked on Balthild, Thérasse had contributed a statue of Gregory of Tours for the exterior of the Église de la Sainte-Marie-Madeleine, a colonnaded temple that was being fitted for religious use by the addition to the exterior niches of thirty-eight statues by thirty-seven different sculptors.[40] The Luxembourg Gardens was another public series of this sort: twenty statues of illustrious women of French history to adorn the palace gardens of the palace once owned by Marie de Médici, queen-regent of France in the early seventeenth century. Judging by the dates of Thérasse's known works, the commissions came in slowly.[41] At any rate, at the time of his commission for the Luxembourg Gardens he was in severe financial trouble, and in real danger of having his works put onto the rue de Vaugirard where he had a studio at no. 61, as he informed the director of the Beaux-Arts in February of 1846.[42] The commission for Balthild's statue came at an opportune moment in the artist's life.

Thérasse's commission for a statue of Balthild came in the form of an Arrêté issued by the ministry of the interior on December 20, 1845. It commissioned the sculptor to provide a marble statue for the Luxembourg gardens whose subject would be communicated to him afterwards, and for which he must first submit a plan for the ministry's approval. He would be paid twelve thousand francs for this work, drawn from the ministry's account for works of art and decoration for public buildings.[43] This was a sizeable sum.[44] Thérasse's plea for financial help came thirty-seven days later. He had not yet received the subject of the commission and so had not submitted a sketch, but he needed the money immediately. He wrote to the director for the commission noting that eminent artists visited his workshop and reminding the director of his recommenders. Furthermore, he states, he had not earned money in four years. The minister responded by supplying Thérasse with a new copy of the original arrêté dated 2 April 1846 but with the additional request that he present himself to the palace architect (who at his time would have been De Gisors), where they would discuss the proposed work. Two days later Thérasse wrote back asking the minister to give him Balthild as his subject. He included an outline of Balthild's life that indicated her suitability for this honor (discussed further below). And two days later, on April 6 he wrote again to the minister to indicate that his model of Balthild was finished, and could he have 6,000 francs on account so that he can continue his work? On April 7 he was given access to half that sum, 3,000 francs. On April 22 came final approval of this "choice." On July 6 Thérasse sent a note to Monsieur Cavé to give him the dimensions for the block of clean white marble that he would need: 2.5 meters high (8'20"), 82 × 82 centimeters (27") wide and deep. The estimate was accepted. On July 16 the requisition order was approved, and on July 18 the order was placed for a cubic block of 1.68 meters (5'5"). Throughout all this documentation in which Thérasse was paid in installments for his work, Balthild was described as regent, "Régente de France." The work was completed, and final payment made on January 3, 1848. Thérasse completed his work just under the wire. Just seven weeks later, on February 23, 1848, the king, the royal commissioner of the beautification program, was removed from power and fled into exile.

However, from the documentation in the national archives it is still unclear exactly how Balthild was to be represented in the Gardens. Although the initial commission communicated to Victor Thérasse did not specify the subject, it is possible that it was not so much doubt about the subject as it was the apportionment of the work that had not yet been resolved, and that Thérasse's "request" to work on Balthild may have been because this subject had been suggested to him. The palace architect with whom Thérasse met is not named but would have been Henri-Adolphe de Gisors. It is possible that Thérasse's letter and enclosed brief description of Balthild's life was fulfillment of a kind of homework, showing that he was familiar with the subject and her importance to France's political life. Indeed, the letter opens with an outline of the important features of Balthild's rule, and her status as regent, suggesting that this information had been specifically required of him. It is clear from the documentation is that Thérasse was keen for the commission and to have Balthild as its subject.

How did someone in the 1840s quickly find information on a Merovingian queen of France? The proposal written in Thérasse's hand drew on information quickly and readily to hand, as he sent it back to the minister in only two days. Thérasse informs us that one of his sources was Charles-Jean-François Hénault (1685–1770) whose *Nouvel Abrégé chronologique de l'Histoire de France* had been wildly popular under the *ancien regime* and had been published in many editions over the decades. The section on Balthild referenced by Thérasse in his proposal indicates that he must have been using the expanded edition of 1768 or later. The second unnamed source appears to have been Jean François Dreux du Radier (1714–80), *Mémoires historiques, critiques, et anecdotes des reines et régents de France* first published 1763–76 but available in a revised edition in 1782 and 1808. This was an account of the queens and queen-regents of French history. Volume 1 contained the queens of the Merovingian dynasty.[45] The restoration of the monarchy sent artists scurrying back to older sources. That Thérasse drew on second-hand sources rather than intimate knowledge of his subject is suggested by the fact that he reported that Balthild's relics were in place under the abbey's main altar whereas in fact the convent had been destroyed half a century earlier.

Thérasse outlined Balthild's importance and suitability for a statue in his proposal. On the sheet of paper that he enclosed with his letter to the minister, he outlined the essential facts of Balthild's life: she was wife of Clovis II, a slave of the mayor of the palace, had three sons, ruled wisely as regent for Chlothar III during his minority, died at Chelles, and founded the monastery of Corbie. Hénault had stated that once a nun she never again recalled that she was a queen, a phrase that Thérasse repeated verbatim. Thérasse noted that Balthild had abolished slavery "that still existed at that time" and that another historian (this must be Dreux du Radier) states that she was perfectly beautiful, her physiognomy pleasing, her spirit just and delicate, her charms supported by her graces and her virtues.[46] Finally, Thérasse noted that Balthild was canonized by Pope Nicolas I, her feast celebrated on January 30, and her relics rest under the abbey's altar with those of Saints Genesius and Bertilla.

Although Thérasse finished his outline with conventional information about Balthild's cult it was not Balthild's sanctity that was to be on display in the gardens—it was Balthild as a policy-driven queen and as a "regent of France." This conformed with the purpose of the commission for the Luxembourg Gardens which adorned the parliamentary seat of government, the Luxembourg Palace (the house of peers in Louis-Philippe's day), and named for Marie de Medici herself a regent of France and progenitor of the Bourbon dynasty.[47] The statues in the garden were thus to reflect the political nature of the space by highlighting notable female protectors and rulers of France, "Reines de France et femmes illustres."

In his cover letter to the minister, he listed her policies, although not entirely accurately: She abolished slavery ("What characterizes Balthild's government is the abolition of slavery which still existed"); she suppressed the taxes that forced people to sell their children (Balthild did not do this—she forbade infanticide); she made war on simony, and "her rule was one of gentleness, of prudence, and of justice" he concluded.[48]

Balthild's fight against simony (read, government corruption) and debilitating taxes was an appropriate warning for any government. It may have seemed particularly apt in 1846, a year that saw an economic downturn and increased poverty in France, two years before revolution erupted. For Thérasse, as part of the artistic community, Balthild's policy against corruption may also have resonated close to home. The director of the Académie des Beaux-Arts, Hygin-Edmond-Ludovic-Auguste Cavé was a royal appointment made by Louis-Philippe and there was discontent in some quarters about perceived nepotism in the assignment of commissions; Cavé's wife was an artist who was thought to show favoritism to her friends.[49] As an artist often starved of commissions, Thérasse may have had some pleasure in penning those lines about Balthild's prohibition of the related corruption of simony!

When Thérasse accepted his commission and framed Balthild as an abolitionist (Fig. 7.3), the anti-slavery position it espoused reflected the majority sentiment of people in the Paris region even if it was not yet clear how emancipation in the colonies would proceed. As we see from Thérasse's letters, it was Balthild's record of anti-slave trafficking that was paramount to her choice as an example of good government. Indeed, Balthild's policy reflected France's current anti-trafficking position, but not the full emancipation of slaves. But in inscribing *Abolitio servi tutis* on the book she held,

Fig. 7.3 Victor Thérasse, "Sainte Balthilde." Luxembourg Gardens, Paris.

Thérasse sent a pointed political message that full abolition of slavery was the desired outcome, and in crediting Balthild with the abolition of slavery he surely revealed his own political sympathies. Furthermore, Thérasse's decision must have been made as early as the spring of 1846 as the design of the statue must already have been determined at that point with a book as part of the design because he needed to secure the dimensions of the block of marble. I have been unable to find the model that Thérasse submitted to the minister in that year, or any other preliminary works that could inform us on how early in the design process for Balthild she was to be portrayed as an abolitionist. The marble book could be made to bear a script to be added later, but in view of Thérasse's synopsis of her Life there is no reason to think that the script was purely an afterthought.

In contrast to Ingres' seductive portrayal (seen on the cover image), Thérasse's statue of Balthild is solid, emotionless, and erect. She stares straight ahead across the garden to where the statue of Chlothild is positioned on the opposite side. There is nothing to suggest a saint—this statue is all about Balthild as a ruler.[50] Her braids are neatly wrapped around her ears in a fashion made popular by Queen Victoria. Her head is covered in the back with a veil, secured by the weight of the crown above. Her tunic dress is cinched high with a belt, and she wears a simple cross pendant. Clasping her cloak with one hand, her left hand is raised to hold open a soft-covered book to show the inscribed page: *Abolitio servi/tutis*. The stark difference between Ingres' portrayal of Balthild and that of Thérasse can be attributed in part to the context in which the portrait was to be seen (chapel versus public space) but it may also be an argument for not dismissing the direct influence of the artist in rendering his subject. It would have been possible for Thérasse to depict Balthild in a less stridently political manner, but it was evidently an opportunity not to be missed.

The statue occasioned scant attention from the critics when it was exhibited. Some of this neglect may have been due to disruptions of 1848 and the fact that his statue was a commission of the recently deposed king. (His was not the only statue exhibited that year that was destined for the Luxembourg gardens.)[51] What small attention the statue received was unflattering. The *Journal des débats* (Jan. 1, 1848) thought the work conscientious but unbalanced, comparing it (unfairly, it must be said) with the strangely off-kilter statue of Anne de Beaujeu in the same series. When the statue was mentioned in Thérasse's obituary in 1864, it was not considered one of his best.[52] Pierre-Armand Malitourne, who reviewed the sculpture exhibits for *L'Artiste* in its June issue that year was also not very impressed by artistic talent being put to the use of commissioned "mannequins" and while Thérasse's statue had at least the honor of being mentioned, Malitourne's verdict on Balthild as its subject was hardly positive: "Queen Balthild (another of these obscure queens! What's the point?)"[53] He makes no mention of its inscription. However, in terms of what this meant for Thérasse personally, he came away with an honorable mention when prizes were given out by the minister for the interior after the work was exhibited at the Salon of 1848.[54]

In the sporadic reviews of his work in the French press there is a discernable lukewarmness about Thérasse's work in general, including his statue of Balthild. Not a single review mentions the inscription on the book, but equally not a single review mentions any other element of the work. It seems the opinion-makers of the artistic community had assigned the statue to obscurity right from the start. This must have been a blow to Thérasse who was often underemployed and who struggled financially. At some point in his later years he married a woman of means and, as his obituary explained, he lived for some years in comfort. But then his wife died. They had no children and he suddenly found that he had to repay her dowry. This required him to return to his profession, which may not have been easy at his age as it was physically demanding work. By the time of his death he had been living almost eighteen months in a hospice for the aged poor in the 16th arrondissement, the "maison de Sainte-Périne."[55] He died "poor and obscure" as one commentator put it who also noted that only one publication had published an obituary, the *Chronique des Arts*.[56] Indeed, the author of the obituary lamented the tardy recognition of a sculptor of merit who had not exhibited in some time and whose death no one seemed to have announced.[57] It was a sad end for an artist who had lived through personal difficulties and whose work had always been judged competent but somehow also second tier.

Still, in 1848 Thérasse's statue had been awarded an honorable mention by the critics. The statue's commission was a moment of hope for the sculptor, yet the timing of its exhibition was inauspicious. The date of its commission in 1845 reflected a particular moment in time when Balthild's story was known to Parisians. Indeed, the statue's commission coincided with a spate of interest in Balthild's life as can be seen in devotional publications published in 1847. And it was also a time when the abolitionist movement in Paris was combined with anti-royal sentiment, yet the abolitionist sentiment could still find expression in a public space. On the other hand, the statue was exhibited at the Salon in a year of political upheaval after its royal patron had been exiled, and rather than abolition, the most pressing concern to those involved in French political life was now domestic electoral reform.

The Pleasures of Light Reading

While the king, Monsieur Cavé, and Thérasse were planning for Balthild's entry into the female pantheon of illustrious rulers, Balthild was being presented to the public in a steady stream of religious and romantic literature. The French Revolution saw the end of Balthild's convent, but it did not extinguish her cult and she remained a person of interest to Parisian readers. She appeared in mini-biographies in a swath of religious reading, especially in journals targeted at young readers like *Le Myosotis*.[58] Often shorn of the political dimension of her reign, these stories lauded her beauty and piety and the rewards of placing God's will before that of earthly suitors.[59] Further, she took her place in the many "Galleries" of famous and pious women.[60] And in publications favorable to monarchy, and in an age when such advice could be given without irony, in 1829 Balthild was one in a series of princesses whose virtue could serve as a model for the young reader.[61]

For the novelist, Balthild's story held irresistible opportunities for imagination and even gothic horror. Somewhat surprisingly, earlier in the century, Balthild's story had been the subject of a quarrel within Napoleon Bonaparte's inner circle. The case involved the wife of Napoleon Bonaparte's younger brother Lucien who had written a poem on Balthild, and the hasty publication in 1814 of a two-volume novel about Bathild by Madame Julie Simons-Candeille (1767–1834). The startling circumstance of these compositions was related in the waspish memoirs of Laure Junot, the Duchess of Abrantès, wife of Napoleon's general Duke Jean-Andoche Junot.[62] Alexandrine Bonaparte, Napoleon's sister-in-law, also known as Madame Lucien and later by her title Princess Canino, had written a poem in six verses on Queen Balthild and she was very pleased with her efforts. In 1811, when the emperor came to hear of this, the poem was almost complete but not yet published. Napoleon was on very bad terms with his brother, having forced him into exile, and he also disapproved of Lucien's marriage to Alexandrine almost a decade earlier. He expressed his displeasure at his sister-in-law's aspirations and plotted to steal her thunder before she could publish her verses. On Napoleon's command, Madame Simons-Candeille was summoned to the ministry of police where she was ordered to write a novel in epic style with the subject of "Bathilde, reine des Francs"; furthermore, this was to be done quickly! Three months later the novel appeared in print, and it was immediately evident among those who knew the case that it drew heavily on Madame Lucien's poem in both structure and detail: in essence, the new novel had plagiarized the poem. The Duchess of Abrantès notes that this was hardly surprising as, without her knowledge, Madame Lucien's notes had been provided to Madame Simons-Candeille for this purpose! The resulting novel, the duchess noted, was not very good, in part because Simons-Candeille was not very good at this sort of work, but with imperial will behind it the volumes were produced in beautiful typeface and with illustrations by Girodet. The emperor's spiteful ploy had worked. As the duchess pointed out, Madame Lucien's poem could no longer be published because it would now be viewed as if Madame Lucien had plagiarized Madame Simons-Candeille's novel, whereas it was Madame

Lucien who had been the victim. In fact, the poem, in ten verses, was eventually published, in 1815, to some acclaim.[63]

Was Laure Junot's assessment of Madame Simons-Candeille's novel correct when she said it was not very good? Frankly, yes. The story of Balthild that she told was fanciful, verbose, inaccurate, but admittedly imaginative. The novel introduced a new character, Marcolm, Balthild's nemesis, and introduces new places into the story, for example, Notre-Dame-des-Bois where Balthild is taken in her baptismal clothes and confronted by evil magicians. The novel revolves around the secret of her birth, an engraved bracelet that claims she is a love child, and the predictable denouement that Balthild was not born into slavery but was rather the niece of the Anglo-Saxon King Edwin. Rather unusually, Simons-Candeille tackles Balthild's religion, depicting Balthild as a pagan who must be given religious instruction and baptized (so that the "blood of Woden" will mix with the "blood of Merovech"!).[64] A veneer of historicity is enabled through endnotes in which Simons-Candeille credited her sources (although not Madame Lucien's poem!).

Not all accounts of Balthild's life were as "Eyes Wide Shut" as that of Simons-Candeille, but the temptation to introduce extraneous material and unwarranted interpretation had been long-standing. Some of it was not innocent. One of the interpolations in Simons-Candeille's account was that the slave trade that engulfed Bathild and others in the seventh century was organized by Jews who then sold the captives on to slave markets in Italy.[65] In an era of slave-trading it was inaccurate to single out the Jewish population. Frankish sources show that Christians were involved.[66] The added detail about Italy may have been prompted both by anti-ultramontane feeling in France and also by the fact the Prince and Princess of Canino had been taking refuge in Italy where they befriended the captive pope and were given their titles by him. Simons-Candeille was drawing on what were considered at the time to be reputable sources. In the work of Sieur François Eudes de Mézeray, *Histoire de France depuis Faramond* (1643–51), a source often mentioned by nineteenth-century writers, and in the many printings of the abbreviated edition of this work, Jews and infidels are singled out as being responsible for the early medieval slave trade.[67] While some eighteenth- and nineteenth-century works on Balthild ignored this, the accusation continued to be repeated in others.[68]

Another characteristic of this literature is its emphasis on Balthild's physical appearance, especially her beauty. This was a claim that originated in the seventh-century Life, and it was given full rein in the early modern era. We have seen that Balthild's physiognomy was a detail that Thérasse extracted from the literature on Balthild that he was reading. For a sculptor this might be some excuse, because it promised an aesthetic option for the sculpture, but in reality there was never any impediment to sculptors beautifying their subject. In the eighteenth and nineteenth centuries, the connection of a pleasing physiognomy with personal virtue was still given scientific credence.[69]

Perhaps as a result of this continuing interest in Balthild as a figure of romance, in the nineteenth century the name "Bathilde" was a popular given-name and was used for heroines in novels and theatrical works. For example, in 1856 a play in two acts was published titled *Bathilde, reine des france, ou, la vertu sur la trone*, an "historical drama in two acts" by an otherwise unidentified Monsieur H. A. The play booklet cost 75 centimes. In this play the slave girl Bathilde is bought by the mayor of the palace, Saint-Gontran. A note tells us that she was bought by Erchinoald but that the name Saint-Gontran has a "more agreeable pronunciation," that is that it was better for the actors. Some Merovingian names were hard to enunciate even in French!

Devotional Reading

As in the other areas we have examined, the 1840s were a high point for devotional interest in Balthild's story. With no originality in their titles, and little in their contents, accounts of the *Vie de Sainte Bathilde, reine de France* proliferated in low-cost, low-production booklets published in Paris, Lille, and Limoges; 1847 saw a bumper crop of these.[70] Sometimes, an author took a little more care and they rose above the rest. Élisabeth Brun's *Vie de Sainte Bathilde, reine de France* is tolerable. These publications relied on a readership that still viewed Balthild as an important saint whose life provided "virtues" worth emulating. The short devotional plays provided material for young boarders at schools and convents to act out. But without the convent, Balthild's cult now relied on popular knowledge of her story. In the Ville de Chelles, the efforts of the local clergy to reanimate popular aspects of her cult led to the reintroduction of the distribution of bread loaves, the "pain de Sainte Bathilde" in the hope of attracting attention. Her feast day was celebrated in the parish church of Chelles on January 30 each year. Some of the *Vie de Sainte Bathilde* publications had the liturgical prayers and notices associated with her cult included in their final pages. Her role in "freeing" slaves was mentioned as an example of the benefits of Christianity in catechetical literature.[71]

Histories and Critical Editions

We have seen that Balthild's Life was accessible in French versions as well as in Latin, providing novelists, playwrights, and devotional authors with the material they needed to pen their works. From the 1830s to the end of the century, the academic study of history together with a growing interest in archaeology garnered renewed interest in the Middle Ages, its history, fashions, architecture, and its artistic aesthetic. The Merovingians were considered "le premier race," the first race (roots, dynasty, founding peoples), and interest in the Merovingians was strong among liberal scholars opposed to the imperial politics of the day that conversely found its model in the emperor Charlemagne.[72]

Most famously, between 1833 and 1840 Augustin Thierry published his *Récits des Temps Mérovingiens*. The work was widely read having been first serialized in 1833 in the *Revue des deux mondes*, and then published with a lengthy historical introduction in two volumes in 1840. The work fed the reading public with an interest in the Merovingian era.[73] Thierry's *récits* drew heavily on some of the core stories of the sixth-century *History of the Franks* by Gregory of Tours, highlighting the violence of the sixth-century Franks by including the dramatic tale of the feuding queens Fredegund and Brunhild. As a seventh-century queen, Balthild lived a century after the events which Thierry related in this work, but the Merovingians existed in the public imagination as a result of his work and knowledge about Balthild could ride the general interest in Merovingian kings and queens that had been awakened by Thierry's publication. The traditions that kept the cult of Saint Balthild alive offered a stark contrast to the "evil" queen Fredegund found in Thierry's volumes. Unlike the violent Merovingians of the previous century, Balthild had the reputation for keeping peace among warring factions. She was also Anglo-Saxon which may have been useful way to distinguish her from other Merovingians at a time when French readers were being taught to see themselves as successors to the Gallo-Romans rather than as latter-day Franks.

From the 1830s the modernization of transportation, especially the laying of railway lines, resulted in increased finds of early medieval artefacts, and for the first time, scholars and artists had access to visual information that could be used to depict the Merovingian elite. Yet for reasons to do with artistic fashion these clues were rarely taken up before the end of the century. Engravings of Balthild in nineteenth-century publications depict her as a nun or as a generic medieval queen with a crown, veil, and flowing robes just as Thérasse depicted her in the gardens.

General reliance on French language versions of her story meant that Balthild's story maintained the viewpoint of the second, Carolingian "B" version of her biography.[74] In these publications Balthild was an aristocratic captive whose looks and deportment singled her out as a woman of good birth despite her temporary servile condition. Dissenting views on Balthild's origins were rare because they would have had to draw on the Latin editions of Johannes Bollandus and Godfridus Henschenius, or Johannes Mabillon that provided the less accessible "A" version. Thus Bernard de Montfaucon in 1729 was unusual in acknowledging that Balthild could have been "une Princesse de basse extraction."[75] However, for those willing to consult the Latin in the 1840s, the earliest version of Balthild's Life was available in the *Acta Sanctorum* of the Bollandists and of Mabillon, and in abridged versions of the former such as the "Little Bollandists."[76]

Renewed interest in the medieval origins of the nations of Europe led to the founding of what later became the Institute of the *Monumenta Germaniae Historica*, which published (and continues to publish) critical editions of medieval texts in a series of the same name. The seven volumes dedicated to Merovingian texts, the *Scriptores rerum Merovingicarum*, were replete with hagiographic texts. As a queen, Balthild's two hagiographies were among the earliest to be edited by Bruno Krusch in 1888 alongside other royal biographies including those of Queens Radegund and Chlothild in Volume 2.[77] Bruno Krusch's side-by-side edition of the "A" version of the Life and the "B" version, with its introduction to the manuscripts and a critical apparatus has provided later scholars with a useful reference. It is Krush's edition that underlies most modern translations and is the preferred reference point in modern scholarship.[78]

While those in the Paris region in the mid-nineteenth century were exposed to Balthild's story in some form or another, it was through the school curriculum that Merovingian history was transmitted nationwide. Early in the nineteenth century, histories of France designed for schoolroom instruction tended to follow the pattern of seventeenth- and eighteenth-century chronologies with its lists of kings. The Merovingian dynasty comprising twenty-two kings (starting from Pharamond in these works) did well in publications on this model. In Laure Saint-Ouen's prodigiously successful *Histoire de France depuis l'établissement de la monarchie jusqu'à nos jours* published in 1827 the Merovingians merited thirty-one pages, although much of each page was taken up with portrait medallions.[79] Laure Saint-Ouen's work was a direct descendant of chronological histories like Mézeray's immensely popular *Abrégé chronologique* which also gave considerable space to the Merovingians and contained "portraits" of kings.[80] Before a standardized school curriculum came into being, narrative-style textbook histories of France might include a few pages on the Merovingians drawing on Gregory of Tours, Auguste Thierry, and other works; Clovis II and Balthild were included in some of these. For example, L. Girault, *Histoire de France (420-1849)* published in 1850 included nine pages on the Merovingians.[81] However, by the turn of the twentieth century, as Edward James has noted, most French school children came to know of the Merovingians through the works of Ernest Lavisse (1842-1922) and in these textbooks French schoolchildren learned less about the Merovingians than before. What did they learn about Balthild in these new textbooks? Nothing. In 1882 the Council for Public Instruction outlined the framework for teaching history; Lavisse's *Récits et entretiens familiers sur l'histoire de France jusqu'en 1328* (1884) was a response to this directive to provide historical instruction for children aged seven to nine, and he explained in his preface that he wanted to instill historical images into the imagination of young children so that they could build on these and learn about national history.[82] The nine pages on the Merovingians were based on *récits* or vignettes having to do with Clovis, the murder of Galswinth, the Irish monk Columbanus who confronted Queen Brunhild and some bad bishops, and good monks who brought prosperity to the land through hard work and education. By 1884, in elementary school, Clovis and Chlothild were the only Merovingians mentioned.[83] In the second year, Saint Eligius merited a short entry relating his time as a skilled metalworker and goldsmith to Kings Dagobert and Clovis II, ending with only the brief comment that he gave away his riches to relieve the poor and to ransom captives.[84] In the second year of the curriculum Clovis' wife Chlothild was mentioned alongside her husband, and Fredegund and Brunhild were relegated to a note about the civil war of the late 570s.[85] But Balthild's record as queen regent and her policy of forbidding the slave trade was ignored in the curriculum. This oversight was due in part to the tendency of textbooks to skip from king Dagobert (the last king of "merit") to the early Carolingians, lumping together kings after Dagobert (d. 639) as "do-nothing kings," "rois fainéants," and thus not worth mentioning. To include a policy-driven queen like Balthild was evidently not worth the trouble of interrupting this convenient scheme.

Christian Cult and Relics after the French Revolution

The public cult of the Christian religion had ceased by decree of the Legislative Assembly on August 10, 1792, and the convent of Chelles was ordered to close its doors by October 1 of that year. By this time the convent had already been stripped of its precious metals but the nuns and some of the inhabitants of Chelles sought to save the precious relics by distributing them among themselves or hiding them in the parish church. Eventually the public cult was re-authorized but the convent was not reconstituted. The nuns held on to the relics that they had divided among themselves: each took a piece of Balthild's skull together with other relics.[86] As they aged and died the relics were gifted to relatives or to local churches. But the bulk of the relics stayed safe within the reliquary of Saint Florus in the parish church of Saint-André.

The process of recovering lost relics began in earnest with Abbot Pruneau's visit to Chelles in 1826. He ordered an inventory of surviving relics and interviewed some of the surviving nuns. As noted by Jean-Pierre Laporte, the resulting document now serves as a baseline record for authenticating the relics of Chelles after the Revolution.[87] In the second half of the nineteenth century the presence of relics and descriptions of reliquaries were noted by visitors to the town, including clergy and antiquarians (who were often one and the same) and from these we know that the relics of Chelles were soon caught up again in the age-old practice of religious institutions gifting relics to other religious institutions, especially to monastic communities that had been able to recover. For example, the community of Jouarre obtained two small bones from Balthild's remains in 1849. When Mgr. Allou inspected the remains of Balthild and Bertilla in 1853 and in 1855, he took bone fragments to gift to various institutions, and on each occasion he also removed additional pieces for later distribution. It was considered an honor in Chelles when Louis-Etienne Pougeouis and his brother were able to gift relics of Balthild and Bertilla to Pope Piux IX. It is reflective of Balthild's second-tier status at this time that the pope had originally wanted relics of Saint Chlothild but, being unable to locate them, relics of Balthild and Bertilla were gifted instead. However, it was with the appointment of Abbé Clément Torchet as curé of Chelles in 1860 that serious efforts were made to record the convent's illustrious history and revive Balthild's cult. It was Torchet who wrote the lengthy history of the convent with its detailed biographies of the abbesses referenced earlier in this chapter, in addition to other works on the history of relics. It was also Torchet who in 1861 celebrated Balthild's feast day with a procession of the relic caskets that were then deposited around the altar. And it was Torchet who in 1867 sent the "Louis XIII casket" containing the so-called "sandals of Saint Balthild" to the Universal Exposition where it won a medal. During the Franco-Prussian War in 1870, Torchet hid the relic caskets and parish registers in the cemetery, in the vault of a local family, wrapped up in a carpet. With the arrival of German soldiers, Torchet went into hiding, surfacing only occasionally to celebrate mass. When he was finally able to return to the parish in January 1871 he found the church vandalized, but his brave actions had saved the relics from destruction. In 1898 he provided a new reliquary for Bertilla's remains in celebration of his own sacerdotal jubilee, an identical casket being paid for Balthild's remains by the widow of a former mayor of Chelles. When Torchet died in 1899 at the age of seventy-six, he had overseen an impressive restoration of the cult of Balthild and associated saints in the Ville de Chelles. His efforts had saved the relics from destruction and he had restored Balthild to the center of religious life in the town. While this was largely a local success story, it was the necessary ground in which a saint's cult could thrive. The Parisian authors of the many writings on Balthild in the mid-nineteenth century knew that Balthild's cult was surviving in their peripheral vision.

Torchet's successor was the Abbé Alfred Bonno, the priest and scholar for whom the current museum is named. His interest in the relics in the parish church took a curious turn when, in 1906, church relics were announced to be the property of the priest in charge. Bonno took advantage of this development to remove the relics, secretly, from their caskets in the church and took them to a new location where he could inspect them. The following year he had all the relics returned to the church, again secretly, but retained the beautiful embroidered "chasuble of Chelles" as part of his personal collection of antiquities. When Bonno received a preferment and became a canon of Meaux cathedral he left Chelles, taking the chasuble with him along with his other treasures. These items returned to Chelles only in 1921 at Bonno's death but ended up in an attic. It was only with the appointment of André Clement in 1942 that Bonno's collection was put into order, and temporarily exhibited in 1952. By then, the chasuble was in a parlous state. Clement had found it tacked to a wooden board. (The brown spots left by the rusting nails are visible on the chasuble today.) But crucially, Clement had the chasuble authenticated as Merovingian by Jean Hubert, a respected scholar of the early Middle Ages. The first modern exhibition of the chasuble and other items in the relic collection was organized by Clement in 1961. The following year saw the last procession of the relics through the town, an event preserved in a photograph with André Clément visible at its right-hand edge.[88]

In 1983 the relics were inspected by an archaeological team headed by Jean-Pierre Laporte whose subsequent publications on the relics provide the definitive account of the activities of the team, analysis of the remains, and the history of the relics and their authentications over the centuries. Laporte's *Le Trésor* did two important things: it provided a forensic account of the location of the relics over the centuries providing a chain of evidence—a new kind of authentication process in the service of scholarship to add to the literature of authentication that had survived across the centuries—and he used this analysis to back up the scientific analysis of the bones and textiles associated with the burial of the saints. The burden of proof is met in his work, establishing the process by which a cache of authentically Merovingian items survived into the late twentieth century. His work forms the basis of modern analysis and underlies much of the relic information provided here.

Balthild in Modern Art and Memorialization

The impact of the painting "Les Énervés de Jumièges" by Évariste-Vital Luminais at the salon of 1880 has been examined in Chapter 6 (pp. 137–39). It drew on the twelfth-century legend of the hamstrung sons of Clovis II and Balthild that had no basis in any historical reality. However, this image came to dominate public associations of Balthild after its exhibition. The painting went on to inspire numerous other works of art and performance.

Only three years after the painting was exhibited, and clearly inspired by it, Marie-Eugenie Chervet, under the pseudonym Raoul de Navery, published *Les mystères de Jumièges* which added further fantastic elements to the story.[89] In 1983 French filmmaker Claude Duty aired an eighteen-minute film in which two young men floated on a barge downriver, only to confront a woman who handed them a knife and was murdered on the river bank.[90] In France today the story of *les enérvées* is a meme.

The statue of Balthild as abolitionist that Thérasse produced in the hungry final years of the July monarchy was not duplicated, as far as I have been able to discover. Monuments to colonial actors are deservedly suspect, even when they commemorate abolitionists. A modern (1996) statue on the island of Martinique commemorating the nineteenth-century French abolitionist, Victor Schoelcher, who declared slaves free in the West Indies in 1848, was vandalized in 2021. In fact, France has been slow to recognize its role in the slave trade and there is little in the public space to recognize and acknowledge France's role. This deficiency has been recognized. A memorial to the victims of slavery at the Quai de la Fosse in Nantes was dedicated in 2012. Another memorial for the victims of slavery, originally announced in 2017 by President Macron and intended for the Tuileries Gardens will now reportedly be erected in the Trocadero Gardens close to the Eiffel Tower in Paris. The competition for a design currently underway is expected to include the names of two hundred thousand slaves from the colonies freed in 1848, and recognizing four million enslaved in the former French colonies.[91]

But what about a statue commemorating an historical queen who was herself a slave and who did much to ameliorate the plight of those caught up in the human trafficking endemic in her own era? On the one hand, she represents the myth of the French people that slavery had been effectively abolished in France in the seventh century. On the other, there are few statues of female rulers in the public space that commemorate hard policy. Balthild and many other women like her were victims of harsh circumstances in which the dignity of human life and individual purpose was denied by those who sought, at the expense of the lives of others, to prosper financially and seek material comfort within a power structure of inhumanity and discrimination. Both as historical figure and as cultural icon, she earns our attention.

And what about Balthild the woman who lived her life in the seventh century? She exercised royal power and she rescued the stranded. Her life, as lived and as written, challenges us to consider the limits of ancient sources to evoke and convey notions of human trauma, compassion, and empathy within a worldview that accepted servitude as a condition of life. There may be limits to biographic and historical certainty, and to imaginative conjuration, but her life inspired later generations to dream a life of compassion and virtue through her. That is a meaningful legacy for a seventh-century queen.

APPENDIX

The Baldehildis Seal Matrix

In 1998, a metal detectorist operating in Postwick in Norfolk uncovered a gold seal matrix, presumably from a finger ring, bearing a face and female name, Baldehildis, on one side and two full-size figures on the other; a bearded male figure and a figure, presumably female, with the same long hair as on the named-side. The seal matrix was found without a finger band but the mounts on each side indicate its use as a swivel ring, a ring-type known from Merovingian Gaul. The seal diameter is 12 mm, less than half an inch, and with a gold content of 98 percent. The seal matrix is now housed in the Norwich Castle Museum and Art Gallery.

From the beginning the name on the seal, Baldehildis, raised the possibility that the ring had belonged to Queen Balthild. This possibility was strengthened by the object's date being consistent with a late seventh-century date on stylistic grounds. However, any identification of the ring with Queen Balthild is at present purely conjectural, and the engraved images, especially of the two naked figures on the reverse, have yet to be adequately explained.

Women wore rings, including name rings and seal rings, in the Merovingian period.[1] Balthild undoubtedly owned a seal ring and wore it alongside the other jewelry she is known to have favored. A seal ring was a useful item as it could be used for a variety of purposes. It could be used as an authentication device for important documents or for securing correspondence. A seal could be used to secure household goods. A ring's name or image could gesture to family ties or religious identity. In short, a ring that could be used to identify its bearer was a useful item. In using these rings the Merovingians continued late Roman practices, and a fairly large number of name rings or monogram rings have survived from the Merovingian period.

The case for and against this being a ring that belonged to Queen Balthild is usefully discussed by Paul Fouracre.[2] The strong connections between Merovingian Francia and Anglo-Saxon England are well known and may provide a context for the ring's discovery. What that connection is, however, remains a mystery. As the ring was found as a loose find, without archaeological context, we cannot know when or how the ring found its way into a Norfolk field.

Is there any reason to think that this looks like a royal seal, or the seal of a queen who had entered a convent? The absence of the royal title "regina" makes it unlikely to have been used by a queen or queen-regent in an official capacity. Merovingian kings used their title, "rex," on their seal ring and the wax impressions sometimes included hair to emphasize authenticity. A queen-regent would want her title to be displayed as this was the source of her authority. Those rings sometimes ascribed to Merovingian queens may not, in fact, be rings of queens, and so do not provide a useful comparison for the Baldehildis ring.

In view of the prominent display of a cross on each side, could the seal ring have been used by the queen during her retirement to Chelles (Fig. A.1)? The presence of a cross suggests something religious and legitimate is being represented. However, no known examples, or written documentation, exist to ascertain whether abbesses or women in

178 APPENDIX: THE BALDEHILDIS SEAL MATRIX

Fig. A.1 Gold seal matrix found near Norwich. It bears the name of Baldehildis. There has been much speculation as to whether this could have belonged to Queen Balthild or an associate. On the reverse side is an image of a naked man and a naked woman. © The Trustees of the British Museum/Art Resource, NY.

the religious life wore rings of any kind in this era. Of course, Balthild was not an abbess, nor was she an ordinary nun until the end of her life (see Chapter 5, pp. 93–97); she may have had property transactions to oversee. However, if Balthild used this ring in connection with her life at Chelles there is the immediate problem of identifying the people on the reverse, and what they are doing. The two figures represented are naked. This is a deliberate choice. Yet the figures are not clearly sexed above the navel and present a rather androgenous appearance. The male figure has a beard, whereas Merovingians were clean shaven, and the head is bald. Is this Balthild's husband, Clovis II? This seems unlikely. Clovis died in his early twenties and any official representation of him would have shown the long hair that was essential to the king's power to rule. Was this her son? Again, for the same reasons, this seems unlikely. The figures are the same size. They gaze directly into each other's eyes. They appear involved in some kind of mutual activity. Between the figures is a cartouche that contains within it a minute etching that has been variously identified as a penis within a vulva, or a symbol of holding hands. However, whether the figures are holding hands, dancing, or having sex, the image does not correlate to a known context in Balthild's life. The item is extremely small, hampering better identification of what is going on. For the present the ring and its owner remain an enigma.

Endnotes

Preface

1. Effros and Moreira, *OHMW*.
2. F&G *LMF*; McNamara, *Sainted Women*; Krusch, *MGH*, *SRM* II.
3. Couturier, *Sainte Bathilde, reine des Francs*. Sixteen chapters supplemented by seven appendices with documents. There are modern editions and discussions of most of these texts.
4. Bellessort, *Sainte Bathilde*.
5. *VB* I. 2. On terminology, see Wilton, "What Do We Mean by Anglo-Saxon."
6. Davis, *The Problem of Slavery in Western Culture*.
7. D'Andilly, *Vies de plusieurs saints illustres*, p. 357 (discussed in Chapter 7, pp. 144, 152–53).

Chapter 1

1. Sources do not agree on the birth order of the sons of Clovis II and Balthild. The *LHF* ch. 44 lists Clovis II's sons as Chlothar, Childeric, and Theuderic. A more contemporary work, the *Passio Leudegarii* ch. 5 explains that Theuderic should have been raised to the throne after the death of Chlothar, but instead was displaced by Childeric of Austrasia, making it sound as though Theuderic was the second son. However, primogeniture was not in force in this era, and it is possible that it was thought Theuderic should have succeeded Chlothar because Childeric was already king of Austrasia. We do not know the details of the succession arrangement that was made in the aftermath of the Grimoald coup, and so the full meaning of this passage remains unclear. Unless otherwise indicated, translations from the LHF are from Bachrach, *Liber Historiae Francorum*.
2. *VB* I. 2. *De partibus transmarinis....ex genere Saxonum*. Unless otherwise indicated, English translations of the first Life of Balthild are from Paul Fouracre and Richard Gerberding, *Late Merovingian France: History and Hagiography, 640–720* (Manchester: Manchester University Press,1996), 118–32.
3. As, for example, when Dagobert I's brother Charibert was given Aquitaine and Gascony to rule until those territories passed to Dagobert on Charibert's death. Fredegar, *Chronicle*, p. 57.
4. The hagiographer states (*VB* I. 3) that her progeny currently rules (this would be Theuderic III), so the biography must have been written sometime between Balthild's death in 680, and Theuderic III's death in 690/91.
5. Nelson suggested the author was a nun at Chelles, "Queens as Jezebels," p. 46, n. 83. Arguments in favor of this view are explored at some length by Wemple, *Women in Frankish Society*, pp. 182–85, and accepted by McNamara, *Sainted Women*, pp. 264–65. F&G *LMF* notes that "there is no other indication of the sex of the author one way or another," and therefore takes the "beloved brothers" to whom the work is addressed to indicate a male author. I agree with this latter view. I am not convinced by Wemple's argument that the roles of mother and peacemaker are indications of female values and authorship in the hagiography. The influence of Baudonivia's work on Balthild's Life is clear, but the differences between the two works, especially relating to how much attention is given to life in the convent, argues against the view that the first Life of Balthild was written by a nun. Absent stronger arguments for female authorship in this case, the dedication of the work to monastic brothers suggests the author was male.
6. As we know from Baudonivia's Life of Radegund, a female author could find a rich source of edificatory stories in convent life. By contrast, the author of the Life of Balthild largely glosses over Balthild's convent years and leans heavily on the hagiographies of Queen Radegund to supply images of convent life.
7. *Vita Sanctae Balthildis*, ed. B. Krusch, *MGH*, *SRM* II (Hannover, 1888), pp. 475–508. The Merovingian Life ("A," hereafter *VB* 1) is contemporary with Balthild's death or within a decade

thereafter, between 680 and 691. This is an important source for her life because, although we do not know if the author had ever met her, the author could tap contemporary knowledge about the queen's career and could fashion a model of the queen-saint that made sense to his audience. No Merovingian manuscripts of the Life survive: the text has been reconstructed from later medieval manuscripts. For more information on the manuscripts see Krusch's introduction to *VB* I and *VB* II; F&G *LMF*, pp. 115–16.
8. De Jong, "Queens and Beauty."
9. Moreira, "Procuratrix Optima"; McNamara, "*Imitatio Helenae*"; Hillner, *Helena Augusta*.
10. Shroeder argues that the first hagiographer promoted a new view of a Christian Francia with the pious Balthild at its center; "Francia as Christendom."
11. The *LHF* mentions Balthild in chs. 43 and 44. Fredegar, *Chronicle*, p. 80 (drawing at this juncture on the *LHF*): "Now Clovis, son of Dagobert, chose for his queen a foreigner named Baldechildis, a sensible and attractive woman. By her he had three sons—namely, Chlothar, Childeric and Theuderic. And the mayor of his palace, by name Erchinoald, was forceful and intelligent. So peace reigned in the kingdom of Clovis, and there were no wars. In his latter years, it is true, his mind became affected, and he died after reigning for eighteen years. The Franks thereupon made his eldest boy, Chlothar, king, with the queen-mother by his side."
12. Fredegar, *Chronicle*, p. 80. "In extremis vero vitae annis amens effectus vitam caruit regnavitque annis xviii."
13. Works cited individually in the bibliography.
14. Life of Wilfrid, ch. 6; Bede, *History* 5.19.
15. VB II. 3. The Carolingian Life ("B") was composed in the late eighth or early ninth century, probably before the translation of her relics in 833 as it does not mention that important event. George Sanders' study of the Carolingian Life of Balthild notes some occasions when the later author glossed over episodes in Balthild's political life that were no longer comfortable, or relevant, to his audience, and that rather than rewriting the work, the second author amplified the biblical gravitas of the saintly ideal: "Le remaniement Carolingien." Balthild's will is mentioned in VB II. 7.
16. Binet, *La vie excellente*.
17. Many of these studies can be found in the OHMW (2020): Pion, Gratuze, Perin, Calligaro, "Bead and Garnet Trade"; Tys, "Maritime and River traders"; Theuws, "Long-Distance trade"; Squatriti, "Good and Bad Plants"; Yvinec and Barme, "Livestock."
18. *Le Trésor des saints*.
19. Hannah, "Anglo-Saxon Diet," p. 26.
20. This scientific approach has been around for a while and an increase in archaeological use has yielded important information about diet from Anglo-Saxon graves. Most notably isotopic analysis has been used to contribute to debates concerning immigration of Saxons into post-Roman Britain. Hughes, "Anglo-Saxon Origins...Isotopic Analysis."
21. See Hemer, "Evidence of Early Medieval Trade...Wales," p. 2355, on the geological "fingerprint" of water and bedrock and thus geographical location in childhood.
22. The change from primary to secondary consumption is marked by a nitrogen "signature." See Haydock, "Weaning at Anglo-Saxon Raunds," p. 605: "When an infant is exclusively breastfeeding they are one trophic level above their mother and this dietary difference is reflected in their nitrogen isotope signature...."
23. Hannah, "Anglo-Saxon Diet." Furthermore, if she were of elevated status, she may have been weaned earlier to reduce child spacing or had a wet nurse thus prolonging her breastfeeding. It would be interesting to know Balthild's own weaning practices as a mother to her sons. One of her sons was buried at Chelles but his remains are no longer extant.
24. Balthild's skull, fragmented since the seventeenth century, was distributed among the nuns when the monastery was ordered to close on October 1, 1792.
25. Crawford, "Overview: The Body and Life Course," p. 625.
26. Kemp, "Where Have All the Children Gone?" On childhood studies: Crawford and Lewis, "Childhood Studies."
27. Fleming, *Britain after Rome*, pp. 356–57.
28. Hannah et al. "Anglo-Saxon Diet."
29. Penal slavery was a real threat and in some circumstances all members of that household could be subject to the penalty.
30. Law Code of Ine, ch. 11.
31. "Sainte Bathilde: Étude Historique," *Le Correspondant*, pp. 227–46. May 25, 1853.

Chapter 2

1. Early medieval slavery has been the subject of a number of important studies in recent years that have challenged older assumptions about issues of status, slavery as commerce, and slavery within Christianity. See Rio, *Slavery after Rome*; Harper, *Slavery in the Late Roman World*; McCormick, *Origins of the European Economy*; Wickham, *Framing the Early Middle Ages*. The insights of Jennifer Glancy, *Slavery in Early Christianity*, are especially pertinent to slave bodies and sexuality within Christianity. Bailey, "Handmaids of God," examines the language of female servitude in the Merovingian period; Flechner and Fontaine, "Admission of Former Slaves."
2. Manumission documents from tenth-century Bodmin (Cornwall) provide graphic examples of the integration of slaves into religious thinking, the ecclesiastical economy, and the comfort of individual clerics; see Whitelock, ed., *English Historical Documents*, pp. 561–64. See now the study by Sommar, *The Slaves of the Churches*.
3. Rio, "Self-Sale."
4. See Pelteret, *Slavery in Early Medieval England*.
5. *VB* I. 2: "vili pretio venundata."
6. As described in Fredegar, *Chronicle*.
7. F&G *LMF*.
8. The case for such a context is provided by Fouracre in F&G *LMF*.
9. Eighteenth- and nineteenth-century writers linked her with King Edwin of Northumbria—a fiction we can probably attribute to familiarity with Bede's *History*.
10. Theodora's biography can be read in this series. Potter, *Theodora*.
11. See Urban, *Conquered Populations*.
12. Fredegar, *Chronicle*, p. 23.
13. Fredegar, *Chronicle*, ch. 37, p. 30.
14. Sivan, *Galla Placidia*.
15. Moreira, "Hector of Marseille."
16. Two Lives of Radegund were written in the sixth century: The first was by Venantius Fortunatus, who later became bishop of Poitiers; a second is by a nun at her convent, Baudonivia, *Vita s. Radegundis*, ed. Krusch, *MGH*, *SRM* II, 1888; trans. McNamara, *Sainted Women of the Dark Ages*, pp. 60–105. Her marital situation and withdrawal to a convent is described also by Gregory of Tours in his *History*.
17. Life of Bertilla, ch. 4.
18. The value of a servant was directly attached to the value of the owner. Law of Ethelbert of Kent, 14: If anyone lies with a nobleman's female cupbearer, he is to pay 20 shillings compensation. Modified from Whitelock, *English Historical Documents*, vol. 1, p. 358 (see n. 1).
19. In *Beowulf*, Queen Wealhtheow serves as cupbearer at her husband's table and her role has been set against the Celtic and Germanic background of female ritual within a warband culture; see Enright, *Lady with a Mead Cup*. However, the Merovingian context was also Roman, or Mediterranean, in which cupbearers were beautiful (and available) women at imperial feasts.
20. This phenomenon in western narrative is analyzed by During, *The Chastity Plot*.
21. Erchinoald's wife died in 649, but according to some calculations Balthild's marriage may have been that early also.
22. Echoing Roman legal opinion, Frankish laws and formularies, and Anglo-Saxon law codes, spell out the many negative ramifications of liaisons between free and unfree.
23. Nantechild died in 642, eight years before the royal marriage, but such thoughts would be paramount to the mother of a king.
24. *VB* I. 3: *astuta*.
25. *LHF* 43.
26. *LHF* 43. On the term *strenuus*, see Sarti, "The Military," *OHMW*, p. 265.
27. Laporte and Boyer, *Trésors de Chelles*.

Chapter 3

1. The Fredegar *Chronicle* and the *Liber historiae Francorum*, the main narrative sources for seventh-century Frankish history, are available in English translation.
2. Written sources indicate that boys were considered legally responsible from the age of twelve to seventeen. Perez, "Children's Lives and Deaths," p. 191. Burial archaeology indicates that young men were given a fully masculine burial from the age of twenty, see Guy Halsall, "Gender in Merovingian Gaul," *OHMW*, p. 171. Clovis was thus ready for marriage.

3. On the Merovingian court system in the seventh century, see Hen, "The Merovingian Polity"; and Barbier, "Le système palatial Franc."
4. I rely on the revised dating of these events as argued by Gerberding, *The Rise of the Carolingians*. On the importance of the testimony of the *LHF* on Grimoald's coup, see esp. pp. 47–66. Alternatives dating suggested by Becher has Sigibert's death five years later on February 2, 656; "Der sogenannten staastsstreich Grimoalds."
5. For overviews of the historical geography of the Merovingian kingdoms and their regional interests, see James, *The Franks*; Wood, *The Merovingian Kingdoms*.
6. Ian Wood, "The Merovingian North Sea."
7. On medieval polygyny, see D'Avery, *Papacy, Monarchy and Marriage*. Merovingian royal polygyny is challenged by Daily, *Queens, Consorts, Concubines*. On women and marriage in early medieval Europe, see Bitel, *Women in Early Medieval Europe*; Stafford, *Queens, Concubines, and Dowagers*; Wemple, *Women in Frankish Society*.
8. Loseby, "The Role of the City."
9. Heidrich, "Les maires du palais."
10. Chlothar II ruled Neustria (584–629), Burgundy (613–29), and Austrasia (613–23); Dagobert ruled Austrasia (623–32) and Neustria and Burgundy (629–39).
11. Fredegar, *Chronicle*, p. 58.
12. Fredegar, *Chronicle*, p. 59.
13. Fredegar, *Chronicle*, p. 60.
14. Fredegar, *Chronicle*, p. 75; *LHF* 42 says it was with Pippin.
15. Fredegar, *Chronicle*, p. 76: "terrorem Dagoberti."
16. Fredegar, *Chronicle*, p. 59.
17. Samo, a Frank, was an entrepreneur whose military successes resulted in his becoming king of the Wends, ruling them thirty-five years, according to Fredegar, and eventually becoming a military threat to Austrasia in Dagobert's time.
18. Fredegar, *Chronicle*, p. 75.
19. On Aega, mayor of Neustria (ca. 639–641), Ebling, *Prosopographie*, #XII, pp. 38–40.
20. Sources are vague on Merovingian marriage procedures.
21. Hen, *Culture and Religion*, pp. 122–37.
22. The case of Chlothar I's reputed son, Gundovald, was a case in point. His father rejected him as an heir, but others were willing to identify him as Chlothar's son. Gregory of Tours, *HF* VI. 24.
23. Scholars differ on how disposable wives were, but in this era Frankish kings were able to negotiate marriages on their own terms with little the church could do about it beyond express disapproval. See discussion in Dailey, *Queens, Consorts, Concubines*, pp. 113–17.
24. Gregory of Tours, Histories, IV. 26; Venantius Fortunatus, *De domno Sigibertcho rege et Brunichilde regina*. Opera Poetica, Carmina 6.1. ed. Fridericus Leo, MGH, Auctores Antiquissimi, vol. 1V. 1. pp. 129–30.
25. *VB* I. 3.
26. *VB* I. 4.
27. *VB* I. 4.
28. *VB* I. 4.
29. Brown, *Holy Treasure*.
30. Population estimates for Paris vary immensely, based on different views of what happened after the Germanic invasions. One view is that Paris was decimated by the invasions, that the population retreated to the protection of the Île de la Cité, and that reconstruction was slow until the ninth century. People who take this view consider Paris to be a city of about 2,000 inhabitants in the Merovingian period. However, archaeologists continue to find evidence of churches, cemeteries, activity on the left bank, and construction beyond the fortifications of the Gallo-Roman period. Derens notes that Michel Fleury argued that Paris saw a renaissance in the Merovingian era, and that Michel Roblin, another archaeologist, argued for a population around 20,000; see Jean Dérens, "Note sur la topographie," p. 49. Dérens identifies seventeen churches in Paris that date from the Merovingian period. Gregory of Tours tells us that Paris had six suburban churches in his time, and Merovingian kings were building churches regularly through the seventh and early eighth century. This activity does not suggest a small or static population. I am persuaded by the arguments for greater continuity from the late antique city, and for stable or slightly expanding population growth. Dérens concludes (p. 50), "Les invasions du Bas-Empire n'ont pas detruit la ville gallo-romaine; elles l'on ravagée, mais réparée, elle a subsisté jusqu'aux invasions normandes." On the archaeology of Paris, see Busson, *Paris*.

31. Duval, Périn, Picard, "Paris," in Picard et al. *Province ecclésiastique de Sens*, pp. 108–9. On Genovefa, see Bitel, *Landscape with Two Saints*.
32. *HF* VI, 9.
33. Gregory of Tours, *HF* V, 17. Chilperic was building (or repairing) an amphitheater in Soissons, also.
34. Inrap (Institut national de recherches archéologiques preventives): "Paris retrouve sa première enceinte médiévale," at the rue Rivoli: https://www.inrap.fr/paris-retrouve-sa-premiere-enceinte-medievale-5044.
35. On the terminology of "palaces" and their use in the Merovingian period, see Barbier, "Le système palatial Franc."
36. Samson, "The Merovingian Nobleman's Home: Castle or Villa?," at p. 304.
37. Barbier, "Le système palatial Franc."
38. Vierck, "La 'chemise de sainte-Bathilde'."
39. Moreira, "Rings on her Fingers."
40. *VE* I. 12.
41. *VE* II. 68.
42. Life of Audoin, ch. 3; *VE* I. 12.
43. *VE* I. 12.
44. *VE* I. 13. The camel in this case was used for carting goods. The more useful pack-animal, the donkey, was not introduced into northern Gaul until the seventh to eighth centuries, but thereafter grew in importance. See Yvenic and Barme, "Livestock and the Early Medieval Diet."
45. The monastery of Corbion was founded in the sixth century by the hermit Saint Laumer (Lomer) in the deep forests around Moutiers-au-Perche (Orne).
46. Chevalier, "Merovingian Religious Architecture. Some New Reflections," *OHMW*, 657–92.
47. Altet, "Le décor." The Marquise de Maille judged the columns (but not the capitals) to be spolia, *Les cryptes de Jouarre*, a view no longer current.
48. Vieillard-Troiekouroff, "La sculpture en Neustrie."
49. Gaborit-Chopin, "Les trésors de Neustrie."
50. The use of cushions is mentioned in sixth century. Some still reclined at table in the seventh century: Passion of Praiectus, ch. 18.
51. According to the account of miracles kept by Nivelles, Saint Gertrude's bed was particularly efficacious as a healing relic. Life of Gertrude, Miracles, Chapters 5, 6, 10, and 11.
52. Yvenic and Barme, "Livestock."
53. Anthimus, *On the Observance of Foods*, ch. 10.
54. Yvenic and Barme, "Livestock," *OHMW*, pp. 743–44.
55. Yvenic and Barme, "Livestock."
56. Anthimus, *On the Observance of Foods*, ch. 67.
57. Anthimus, *On the Observance of Foods*, chs. 83ff.
58. Anthimus, *On the Observance of Foods*, ch. 25.
59. Effros, *Creating Community*.
60. Yvinec and Barme, "Livestock," pp. 755–57.
61. Depreux, "Princes, princesses et nobles étrangers."
62. Hen, "The Merovingian Polity," p. 217.
63. Hen, "The Merovingian Polity."
64. Sarti, "The Military," p. 267.
65. Although there are divergent opinions on this, current scholarship argues that the Merovingians did not have a standing army: Sarti, "The Military," p. 261 cautions against considering *milites* to be soldiers; rather they were armed personnel in cities in a judicial capacity or as leaders of armed retinues. It was this latter group that must have attended Eligius' funeral.
66. Fouracre, "Why Were So Many Bishops Killed?"; Fouracre, "Merovingian History and Merovingian Hagiography."
67. *VE* I. 10. We hear less of Saxons in the sixth century, but the Saxon Chulperic is mentioned by Gregory of Tours; *HF* VII.3, VIII.18, X.22.
68. Fredegar, *Chronicle*, p. 73.
69. Drews, "Migrants and Minorities."
70. Eddius, Life of Wilfrid, ch. 12.
71. Drews, "Migrants," pp. 122–24 and 130.
72. Notably, Irish views on purgatory ruffled feathers. See Moreira, "Visions and the Afterlife" pp. 1004–06.

73. *VB* I. 11.
74. *VB* I. 3.
75. *VE* II. 32.
76. *VE* II. 32. Trans. McNamara in Thomas Head, *Medieval Hagiography*, pp. 161–62.
77. Moreira, "Dreams and Divination."
78. Gerberding, *The Rise of the Carolingians*, p. 49, argues that Sigibert II's death was in 651, however, the date continues to be debated.
79. See Hen, "Changing Places."
80. *LHF* 45.
81. See Hofmann, "The Marriage of Childeric II."
82. Esders, "The Merovingians and Byzantium," p. 359.

Chapter 4

1. Between 26 and 31 of October.
2. Fredegar, *Chronicle*, continuator, ch. 1: "Franci quoque Chlotharium filium eius maiorem in regno statuunt cum praefata regina matre." *LHF* ch. 44: "Franci vero Chlotharium, seniorem puerum ex tribus, regem sibi statuunt, cum ipsa regina matre regnaturum."
3. Fredegar, *Chronicle*, ch. 58, p. 49. Nantechild is described as one of the servants of the bedchamber: "Unam ex puellis de menisterio." Balthild is described as a *puella*, *VB* I. 3. On the prevalence and challenge of this terminology in hagiography see Bailey, "Handmaids of God."
4. Fredegar, *Chronicle*, chs. 79 and 80.
5. Flaochad, mayor of Burgundy from 642 (Ebling, *Prosopographie*, #CLXXIV, pp. 150–51). Fredegar, *Chronicle*, pp. 75–76. Erchinoald and Flaochad "had a single aim and were of one mind: and so they supported one another and prepared to exercise their high office in friendliness." Flaochad's activities in Burgundy, his feud with Willebad, and his subsequent death by God's judgement, are related in Fredegar, *Chronicle*, chs. 89–90, pp. 75–79.
6. It has been suggested that Emma, wife of Eadbald of Kent, was Erchinoald's daughter, see Wood, "Frankish Hegemony," p. 239.
7. *VB* I. 5.
8. *VB* I. 5.
9. *VB* I. 5.
10. *VB* I. 5. On this marriage alliance as a response to Grimoald's coup, see Hofmann, "The Marriage of Childeric II."
11. *VB* I. 5.
12. The Council of Mâcon I (581–83) canons 16–17 gives most attention to this issue in a council dominated by regulating Jewish activity and sets a repurchase or liberation price of 12 solidi. Similar prohibitions are found in Orléans III (538) canon 14 citing a fair price; Orléans IV (541) canons 30–31. See the Theodosian Code 16.9. In the early fourth century, imperial law was mostly concerned about Jews forcibly circumcising Christian slaves (16.1 and 2), but accepted Jewish ownership of Christian slaves in some circumstances. However, prohibitions became more absolute and antagonistic to Jewish ownership over time. In 423 the emperors Honorius and Theodosius pronounced that "No Jew shall dare to purchase Christian slaves. For we consider it abominable that very religious slaves should be defiled by the ownership of impious purchasers" (16.9.5). Trans. Pharr, p. 472.
13. Council of Clichy, 27 September 626 or 627, canon 13; ed. Gaudemet and Basdevant, *Les Canons*, pp. 526–47.
14. Council of Chalons-sur-Saône, canon 9; Gaudemet and Basdevant, eds., *Les Canons*, pp. 554–55.
15. *Pactus Legis Salicae* 39.
16. Council of Chalons-sur-Saône, in Gaudemet and Basdevant, eds., *Les Canons*, pp. 554–55. But see also comments of Pontal, *Histoire*, pp. 216–20. The council was convened by Clovis II and took place on October 24 in a year sometime between 647 and 653.
17. "Pietatis est maximae et religionis intuitus, ut a captivitatis vinculo animae a christicolis redimantur"; Council of Chalon-sur-Saône, canon 9.
18. Pontal, *Histoire*, pp. 280–83, provides a useful overview of slave legislation in Merovingian church councils.
19. *VE* I. 14.
20. *VB* I. 9. Trans. F&G *LMF*; "Et illud commemorandum est, quia ad mercedis eius cumulum pertinent, quod captivos homines christianos ire prohibuit, datasque praeceptiones per singulas regiones, ut nullus in regno Francorum captivum hominem christianum penitus transmitteret.

Sed magis et ipsa, dato pretio, captivos plurimos redimere precepit et liberos relaxavit et alios ex ipsis in monasteria intromisit et precipue de gente sua viros et puellas quam plures denutritas suas. Quantas enim adtrahere potuit, eas per sancta coenobia commendavit et, ut pro ea exorarent, eis precepit." The Frankish realm was synonymous with Neustria.
21. Canon 9 of the Council of Chalon-sur-Saône identifies this prohibition with Clovis' realm, and affirms again the danger that Christian slaves sold abroad might end up being sold to Jews.
22. This passage does not indicate that Balthild was arranging for prayers for her soul after her death—the prayers she requested were in support of her present situation. Indeed, Merovingian churchmen resisted novel ideas about post-mortem purgation (purgatory) that were developing slowly in other areas of Europe at this time. See Moreira, *Heaven's Purge*, and "Visions of the Afterlife."
23. Law Code of Ine, 11.
24. Although the two Lives of Saint Eligius are anonymous, the attribution of both to Audoin of Rouen is generally accepted. Eligius died in 660. Audoin died in the 680s and was writing contemporaneously with the hagiographer who wrote the Life of Balthild. The Latin text edited by Bruno Krusch in 1902 is in *MGH, SRM* IV, 634–761. A substantial translation of Krusch's edition by Jo Ann McNamara is published electronically as part of on Fordham University's Medieval Sourcebook and in Thomas Head, *Medieval Hagiography: An Anthology* (New York: Routledge, 2000), pp. 137–68.
25. *VE* I. 10.
26. *VE* I. 10.
27. *Pactus Legis Salicae* 26.2.
28. *VE* I. 10.
29. *VE* I. 12.
30. *VE* I. 10.
31. *VE* I. 10.
32. *VE* I. 10.
33. *VB* I. 9.
34. McNamara suggests that Eligius' convent foundation in Paris under the abbess Aurora was intended to serve the same purpose of providing refuge for female slaves, "Dado of Rouen," n. 17 in Head, *Medieval Hagiography*, pp. 165–66.
35. The source for this aspirational comment is a provincial council at Eauze (Dep. Midi-Pyrénées) in the Vasconia (Gascony) region of Merovingian Aquitaine. Council of Eauze (551) canon 6. Gaudemet and Basdevant, *Conciles*, pp. 334–35.
36. Miracles of Austreberta, ch. 4 (appended to the Life of Austrebertha); trans. McNamara, *Sainted Women*, p. 320.
37. On Theodora's institution meant for the relief of trafficked sex workers, Metanoia, as described by Procopius, *Concerning Buildings*, see Potter, *Theodora*, pp. 182–83.
38. Perpetual prayers (*laus perennis*) were instituted at the royal Burgundian monastery of Saint Maurice of Agaune in 515 for the praise of God and for the royal dynasty.
39. *VB* II. 9: "Ut pro ea viroque eius defuncto ac filiorum salute nec non et regni pace pium dominum exorarent, precepit."
40. *VB* I. 6.
41. Garver, "Childbearing and Infancy"; *Pactus Legis Salicae* LXVe. 1 and 2. On imperial legislation on the family see Grubbs, "Constantine and Imperial Legislation."
42. Penitential of Theodore, ch. 25.
43. Archaeologists have long noted the underrepresentation of children in Merovingian cemeteries, and in recent years considerable attention has been given to exploring models that can help explain the phenomenon. However, widespread infanticide does not appear to be a sufficient explanation for this phenomenon, so the level of danger to infants or young children is not easy to determine. See Coleman, "Infanticide"; Garver, "Childbearing and Infancy"; and Kemp, "Where Have All the Children Gone?"
44. This is unusual—simony and infanticide are not categorized as avarice in penitential literature.
45. *VB* II. 6.
46. Augustine's views on this matter were distinctly out of alignment with general views about burial and religion in late antiquity. In his letter-treatise *De cura pro mortuis gerenda* (*On Care for the Dead*) he made a provocative contribution to debates about the value of specific burial practices. While recognizing the importance of providing comfort to the grieving, he denied burial practices any role in the salvation of the deceased.

47. *Pactus Legis Salicae* LV prohibits despoiling or digging up dead bodies.
48. Effros, *Caring for Body and Soul*; Paxton, *Christianizing Death*; Rebillard, *In Hora Mortis*; Moreira, "Purgatory's Intercessors."
49. *VE* I. 31.
50. *VB* I. 4: "Sepelire ordinabat mortuos." Merovingian councils were not greatly concerned by matters relating to burial unless it infringed on the sanctity of church spaces. The disputed Council of Nantes (ca. 660) sought to prohibit burial within churches. Anxiety about improper burial was more common in other written sources; see Effros "Beyond Cemetery Walls."
51. Life of Anstrude of Laon, chapter 4.
52. A sense of the charitable activities of this society can be gained by reading the commemorative booklet of 1876, Coquidé, *Confrérie.*
53. Chalon-sur-Saône, canon 16: "Ut nullus episcopus neque presbyter vel abba seu diaconus per praemium ad sacrum ordinem amodo penitus non accede. Quod qui fecerit, ab ipso honore, quem praemiis comparare praesumpserit, omnino privetur."
54. Including the Councils of Orléans, in 533 and in 549, and of Tours.
55. "The holy men Eligius and Ouen [Audoin] in common council with certain other Catholic men, warned the prince and his optimates that this death dealing virus must swiftly be eliminated from the body of Christ which is the universal church. Their pious petition had its effect and they freely obtained what they had requested devoutly. Thus a single counsel was pleasing to all, accepted in the Holy Spirit and by royal order, that no one who had paid a price should be admitted to sacerdotal offices, nor those who, like rapacious wolves, profited by putting the gifts of the Holy Spirit up for sale. But only men of good reputation and irreproachable life should be chosen for the pontifical offices." *VE* II. 1.
56. *HF* VI. 7. We have a good example of this in Gregory of Tours' account of Cato and Cautinus of Clermont. Gregory was himself a royal appointment.
57. Prinz, *Frühes mönchtum.*
58. Dunn, *Emergence of Monasticism* for an overview.
59. *VB* I. 9. Folz suggested that these basilicas had followed a Martinian style of life hitherto and that Balthild introduced a mixed Benedictine-Columbanian rule. Folz, "Tradition hagiographique."
60. Wood, *Merovingian Kingdoms*, p. 200.
61. They are for Saint Denis, Saint-Pierre-le-Vif, Sithius (Saint Omer), and Corbie.
62. Prinz, *Frühes Mönchtum*, see on the monastic foundations of Clovis II and Balthild, pp. 171ff. Erchinoald, Clovis, and Fursey worked together in founding Lagny (dép. Seine-et-Marne), and Péronne (dép. Somme).
63. Further information on Clovis II's monastic patronage, Prinz, *Frühes Mönchtum*, pp. 171ff.
64. Life of Philibert, ch. 6, *MGH, SRM* V, 587–88. This joint royal connection gave rise to the stories told of Clovis and Balthild in the medieval era, examined in Chapter 6 (pp. 132–35).
65. "Signs" or "seals" on the walls are noted in the description of a small church built to honor Saint Austrebertha in Le Mans, and also as decorative ornaments in the interior of the mystical church seen in Aldegund's vision. Miracles of Austrebertha ch. 24; Life of Aldegund, ch. I. 5. These may have been signs of the cross, or Chi-Rho monograms, but not necessarily; see also the image of the seals in the Book of Revelation. On the Christian appropriation of Hellenistic and Roman architectural interiors for the mystic's palace of Love, see Moreira, "Living in the Palaces of Love." On the use of graphic signs, Garipnazov, *Graphic Signs of Authority*; on the use of seals and seal-rings in religious and eschatological contexts in Merovingian Gaul, see Moreira, "Rings on her Fingers."
66. *VB* I. 8.
67. *VB* I. 8.
68. *VB* I. 8.
69. *VB* I. 8.
70. *Testament of Burgundofara* (26 October 633/34), clauses 4, 5, 6, 7, 9. Edition and historiography by Guerout, "Le testament de Sainte-Fare." Translated pp. 311–14 in O'Hara and Wood, *Jonas of Bobbio*. This was not a deathbed bequest but rather a donation made during her lifetime: Burgundofara asked that it be read out to her periodically. On the document's authenticity, see Levillain's arguments in his review of Maurice Lecomte's *Le Testament de Sainte Fare* in *Bibliothèque de l'École des Chartes*, vol. 60 (1899), pp. 95–100, and Guerot, "Le testament." On the testamentary types and the importance of living donations, see Barbier "Testaments." Also, Joye and Bertrand, "Les 'testaments de saints'."

71. Ganz, *Corbie*.
72. The Merovingian documents for Corbie include the foundation charter and privileges given by Balthild and Chlothar III, by Theuderic III, and by her grandson Chilperic II, edited by Levillain, *Examen critique*. See also Ewig, "Das Privileg." Her grandson's hair (dark brown with strands of blonde) survives in the wax seal of one of his charters and has been analyzed. Charlier et al., "Into the Wax."
73. *VB* I. 7.
74. On the archaeology of Chelles from the Neolithic to the tenth century CE, Charamond, "Chelles."
75. Charamond, "Chelles," p. 421, #23.
76. Berthelier and Ajot, "Chelles," suggest a location around the rue Pont-Saint-Martin, to the east of the monastic complex.
77. *HF* VI.46. "…Chilperic, the Nero and Herod of our time, went off to his manor of Chelles, which is about a dozen miles from Paris. There he spent his time hunting. One day when he returned from the chase just as twilight was falling, he was alighting from his horse with one hand on the shoulder of a servant, when a man stepped forward, struck him with a knife under the armpit and then stabbed him a second time through the stomach. Blood immediately streamed both from his mouth and through the gaping wound, and that was the end for this wicked man."
78. Gregory relates that it was to Chelles that Chilperic and his wife, Queen Fredegund, repaired after the death of two of their two sons from "pestilence." Gregory of Tours tells us a horrible story about the viciousness of the grieving queen, *HF* V.39. Clovis, Chilperic's son by another wife, Audovera, began to boast of his expected inheritance now that his stepbrothers were dead and reportedly threatened his stepmother Fredegund. Fredegund took her revenge, first on a young woman with whom Clovis was enamored, a daughter of one of Fredegund's serving women. We are told that Fredegund ordered the girl to be thrashed/whipped, her hair cut off, and bound to a stake positioned in front of Clovis' residence. The girl's mother, a servant in Fredegund's household, was tortured until she admitted that she had been instrumental in the death of Fredegund's sons. Clovis was apprehended on Chilperic's orders and questioned. Fredegund then had him taken to the nearby estate of Noisy-le-Grand where he was murdered in such a way as to suggest suicide. Clovis' mother, Audovera, was murdered, and the woman who had given evidence against Clovis was burned at the stake.
79. On modern discussions of these connections see Yorke, "Monastic Policy" and literature cited there.
80. Bede, Ecclesiastical History 3.8.
81. Bede, Ecclesiastical History 4.17, relates that Hereswith's son had reigned seventeen years by the time of the Synod of Hatfield in 679, so he had ascended the throne in about 662. It is unlikely that Hereswith would have left her son before securing his succession, and this date would work well since it would give time for news of the new convent to reach England.
82. Life of Bertilla, ch. 5.
83. Diem, *The Pursuit of Salvation*.
84. The councils discussed here are edited with French translation by Gaudemet and Basdevant, *Les canons*; Council of Bordeaux (pp. 566–73), Council of Losne (pp. 575–83), Council of Autun (pp. 585–91).
85. Pontal, *Histoire*, pp. 235–43.
86. Pontal, *Histoire*, pp. 241–43. The text of the sixteen canons of the Council of Rouen can be found in J. D. Mansi, *Sacrorum conciliorum nova et amplissima collectio*, vol. 10, cols. 1199–1206. Pontal (p. 242) notes Mansi's change of heart about the dating of this council.
87. Losne, Canon 12.
88. Council of Nantes in Mansi, *Sacrorum conciliorum*, vol. 18, cols. 165–74. Mansi's edition is from Labbe who used Surius' *Conciliorum omnium*, who included the council without citation but which it is believed to be from Regino of Prüm's collection of canons from ca. 910. Pontal, *Histoire*, pp. 241–43 provides a summary overview of the arguments including those presented by Gaudemet for a ninth-century date, and by Aupest-Conduché for a seventh-century date. Aupest-Conduché provides an edition of the canons of the council reordering the numbers from those used by Baluze, see Aupest-Conduché "De l'existence." By contrast, Gaudemet, "Le pseudo-concile," considers the text a forgery, drawing from Theodulf and Hincmar rather than being their source. The "council" is attested in two manuscripts, Vienne, ms. 2198 (tenth century) and Paris, Bibl. Sainte-Geneviève, ms. 166 (end of eleventh century):

the former contains ninety-eight chapters taken from Regino of Prüm and from the penitential collection of the Capitula Dacheriana; the latter manuscript is a themed collection of canons (see Baluze, *De synodalibus*). Pontal leans in favor of a seventh-century date for the Council of Nantes. Discussions of authenticity based on the content of individual canons have turned largely on those canons dealing with parish organization and the priesthood. Canon 4 on the visitation of the sick is not discussed in any detail by Aupest-Conduché or by Gaudemet or considered in the dating of the council, yet the guidelines on bedside advice and the theology of purgation implied there point to a post-Merovingian date for that particular canon, probably informed by Carolingian reforms of the clergy.
89. The Nantes text concerns where burials can or cannot occur on church property, and not with the problem of providing burial as a charitable act. This is a false correlation with Balthild's policy.
90. A determination about whether this council text is genuine or false would seem to depend greatly on whether one approaches the text as a defined historical document, or a mélange of stray fragments. Ultimately, the history of the canon-list of this council is so complex that it is important to take each canon on its own merit rather than see it as a coherent document attributable to any single century.
91. See Bathrellos, *The Byzantine Christ*, pp. 60–98.
92. On the divisions within the episcopate and the Austrasian and Neustrian kings with respect to the Lateran Council see Esders, "The Merovingians." On the monotheletes and the Merovingians, see now Lin, "Monothelete Controversy."
93. Sarti argues that the "digression" on Pope Martin I in the Life of Eligius can be plausibly viewed as representing a contemporary source and that the passage was introduced into the Life at an early stage; Sarti, "The Digression."
94. Bede, *Ecclesiastical History* 2.1; Whitby, Life of Pope Gregory, ch. 9.
95. The date, authorship, and stages of the work's composition continues to be debated. However, there is general agreement that the text is a Merovingian work by Audoin of Rouen, but with some later editing as was commonly done in the Carolingian era.
96. *VE* I. 14.
97. The role monasteries played in the incarceration of prisoners and political enemies in the seventh century has been explored; see, for example, De Jong, "Monastic Prisoners"; the role of monasteries in mitigating the effects of the slave trade has received less attention.

Chapter 5

1. *VB* I. 10 (on Sigobrand) and the Acts of Aunemund, ch. 11.
2. On monasteries as a means of removing people from public life, see de Jong, "Monastic Prisoners."
3. *VB* I. 10.
4. *VB* I. 11.
5. *VB* I. 11.
6. Caesarius, rule for nuns, ch. 18, trans. McCarthy, *The Rule for Nuns*, p. 175. This rule was written by Bishop Caesarius of Arles for his sister's convent in 512 and was revised and recapitulated in 534. It drew heavily on the so-called rule of Augustine, and on provisions in Caesarius' rule for monks. It was a widely adopted rule for nuns in Gaul including by Queen Radegund for her convent in Poitiers.
7. *Regula cuiusdam ad virgines*, ch. 1, trans. Diem, *The Pursuit of Salvation*.
8. Life of Bertilla, ch. 7.
9. Life of Bertilla, ch. 2.
10. Life of Bertilla, ch. 5.
11. A descendant of King Aethelberht of Kent, Mildreth (ca. 660–ca. 732) was included in the Kentish Royal Legend. According to the story, the abbess who threatened her with this fate was Wilcoma (or Willcome), the second abbess, although given the dates when Mildreth's education must have taken place, Bertilla would still have been abbess. Knowledge of the name of the second abbess, then, must have come from another source. On the history and texts on Saint Mildreth, see Rollason, *The Mildrith Legend*.
12. Life of Bertilla, ch. 6.
13. See Yorke, "Queen Balthild's 'Monastic Policy'."
14. The first indication that monks were attached to the convent is in the Life of Bertilla; in Balthild's time the community may have made use of local clergy.

15. Diem, *The Pursuit of Salvation*. Jonas records having met with Balthild. It would make sense that Balthild wanted a monastic rule for her convent that combined seventh-century values with the ideals of Columbanian monasticism.
16. Council of Orléans V (549) canon 15. On *xenodochia* in Gaul, see Horden, "Public Health," *OHMW*, pp. 299–319.
17. De Jong, "Monastic Prisoners."
18. *VB* I. 12.
19. The *Regula cuiusdam ad virgines* may have been used at Chelles; it outlines the ritual abasement of nuns who were subjected to penance and excommunication.
20. Council of Orléans V (549) canon 19. The council recapitulated Caesarius of Arles' rule for nuns, ch. 4, which specifies one year of probation, but added a longer probation for those in convents that were not as strictly cloistered.
21. Caesarius, rule for nuns, ch. 5; ch. 6 on the damnation of Ananias and Sapphira (Acts 5:1–11) for holding back property; recapitulated ch. 52.
22. *VB* I. 19.
23. Laporte, *Trésor*. Laporte was the lead archaeologist who examined the relics of Balthild and Bertilla and of other saints connected to Chelles in 1983. It is the most comprehensive published study to date on the relics of Chelles and their history. Photographs, analysis, key documents, and summary tables are provided throughout, with an eye to identifying and authenticating the relics from the seventh to twentieth century.
24. Life of Gertrude, ch. 2: Itta used a cutting implement (*ferrum tonsoris*); the crown-shape hairdo replicated the clerical tonsure.
25. Before 840 to Jouarre, to Corbie between 1158 and 1172, and to Jumièges in 1655. Laporte, *Trésor* (1988), pp. 56–57.
26. *The Rule for Nuns*, ch. 56, trans. McCarthy, p. 189.
27. On Chlothar's tomb, Laporte, *Trésor* (1988), pp. 173–76. Chlothar's body would have been moved, as Balthild's was, from the Holy Cross burial to the new church built by Gisela. In the thirteenth century, after a fire required the rebuilding of the church, Chlothar's tomb was upgraded to a recumbent form—at about the time when recumbents became fashionable for royal burials at Saint Denis, and elsewhere.
28. On Childeric II's marriage alliance with Bilichild as a response to the Grimoald coup, see Hofmann, "The Marriage of Childeric II."
29. Fredegar, *Chronicle*, continuator ch. 2; see also *LHF* 45.
30. It is not recorded at what date the relic of Saint Vincent of Saragossa joined the collection at Chelles. It was listed in the 1544 relic inventory. Laporte, *Trésor* (1988), p. 250, no. 71.
31. "nobilis et strenua," according to *LHF* 48.
32. *LHF* 49; Fredegar, *Chronicle*, continuator ch. 6.
33. *VB* I. 19. Balthild's "striving" was a direct allusion to Queen Radegund. Moreira, "Provisatrix Optima."
34. The first, "A" Life of Balthild, ch. I. 18, includes the information about the church of Saint George. The Carolingian (B) version of the life adds the detail about the dedications to Saint George and Saint Stephen in the new basilica dedicated to the Holy Cross.
35. *VB* I. 18. Described as "coenobiolo virginum."
36. Life of Chlothild.
37. The *xenodochium* was protected by provisions in the 5th Council of Orléans: Peregrine Horden, "Public Health," in *OHMW*, p. 307. The royal couple worked with Aurelian of Arles; Diem, "Merovingian Monasticism," *OHMW*, p. 322.
38. *VB* I. 19.
39. *LHF* 44, and reprised in the *Gesta Dagoberti*, ch. 52. The cloak (*cappa*) relic of Saint Martin of Tours has not survived. Ewig, "Das Privileg," p. 112, thought Balthild may have acquired the relic of Saint Martin of Tours for the royal collection. Laporte notes that eventually, after the French Revolution, a relic from Chelles that passed to the church of Busy-Saint-Martin was piously claimed to be a portion of Saint Martin's cloak. It was, in fact, a sleeve from a late medieval garment that had probably been gifted to the convent; *Trésor*, p. 182.
40. *VB* I. 19.
41. On the Helena motif, see Moreira, "Procuratrix Optima"; McNamara, "*Imitatio Helenae*"; Tatum, "Auctoritas."
42. Laporte, *Trésor*, pp. 246–55.
43. Laporte, *Trésor*, p. 118.

44. Laporte, *Trésor*, pp. 51–52, mused that Balthild may have waited for a later, less fraught, occasion to acquire Eligius' head for the convent as it was a treasured relic there.
45. VB I. 12: *viscerum incisione*; the Carolingian Life (VB II. 12) adds that it was what doctors call 'of the illeum' or perhaps ileitis (*quod medici yleos vocant*), which points to an intestinal condition.
46. As in a compilation that includes ancient medical authorities and diet, early twelfth-century manuscript: BL Royal Ms. 12 E XX.
47. Anthimus, *Observance*.
48. Anthimus, *Observance*, ch. 14.
49. *Rule for Monks*, ch. 3, ed. and trans. Walker, *Sancti Columbani Opera*.
50. Chapters 9 to 11 of the *regula cuiusdam ad virgines* addressed food and dining expectations and the hours at which meals were to be served in different seasons.
51. Estimates based on Freemaptools.com and Stanford ORBIS (The Stanford Geospatial Network Model of the Ancient World) Orbis.Stanford.edu.
52. *VB* I. 13.
53. Caesarius, *Rule for Nuns*, ch. 11. This goddaughter is described as a very young child (*infantula*) at the time of her death. Balthild was in the convent for sixteen years, which means she sponsored the baptism of this child during her time at Chelles.
54. *VB* I. 14.
55. A milestone with the ladder is to be found in the collection of the Alfred-Bonno Museum, Ville de Chelles. The convent's seal in 1720 showed the ladder and fleur-de-lys. Laporte, *Trésors*, p. xii.
56. This description follows the order for the burial of the dead that was common both to the Roman Ordo and the later Gelasian sacramentary. Psalm choice and readings could vary; eventually seven penitential psalms were viewed as appropriate. On burial for the dead see Effros, *Caring for Body and Soul*, esp. pp. 169–204; Paxton, *Christianizing Death*. On the liturgy for the dead see Sicard, *La liturgie de la mort*; McLaughlin, *Consorting with Saints*.
57. Unfortunately, episcopal records for Paris at this time are sketchy so that the bishop could have been either Agilbert or his successor Sigefrid. The bishop of Paris in 680 was likely still Agilbert, scion of a Neustrian family whose career included time spent in Ireland and England, and for some years as bishop of Dorchester. However, since he was criticized for not having learned the English language during his time there (according to Bede), it is unlikely that this experience provided much common ground with the queen. If he died in 680, he died in the same year as Balthild, probably about two months later according to their feast days. On Agilbert, see Hammer, "Holy Entrepreneur: Agilbert."
58. *VB* I. 15.
59. *VB* I. 15.
60. "Refecti alimonia caelesti, omnipotens pater, quaesumus pietatem tuam, ut intercessione sanctae Batildis misericordiae tuae gratiam consequi mereamur" (Refreshed by heavenly nourishment, almighty Father, we ask of your godliness that through the intercession of Saint Balthild we may be worthy of your grace), Oratio #4989, in *Corpus Oratonum tomus XII, Calendarium Liturgicum*, ed. Eugenio Moeller and Ioanne Maria Clément, CCSL. Also, Oratio #6033: "Ut haec munera, domine, tibi accepta sint, sanctae Batildis obtineat merita, quae seipsam tibi hostiam vivam, sanctam et beneplacentem exhibuit" (That these gifts may be accepted by you, Lord, that he may obtain the merits of Saint Balthildis, who has presented to you the living host, holy and well pleasing). In the codices of Arbuth and Sarum for the festival of Balthild on January 30.
61. The *Translatio Bathildis* is preserved as Corbie 17, BnF ms. Latin. 18296. The manuscript is digitized and available on the BnF: Gallica website. The Latin text is reproduced in AASS Ian., pp. 747–49, and in Mabillon, AASS OSB, saec. IV, part 1, pp. 450–53. Jean-Pierre Laporte published a French translation of the text by G. Duchet-Suchaux, and added his own editorial notes, in *Trésor* (1988), pp. 151–60. For the connection of this translation with imperial politics, see Caroli, "A Woman's Body."
62. Charamond, "Chelles."
63. *VB* I. 17.
64. Le Forestier, *Archéologie des necropoles*. As noted by the archaeologists at the convent-site of Chelles, stone sarcophagi tend to be sixth century and plaster sarcophagi are a seventh-century innovation, Ajot and Berthelier-Ajot, "Les Fouilles." However, stone would have been more prestigious than plaster; see the tombs at Jouarre. Evidence of plaster was found in the relic packet; plaster could be used to decorate stone, inside and out.
65. Gauthier, ed., *Les premiers monuments*.

66. Bede, *Hist.* 3.8.
67. This account is from Bede, *Hist.* 4.19. Bede was so impressed by Etheldreda that he wrote a hymn to her which he included in *Hist.* 4.20.
68. Laporte, *Trésor*, pp. 59–61.
69. Laporte, *Trésor*, pp. 206 and 241. However, Laporte also reports that a tooth was later found that may have originally belonged to the jawbone.
70. Laporte, *Trésor*, pp. 209–10.
71. The term "gracile" is used by archaeologists to describe skeletons that are small, slender, that show no signs of bone thickening due to hard labor. In the absence of the pelvis which can help determine sex, the characterization of a skeleton as "gracile" can also suggest that it is a woman.
72. Laporte, *Trésor*, p. 152, notes that although Hegilvid's status as abbess is not made clear in the sources, and that she may have held Chelles as a laywoman, she resided in Chelles and was active in its affairs. She was listed as abbess in abbatial lists, and appears as such in the journal of an anonymous nun of Chelles written ca. 1782; Bourbon, *Journal d'une moniale*.
73. The *Translatio Balthildis* is an account of the 833 opening and translation of Balthild's tomb written after the middle of the ninth century, but perhaps taken from an earlier account. The Latin text is in AASS, Ian., pp. 747–49. A French translation of this text by G. Duchet-Suchaux is reprinted in Laporte, *Trésor*, along with Laporte's own annotations partially drawn from Mabillon, AASS OSB, IV, 1, pp. 450–53, and from the Corbie manuscript, B.N., Ms. Lat. 18296.
74. Laporte, *Trésor*, p. 154.
75. Laporte, *Trésor*, pp. 57–58.
76. Laporte, *Trésor*, p. 155.
77. Laporte, *Trésor*, p. 203.
78. On Cuthbert, see articles in Bonner, Rollason, Stancliffe, eds., *St. Cuthbert*. On Theudechild, see Maille, *Les cryptes*, p. 89.
79. Janet Nelson, "Gendering Courts," p. 190, notes that "a royal convent could function...as an outpost of courtliness."
80. Laporte, *Trésor*, pp. 102–13, at p. 113.
81. *VB* I. 19.
82. *VB* I. 2: "venerabilem magnamque feminam, domnam Balthildeam reginam."
83. *VB* I. 16.
84. *VB* I. 16: "per eius sanctam intercessionem."
85. Robert Folz, "Tradition hagiographique," p. 375.
86. Folz, "Tradition hagiographique," p. 375.
87. As suggested by Jean Hubert who cites a nineteenth-century description of her tomb as "pierre brut, rude et impolie" in contrast to more artistic coffins, see Hubert's comments (pp. 383–84) on Folz "Tradition hagiographique," citing the 1883 ed. of Jean Lebeuf's eighteenth-century, *Histoire du diocèse de Paris*, 1883 ed., vol. 2, p. 406 (= *Histoire de la Ville det de tout le diocèse de Paris*). I have not been able to confirm Lebeuf's reference to the tomb. Since Balthild's remains had been removed and the bones of her goddaughter Radegund interred in it, it is unclear what was being referenced.
88. Folz, "Tradition hagiographique," makes a strong argument that the cult of Balthild dated from the time of Louis the Pious' intervention.
89. On the medieval liturgical texts relating to Balthild, see Folz, "Tradition hagiographique."

Chapter 6

1. Eddius Stephanus, *Life of Wilfrid*, Preface.
2. Miscarriages appear in penitential works. For example, a woman who has a miscarriage (and suspected of having caused it) is considered a sinner required to do penance in the Old Irish Penitential, ch. 5.6.
3. *VB* I. 3.
4. Life of Lantbert of Lyon, ch. 2.
5. Life of Anbert, ch. 1.
6. Life of Ansbert, ch. 7.
7. *VE* II. 32.
8. Acts of Aunemund, ch. 2. *Acta Sancti Aunemundi alias Dalfini episcopi*, P. Perrier (ed.), AASS, Sept. VII, Antwerp, 1760, pp. 744–46: "...qui eius de lavacro sacro fontis filiolus fuerat." The oldest Acts of Aunemund is known only in Perrier's edition for the *Acta Sanctorum* as the

manuscript is now lost. A short history of the manuscript and editions can be found in F&G *LMF*, pp. 166–79. Eddius Stephanus attributed Aunemundus' death to Balthild in his Life of Wilfrid, but this source is poorly informed on Merovingian politics.
9. *VE* II. 32.
10. Régine Le Jan, "Personal Names," p. 43 notes that while Merovingians used name repetition for their sons, name variation continued for their daughters alongside most of the rest of the population.
11. *VE* II. 37 (36).
12. *VE* II. 37.
13. *VE* II. 41(40): "insignia auri gemmarumque."
14. *VE* II. 48. Holy relics were often secured with a wax seal.
15. Life of Wilfrid, ch. 6.
16. On the office of the count of the city, *comes civitatis*, see S. T. Loseby, "The Role of the City in Merovingian Francia," *OHMW*, pp. 583–610.
17. Life of Aunemund, ch. 3.
18. Fredegar, *Chronicle*, ch. 42, p. 35.
19. As noted by Colgrave, note to ch. 6, *The Life of Wilfrid*, p. 154.
20. Acts of Aunemund, ch. 11. "a duobus submissis viris."
21. On this incident, see discussion in F&G *LMF*, pp. 168, 172–76.
22. F&G *LMF*, p. 112.
23. On the history of the monastery of Jumièges: Langlois, *Essai historique et descriptif*.
24. Life of Philibert, ch. 6.
25. This legend was preserved carved into two stone corbels of the chapel of Saint-Martin in the church of Saint-Pierre, and a third decoration was inside the monastery. Langlois relates the legend (pp. 15ff.), discusses the corbels, and provides three small illustrations of them in Langlois, *Essai sur les Énervés*. The church was destroyed in WWII.
26. Tassilo and his son were exiled by Charlemagne. The attribution is unlikely. It is unclear why a twelfth-century sculpture would cover a ninth-century grave, and why the robes of two rebels would have fleurs-de-lys. The sculptures were found in 1828 through excavation, the second head added later.
27. Huet, "La légende des Enervés de Jumièges. Texte latin."
28. Merceron, "De l'hagiographie à la chanson d'aventures," notes the great variety of versions of Balthild's name; see n. 1: "Dans cette étude, nous uniformisons le nom français de la reine sous la forme courante «Bathilde». Les formes originales rencontrées sont les suivantes: Baltelt, Baltalt, Batelt, Bauptheur, Bateulz, Baudour, Baudeur (Vies françaises); Bautheuch (*Miracle de sainte B.*); Baudour (*Theseus de Cologne* et *Ciperis de Vignevaux*). Le P. Cahier, *Caractéristiques des saints dans l'art populaire*, Bruxelles, Culture et Civilisation, 1966 [Paris, J. Claye, 1867], p. 806, signale en outre: Bathechilde, Bautour et Bauteur."
29. Merceron, "De l'hagiographie à la chanson d'aventures." See also, Bengtsson, *La Vie de Sainte Bathilde*, pp. xxiii–xxviii.
30. *Miracle de sainte Bautheuch*, ed. Paris and Robert.
31. "De l'hagiographie à la chanson d'aventures."
32. "De l'hagiographie à la chanson d'aventures."
33. "Leur mère adonc, ah! mère sans mercy / Fera bouillir leurs iambes, et ainsi / Tous meshaignez les doit ietter en Seine." Ronsard, *La Franciade*.
34. Langlois, *Essai sur les Énervés de Jumièges*.
35. Seine-Maritime, 6Fi02/76.
36. In 1885, Charles Perkins, who examined the legend, reported that the cloister had been bought by an English nobleman who transported it across the Chanel; "The Abbey of Jumièges," p. 136, n. 12.
37. On Luminais and other nineteenth-century French painters of Merovingian subjects, see Effros, "Artistic, Scholarly and Popular Depictions"; Effros, *Uncovering the Germanic Past*; and James, "The Merovingians from the French Revolution."
38. Described by "H. C." in *Salon de 1880. Peinture*, pp. 76–77; see also *Le Salon: journal*, p. 114.
39. Art Gallery of New South Wales, Australia, Acquisition #712.
40. Musée-des-Beaux Arts, Rouen. Laurent Quevilly's article "Les Énervés de Jumièges" on the website "Jumieges.free.fr" reports that an art collector saw one of the copies in Luminais' studio and demanded as explanation because, he said, he had just seen the very same painting in Australia! The collector appears to have been shocked that Luminais had made a copy of his

celebrated work—it seemed to violate his understanding of what a collector was entitled to when a piece of art was purchased. In the nineteenth century copyright laws were coming into effect to protect artists against copiers, but this was an issue of protecting the collector. In any event, the criticism seems to have struck home because Luminais did not sell the copy he had made of the painting.
41. Reproduced on Quevilly's site. The text reads: "Les Énervés de Jumèges [sic]: Les malheureux cherchent à endormir leurs souffrances en lisant la *Civilisation*."
42. Duty, "Les Énervés de Jumièges."

Chapter 7

1. ABOLITIO/SERVI/TVTIS: "Abolition of slavery."
2. Torchet, *Histoire*, vol. 1, Preface, p. xiii.
3. The engravings of the convent as it appeared in 1688 were among the many engravings of monasteries that were part of an ambitious project to record the physical plans of the monasteries of the Benedictine order. This *Monasticon Gallicanum*, a seventeenth-century project undertaken by Dom Michel Germain, monk of Saint-Germain-des-Prés, was not completed on the author's death and the engravings were not fully published until the nineteenth century: Louis Courajod, *Monasticon Gallicanum*; the two engraved plates of Chelles (plates 64 and 65) were published by Achille Peigné-Delacourt with a preface by Léopold Delisle in 1871.
4. Binet, *La vie excellente*.
5. "Cette rose de Saxe plantee au milieu des fleurs de Lis de la France leur donera & odeur, & bonté, et tout bon-heur ensemble," p. 28.
6. Binet, *La vie excellente*, frontispiece: "Servire Deo regnare est."
7. The composition appears largely indebted to the woodcut by Alexius Lindt (1517) printed by Leonhard Beck. British Museum #1920,0430.7 "St. Balthildis."
8. "La bien-heureuse Reine dont nous écrivons la vie estoit descenduë de la royale maison de Saxe, si ancienne & si illustre que les Rois de France en ont tiré leur origine" (p. 356).
9. "La France est obligé à cette bien-heureuse Reine de ce qu'il n'y a point de Chrestiens esclaves. Car ce fut elle qui abolit cet abus indigne de la sainteté du Christianisme, de faire un trafic honteux de ceux qui on esté rachetez par le sang de Iesus-Christ & regenerez par le baptesme." D'Andilly, *Vies de plusieurs saints*, p. 357.
10. Torchet's *Histoire* remains the most complete history of the convent of Chelles from its beginnings to the French Revolution. Torchet was curé of Chelles from 1860 to 1899. He was a man on a mission—to recover the lost history of the community of Chelles and the history of its institutions that had been "decapitated" during the revolution (p. x) and by so doing to revive French dedication to the saints, and especially to Saint Balthild, that had been such an important element in the religious life of the parish. Taking his cue from the structure of earlier convent documentation, Torchet wrote his history by means of a series of biographies of each abbess in turn. Importantly, he drew on original documentation from the abbey preserved in the seminary library in Meaux, and from parish records. He also had local knowledge of the landscape, and changes made to it, that aided in his discussion of the final centuries of the convent's history. The account I give here of the last abbesses of Chelles draws substantially on his work as it incorporates the earlier documentation at length.
11. Abrégé of 1631. Laporte, *Le Trésor*, pp. 201–2.
12. For a more comprehensive account of the extensive changes to the reliquaries at Chelles in this era, see Laporte, *Le Trésor*, pp. 15–20.
13. The life and travails of Princess Abbess Louise-Adélaïde d'Orléans is well documented. Torchet provides a lengthy account of her tenure in his *Histoire*, vol. 2, pp. 96–120, in the chapter on abbess Agnès, and pp. 121–54. The account of Louise-Adélaïde's life in Torchet is supplemented by numerous documents including the *Confession* that Louise-Adélaïde wrote towards the end of her life. See also the 1963 catalogue of André Clément, *Louise-Adélaïde d'Orléans*.
14. Torchet, *Histoire*.
15. *Élévations sur la concorde des Évangiles*, and *Méditations sur la règle de Saint-Benoît*. BnF Arsenal. Cote 2556.
16. "Les confessions de Mme l'abbesse de Chelles, fille du duc d'Orléans." BnF Arsenal. Cote 6108.

17. Torchet, *Histoire*, vol. 2, p. 174.
18. The journal was published as a photographic facsimile in 2018 by Jean Olivier Bourbon in whose family's archives the work was preserved. The cover and first few pages of the work are lost, as are the author's name and the work's title, if it ever had one. This is termed a "journal" in the Bourbon's published edition. The hand-written text is mostly regular although marred with stains on the opening pages. The rest of the manuscript has survived remarkably well. The journal's author drew material from published works, but it is also likely that she drew on lists of abbesses kept in the convent. One can imagine that writing out a copy of the list of abbesses was a suitable educational exercise for a boarder or novice.
19. Torchet, *Histoire*, vol. 2, p. 206.
20. Torchet, *Histoire*, vol. 2, p. 215.
21. Engraving reproduced in Laporte, *Le Trésor*, p. 16, fig. 4.
22. Torchet, *Histoire*, vol. 2, p. 224.
23. This list is taken from the article by Desthuilliers, "Chelles," *Notre Département: La Seine-et-Marne*. The article includes some wonderful photographic images of inhabitants of Chelles in the nineteenth and early twentieth centuries.
24. There have been extensive excavations in Chelles, in the town, around the church of Saint-André, and to a limited extend within the grounds of the former convent site. Information on excavations can be found in the following publications: Charamond, "Chelles" in Griffisch, Magnan, Mordant, eds., *La Seine-et-Marne*; Ajot and Berthelier-Ajot, "Les fouilles de l'abbaye"; Berthelier and Ajot, "Chelles. Abbaye mérovingienne"; Berthelier, "Chelles à l'époque mérovingienne."
25. Berthelier and Ajot, "Chelles. Abbaye mérovingienne," 184–87.
26. Laporte, *Le Trésor*, p. 48. The relic labels were deposited in the national archives.
27. Binet, *La vie excellente*.
28. "La France est obligée à cette bien-heureuse Reine de ce qu'il n'y a point de Chrestiens esclaves. Car ce fut elle qui abolit cet abus indigne de la sainteté du christianisme, de faire un trafic honteux de ce qui on esté rachetez par le sang du Iesus-Christ & regenerez par le baptesme." D'Andilly, *Vies de plusieurs saints*.
29. D'Andilly, *Vies de plusieurs saints*, p. 357.
30. The Code Noir dealt primarily with slavery in the colony of Louisiana, but later it also encompassed the issue of slaves introduced into France by colonists.
31. Jennings, *French Anti-Slavery*, pp. 10–11, describes the Society as "a liberal, nondenominational philanthropic society, inspired by both universalist Enlightenment and religious principles, which devoted itself to advancing moral and social issues through education, propaganda, and political activism, while in the process indicting the government's retrograde social policies."
32. Jennings, "Slavery and the Venality."
33. De Gisors (1796–1866), Architecte de la Chambre des Pairs, et de l'Université. After the Luxembourg project he was known as the Architecte du Sénat. Hustin, *Le Palais du Luxembourg* provides a short biography of De Gisors and an engraved portrait, pp. 37–38.
34. *Le Palais du Luxembourg*.
35. The king had ordered ornamentation for the chapel in 1843; Ingres' commission for preparatory paintings for the stained-glass windows was formalized July 27, 1846.
36. The commissioning documents for the royal chapel are in the National Archives. AN Cote 20144790/63.
37. Cited by Jennings, *French Anti-Slavery*, p. 270.
38. Lami (1858–1944) is the only source to identify his parents: *Dictionnaire des sculpteurs*, pp. 291–92.
39. *Le Faubourg Saint-Germain*, p. 62. This appears to have been the only issue—or perhaps the only one to have survived.
40. Simon, "Les statues du péristyle."
41. A list of works is provided by *Wikiphidias—L'Encyclopedie des sculpteurs français*. The death of Ajax (1831), busts of Claude Perrault (1833), Duquesne (1834) and La Trouche Treville (1836), a statue of Cydippe (1837) a bust of General Stengel (1838), plaster busts of Admiral André Baptiste de Brancas (1838) and General Montbrun (1839), De la Rochefoucauld (1840), Gregory of Tours, Louis XVI, Balthild (1848), Cicero (1848), Egidio Romauald Duni (1853), Hyacinthe Rigaud (1855), and Napoleon I (1857).

42. February 13, 1846. AN. Cote F/21/57. I thank Pascal Piviale for help identifying the dossier.
43. AN. Cote F/21/57. "Arrêtons ce que suit: M. Thérasse est chargé d'exécuter, pour le compte de notre Départment et moyennant une somme de douze mille francs imputable sur le crédit des ouvrages d'art et décoration d'édifices publics, une statue en marbre dont le sujet lui sera ultérieurment indiqué et dont l'esquisse devra être soumise à notre approbation. Cette statue est destinée à la décoration du Jardin du Luxembourg."
44. Based on gold content, twelve thousand Francs in 1846 is calculated to have the value of about $30,000 U.S.
45. Dreux du Radier, *Mémoires historiques* 1782 ed., vol. 1, pp. 403–16; 1808 ed., vol. 1, pp. 324–35.
46. *Mémoires historiques* (pp. 324–25 in the 1808 ed.), taken verbatim.
47. http://www.senat.fr/lng/en/the_luxembourg_palace/a_republican_palace.html. The gardens are attached to the Luxembourg Palace, formerly the "Medici Palace," and then the "Palais d'Orléans." From the time of the Revolution, the palace was turned to parliamentary use, first of the Directoire, and then as an assembly of peers. Since 1848 the building has housed the senate.
48. Dated Paris, April 4, 1846: "Ce qui signale le gouvernement de Bathilde, c'est l'abolition de l'esclavage qui substitait encore." It is interesting that he thought Balthild had suppressed the taxes that forced people to kill their children, when in fact she prohibited infanticide. But this error can be found in other writings of the time, for example, *Le Myosotis*, vol. 10 (1847), p. 102.
49. Tinterow, "Paintings: Catalogue, 119–149," p. 400.
50. The plaques on the statues' pedestals in the garden are uniform in shape and not the work of the artist. The inscription on Balthild's pedestal reads "Sainte Bathilde, Reine de France—680."
51. The *Journal de débats* lists him.
52. *La Chronique des arts et de la curiosité: supplement a la gazette des beaux-arts*. Jan. 3, 1864, p. 254.
53. Malitourne, "La sculpture en 1848," p. 144: "la reine Bathilde (encore une de ces reines obscures! A quoi bon?)." The critic was only marginally more impressed by another sculpture that year, Etienne-Hippolyte Maindron's "Attila and Geneviève," which he deemed too theatrical.
54. Reported in the *Journal des beaux-arts*. Aug. 27, 1848, p. 3.
55. The establishment still exists as the Hôpital Chardon Lagache-Rossini. It is on land that was originally the property of the Augustinian canonesses of Saint-Geneviève. Confiscated by the state during the French Revolution, it was designated as a hospice for the aged by the Empress Josephine in 1806. By the time Thérasse lived there, the institution was on the rue Chardon-Lagache.
56. "Nécrologie artistique de 1864," p. 132.
57. "Nécrologie: Thérasse (Victor)."
58. Guérin, "Biographie: Bathilde Reine des Francs (960*)," vol. 9, pp. 77–80. The incorrect date was changed to 680 in part II of the biography, vol. 10, pp. 102–4. Another example from 1847, Lamé Fleury, *L'histoire de France*.
59. For example, de Paban, *Année des dames*, where Balthild is a slave, wife, beauty, and then died. There is no mention of her policies, her regency, or even her children!
60. For example, Amory de Langerack, *Galerie des femmes*.
61. Prévault, *Les princesses de France*.
62. Simons-Candeille, *Bathilde, reine des Francs*; Junot, "Duchess of Abrantès, *Memoirs*," pp. 331–33.
63. *Batilde, Reine des Francs*. The poem comprised ten poems with notes. Number seven addressed the plight of slaves and imagined Balthild continuing the work of her mother-in-law Nantechild. Alexandrine continued to write on queens; a letter survives in which she asks Victor Hugo to give his opinion of another poem she wrote on "Mathilde, Reine des Francs."
64. *Bathilde*, vol. 1, pp. 26, and 41: "Que le sang de Woden se mêle au sang de Mérovée."
65. Simons-Candeille, *Bathilde*, vol. 2, p. 199. "...et ses parents, pressés par la misère, le livroient pour un certain prix aux juifs qui alloient revendre en Italie, comme on venoit revendre en France les enfants de Saxe ou d'Angleterre. Défense aux juifs d'acheter ces enfans; défense aux marchands étrangers de continuer avec les nôtres l'odieux commerce d'esclaves...."
66. Drews, "Migrants and Minorities," *OHMW*, p. 127.
67. Mézeray, *Histoire de France depuis Faramond*, vol. 1, p. 249; *Abrégé chronologique, ou Extrait de l'historie de France*. On the role of the Jewish community in the seventeenth-century slave trade, see Hershenzon, "Jews and Early Modern."
68. For example, Dreux du Radier, *Mémoires historiques*, p. 328 in the 1808 ed. Louis-Philippe, Comte de Ségur, *Histoire universelle*, vol. 12, pp. 258–60, the Jews were in charge of selling children. Frantin, *Annales du moyen-âge*, p. 217.

69. In his *Les vies des saints* (1724) Baillet wrote in terms very reminiscent of Thérasse's precis: "car outre qu'elle étoit parfaitement belle, adroite, sage, modeste, douce, agréable, & obligeante; sa bonne mine & une certaine majesté qui paroissoit dans toutes ses action, se ressentoient de la grandeur de sa naissance."
70. Laubie, *La Reine Bathilde*; Anon. *Vie de Sainte Bathilde, Reine de France*; Anon. *Vie de Sainte Bathilde reine de France*.
71. Janvier, *Le Catéchisme en examples*, p. 357.
72. Effros, *Uncovering the Germanic Past*; Wood, *The Modern Origins*.
73. On Augustin Thierry and the reception of the *Récits*, see Bonnie Effros, *Uncovering the Germanic Past*, pp. 6–8, 314–15, 324; Thierry's emphasis on the Franks as oppressors was challenged as the century went on; Effros, p. 7. Thierry published the *Récits* in 1840 in two volumes dedicated to the Duc d'Orléans, King Louis-Philippe's eldest son Ferdinand-Philippe, an enthusiastic patron of the arts. The first volume comprised a long historical essay and the first *Récit*; vol. 2 contained the remaining six. See also James, "The Merovingians from the French Revolution to the Third Republic"; Wood, *Modern Origins*, pp. 97–102.
74. French translations drew from Surius' edition of the "B" version of the Latin text, or on later editions that drew on it: Binet (1624), Modeste de S. Amable (1670), D'Andilly (1675). See also Sanders, "Le remaniement carolingien."
75. Montfaucon (1655–1741), *Les monumens [Sic] de la monarchie Françoise*, vol. 1, p. 170: "C'étoit donc une Princesse de basse extraction; mais dont la piété & les vertus on été celebrées dans tous les tems."
76. Bollandus, *AASS* Ian. iii. Guérin, *Les Petits Bollandistes*. The text was also published in AASS, OSB, ed. Lucas Archery, Johannes Mabillon (Paris: apud Carolum Savreux, 1669), pp. 775–84.
77. *Vita sanctae Balthildis*, ed. Krusch, *MGH, SRM* (Hanover, 1888), pp. 475–508. This edition is the text used in the English translation of version "A" by F&G *LMF*.
78. Migne, *PL* 87, cols. 661–76 reprinted Mabillon's introduction and text of the "A" version.
79. This work is estimated to have sold over two million copies according to James "The Merovingians from the French Revolution," p. 451 citing C. Amalvi, *Répertoire des auteurs de manuels scolaires et de livres de vulgarization historique de langue française de 1660 à 1960* (Paris, 2001), p. 247.
80. Mézeray, *Abrégé chronologique*, vol. 1. On pre-revolutionary histories see section above (pp. 000–000).
81. Girault, *Histoire*, pp. 4–12; Balthild abandons government because of Ebroin's domination (p. 8).
82. Lavisse, *Récits et entretiens*, preface. The book was for elementary course instruction.
83. Blanchet and Pinard, *Histoire de France: cours élémentaire*, for first year of instruction.
84. Lavisse and Dupuy, *Histoire de France*.
85. Lavisse, *La deuxième année d'histoire de France*, in 1884.
86. Laporte, *Le Trésor*, pp. 28–29 lists what happened to the relics when they were reorganized in 1792 and which nuns took possession of which relics.
87. As noted by Laporte, *Le Trésor*, pp. 32–33.
88. Photo reproduced in Laporte, *Le Trésor*, plate XVI.
89. Published in 1883, the novel refers to Balthild and Clovis II while weaving a romantic story about a later prince Carloman and his duchess, 'Bathild,' and the wounding of their two sons, Charles and Thierry (Theuderic), placed on a barge and floated down stream—a scene made famous by the painting by Luminais in 1880 and discussed in Chapter 6 (pp. 137–39).
90. Duty, "Les Énervés de Jumièges," is currently available on YouTube: 18:46 minutes long, uploaded June 17, 2016: https://www.youtube.com/watch?v=VfYRsidhZ4c&t=493s.
91. Machemer, "France Seeks Proposals"; McAuley, "France Confronts Slavery"; "The Memorial to the Victims of Slavery Moves."

Appendix

1. On Merovingian rings used by women see, Deloche, *Étude historique*; Hadjadj, *Bagues mérovingiennes*; Moreira, "Rings on her Fingers."
2. "Balthild and 'her' Seal Ring." The artefact is described in detail in Pestell, "Das Baldehildis-Siegel."

Bibliography

1. Primary Sources and Pre-Modern Works

Abrégé of 1631. Ed. Jean-Pierre Laporte, *Le Trésor*, pp. 201–2.

Acts of Aunemund. *Acta Sancti Aunemundi alias Dalfini episcopi.* Ed. P. Perrier. AASS, Sept. vii, Antwerp, 1760, pp. 744–46.

Amory de Langerak, Joséphine. *Galerie des femmes célèbres depuis le 1er siècle de l'ére chrétienne jusqu'au xvi siècle.* Paris: Mellier Frères, 1847; reprinted 1862.

Anon. *Vie de Sainte Bathilde reine de France.* Limoges: Barbou Frères, 1847.

Anon. *Vie de Sainte Bathilde, Reine de France.* Lille: L. Lefort, 1847.

Anthimus. *On the Observance of Foods: De observatione ciborum.* Ed. and trans. Mark Grant. Totnes: Prospect Books, 2007.

Audoin, Life of Eligius. *Vita Eligii episcopi Noviomagensis.* Ed. Bruno Krusch. MGH, SRM IV (1902), pp. 634–61. Partial translation by Jo Ann McNamara, "Dado of Rouen: Life of St Eligius of Noyon," in Thomas Head, *Medieval Hagiography: An Anthology.* New York: Routledge, 2000, pp. 137–67. Full Latin text: Migne, *Vita S. Eligii*, PL 87: cols. 477–594.

Augustine, *De cura pro mortuis gerenda.* Ed. Joseph Zycha. CSEL 41 (1900), pp. 619–660.

Baillet, Adrien. *Les vies des saints composées sur ce qui nous reste de plus authentique.* 4th ed. Paris: Louis Genneau, 1724 (first published 1701).

Baluze, Étienne. *De synodalibus causis et disciplinis ecclesiasticis.* Paris: François Muguet, 1671.

Baudonivia. *Vita s. Radegundis.* Ed. Bruno Krusch. MGH, SRM II (1888), pp. 377–95. Trans. Jo Ann McNamara, *Sainted Women*, pp. 86–105.

Bede. *Ecclesiastical History of the English People.* Ed. Bertram Colgrave and R. A. B. Mynors. Oxford: Clarendon Press, 1969.

Beowulf. Trans. Michael J. Alexander. London: Penguin Books, 1995.

Binet, Étienne. *La vie excellente de sainte Bathilde royne de France fondatrice et religieuse de Chelles.* Paris: Sebastien Chappelet, 1624.

Blanchet, Desirée and Jules Pinard. *Histoire de France: cours élémentaire, récits et entretiens.* 19th ed. Paris: Eugène Belin, 1879.

Bonaparte, Alexandrine de Bleschamp, Princess of Canino. *Batilde, Reine des Francs: Poëme en dix chants avec des notes.* Paret: Rapet, 1820.

Bonaparte, Alexandrine. "Letter from Alexandrine de Bleschamp, widow of Lucien Bonaparte, princesse de Canino (1778–1855) to Hugo, 15 May (1840–51)." The Victor Hugo Collection. University of Manchester Library. GB 133 VMH/1/65.

Brun, Élisabeth. *Vie de Sainte Bathilde, reine de France.* Lille: L. Lefort, 1847.

Caesarius of Arles, *Rule for Nuns.* Ed. Sister Maria Caritas McCarthy. *The Rule for Nuns of St. Caesarius of Arles: A Translation with a Critical Introduction.* Washington, DC: Catholic University of America Press, 1960.

Columbanus. Rule for Monks. Ed. and trans. G. S. M. Walker. *Sancti Columbani Opera.* Dublin: Dublin Institute for Advanced Studies, 1957.

Coquidé, Victor. *Confrérie des Charitables de Saint-Éloi fondée a Béthune et à Beuvry en 1188: Célébration du jubilé demi-séculaire de M. Vallage Ainé doyen de la confrérie: Compte rendu de la cérémonie du 30 Juillet 1876.* Arras: H. Schoutheer, 1876.

D'Andilly, Robert Arnaud. "La Vie de Ste Bathilde reine de France. Ecrite par un auteur de cetemps-la: & rapportee par Surius au 26 jour de Ianvier." *Vies de plusiers saints illustres de divers siècles choisies & traduites par Monsieur Arnaud D'Andilly.* Paris: Pierre le Petit, 1664, pp. 356–58.

D'Andilly, Robert Arnaud. *Vies de plusieurs saints illustres de divers siècles choisies & traduites par Monsieur Arnaud D'Andilly*. Paris: Pierre le Petit, 1664.

De Gisors, Henri-Alphonse Guy. *Le Palais du Luxembourg, fondé par Marie de Medicis, régente, considérablement agrandi sous la règne de Louis-Philippe Ier*. Paris: Typographie de Plon Frères, 1847.

Des Essarts, Alfred. "Sainte Bathilde, Étude Historique." *Le Correspondant*, May 25, 1853, pp. 227–46.

Dreux du Radier, Jean François. *Mémoires historiques, critiques, et anecdotes des reines et regents de France*, 6 vols. (Amsterdam: Michel Rey, 1782; Paris: Frères Mame, 1808).

Du Breul, Jacques. *Le théâtre des antiquitez de Paris*. Paris: Claude de la Tour, 1612.

Eddius Stephanus. Life of Bishop Wilfrid of York. Ed. Bertram Colgrave. *The Life of Bishop Wilfrid by Eddius Stephanus: Text, Translation and Notes*. Cambridge: Cambridge University Press, 1927.

Fouracre, Paul and Richard A. Gerberding, *Late Merovingian France: History and Hagiography 640–720*. Manchester: Manchester University Press, 1986.

Frantin, Jean-Marie-Félicité. *Annales du moyen-âge, comprenant l'histoire des temps qui sont écoulés depuis la decadence de l'empire romain jusqu'à la mort de Charlemagne*, vol. 5. Paris: Lagier, 1825.

Fredegar, *Chronicle*. Ed. and trans. John Michael Wallace-Hadrill. *Fredegar, The Fourth Book of the Chronicle of Fredegar with its Continuations*. London: Nelson, 1960.

Gaudemet, Jean and Brigitte Basdevant. *Les canons des conciles mérovingiens (VIe–VIIe siècles)*. Sources chrétiennes vol. 354 (2). Paris: Editions du Cerf, 1989.

Germain, Michel. *Monasticon Gallicanum* (1675–94). Paris: Liepmannssohn et Dufour, 1869; engraved plates of Chelles (plates 64 and 65), *Monasticon Gallicanum*. Paris: Victor Palme, 1871.

Gesta Dagoberti I Regis Francorum. Ed. Bruno Krusch. MGH, SRM II (1888), pp. 396–425.

Girault, L. *Histoire de France (420–1849)*. Paris: Philippart, 1850.

Guérin, Aline. "Biographie: Bathilde Reine des Francs." *Le Myosotis: revue dédiée aux jeunes personnes*, vol. 9 (pp. 77–80) and vol. 10 (pp. 102–4). Paris, 1847.

Guérin, Paul. *Les Petits Bollandistes: vie des saints, d'après les Bollandistes, le père Giry, Surius etc.*, vol. 2. 7th ed. Paris: Bloud et Barral, 1876.

H. A. Monsieur. *Bathilde, reine des france, ou, la vertu sur le trône: drame historique en 2 actes*. Lyon: Girard et Josserand, 1856.

Hénault, Charles-Jean-François. *Nouvel Abregé chronologique de l'Histoire de France*. 4th ed. Paris: Prault père, Prault fils, Desaint et Saillant, 1768.

Huet, Gédéon, "La légend des Enervés de Jumièges. Texte Latin." *Bibliothèque de l'École des Chartes* 72 (1916): 197–216.

Hustin, Arthur, *Le Palais du Luxembourg: ses transformations, son agrandissement, ses architects, sa décoration, ses décorateurs*. Paris: P. Mouillot, 1904.

Ingres, Jean-Auguste-Dominique. "Commissioning Documents for the Royal Chapel at Dreux." *Archives nationales*, Cote 20144790/63.

Janvier, Pierre. *Le Catéchisme en examples*. Paris: J. Le Fort, 1870.

Jonas. *Life of John of Réomé*, in *Jonas of Bobbio, Life of Columbanus, Life of John of Réomé, and Life of Vedast*. Trans. with introduction and commentary by Alexander O'Hara and Ian Wood. Liverpool: Liverpool University Press, 2017.

Journal de débats politiques et littéraires. May 31. Paris, 1848.

Journal des beaux-arts: peinture, sculpture, architecture, gravure, théâtres, etc. 1848.

Journal of a Nun of Chelles (ca. 1782). Ed. Jean Olivier Bourbon. *Journal d'une moniale de l'Abbaye Royale de Chelles*. Saint-Witz: Association de reconstitution historique Fabricae. 2018. Facsimile of manuscript with notes.

Junot, Laure, Duchess of Abrantès. *Mémoires de Madame la duchesse d'Abrantès, ou souvenirs historiques sur Napoléon, la Révolution, le Directoire, le Consulat, l'Empire et la Restauration*, vol. 12. Paris: Mame-Delauny, 1833.

La Chronique des arts et de la curiosité: supplement a la gazette des beaux-arts. Jan. 3, 1864.
La reine Bathilde et son temps (exposition Mérovingienne), Jan. 28–March 12. Chelles: Musée Alfred-Bonno, 1961.
Lamé Fleury, Jules Raymond. *L'histoire de France, racontée à la jeunesse*, vol. 1. 8th ed. Paris: A. Allouard et Charles Borrani, 1847.
Lami, Stanislas. *Dictionnaire des sculpteurs de l'École française au dix-neuvième siècle*, vol. 4: N–Z. Paris: Champion, 1914–21.
Langlois, Eustache-Hyacinthe. *Essai sur les Enervés de Jumièges.* Rouen: Ed. Frère, 1838.
Laubie, Antoine (Abbé). *La Reine Bathilde, Drame historique en deux actes mêlé de couplets, spécialement destiné aux pensionnats de jeunes demoiselles, pour les exercises publics d'une distribution des prix, par M. l'Abbé Laubie, principal de Collége de Treignac*, 1847.
Lavisse, Ernest. *La deuxième année d'histoire de France avec récits et dissertations.* Paris: Armand Colin, 1884.
Lavisse, Ernest. *La première année d'histoire en France: leçons, récits, reflections.* Paris: Armand Colin, 1884.
Lavisse, Ernest. *Récits et entretiens familiers sur l'histoire de France jusqu'en 1328.* Paris: Armand Colin, 1884.
Lavisse, Ernest and Paul Dupuy. *Histoire de France et notions sommaires d'histoire générale.* Paris: Armand Colin, 1890.
Law code of Ethelbert. Ed. Dorothy Whitelock. *English Historical Documents*, Vol. I: *c.500–1042*. London: Eyre and Spottiswoode, 1955.
Law code of Ine. Ed. and trans. F. L. Attenborough. *The Laws of the Earliest English Kings.* New York: Russell & Russell Inc., 1963.
Le Faubourg Saint-Germain: journal de la mode, de goût et d'esprit. March 16. Paris: 1844.
Le François, A. B., ed. *Mystères des vieux châteaux de France, ou Amours secretes des rois et des reines, des princes et des princesses, ainsi qui des grands personnages du temp*, vol. 2. Paris: Eugène et Victor Penaud, 1850.
Le Salon: journal de l'exposition annuelle des beaux-arts. June, no. 8, 1880.
Liber historiae Francorum. Ed. Bruno Krusch. *MGH, SRM* II (1888), pp. 215–328. Trans. B. Bachrach. *Liber Historiae Francorum.* Lawrence, KS: Coronado Press, 1973.
Life of Audoin. *Vita Audoini episcopi Rotomagensis.* Ed. W. Levison. *MGH, SRM* V (1910), pp. 536–67.
Life and Translation of Balthild. *Vita et Translatio sanctae Bathildis reginae* (ninth-century manuscript: BnF 18296 = Corbie 17); *S. Bathildis Reginæ Galliæ corporis Inuentio & eleuatio contigisse hoc die dicitur in Historia Translationis post vitam eius edita, AASS Jan.* ii., pp. 742–47. Ed. J. Mabillon. *Translatio Bathildis anno 833*, AASS, OSB IV, vol. 1, pp. 450–53. French translation by G. Duchet-Suchaux, in Laporte, *Le Trésor de Saints de Chelles* (1988), pp. 156–60.
Life of Aldegund of Maubeuge. *Vita s. Aldegundis.* Ed. J. Bollandus. AASS Ian. ii, 1643. Trans. Jo Ann McNamara. *Sainted Women*, pp. 235–63.
Life of Ansbert of Rouen. *Vita Ansberti episcopi Rotomagensis.* Ed. W. Levison. *MGH, SRM*, V (1910), pp. 613–43.
Life of Anstrude of Laon. *Vita s. Anstrudis abbatissae Laudunensis.* Ed. W. Levison. *MGH, SRM* VI (1913) pp. 64–78.
Life of Austreberta. *Vita s. Austreberthae abbatissae Pauliacensis.* Ed. J. Mabillon. AASS, OSB, vol. III, i (1639). Trans. Jo Ann McNamara. *Sainted Women*, pp. 304–18.
Life of Balthild. *Vita s. Balthildis Reginae Francorum*, in AASS, OSB, vol. 1. Paris: apud Carolum Savreux, 1669, pp. 775–84; *Vita sanctae Balthildis, A and B.* Ed. Bruno Krusch. *MGH, SRM*, vol. II (1888), pp. 475–508; J.-P. Migne, *PL* 87, cols. 665–676. Introduction and translation of the first (A) manuscript by F&G *LMF*, pp. 97–132. Translation of the Carolingian (B) manuscript by Jo Ann McNamara, *Sainted Women*, pp. 264–88.
Life of Bertilla. *Vita Bertilae Abbatissae Calensis.* Ed. W. Levison. *MGH, SRM* VI, pp. 95–109. Trans. Jo Ann McNamara, *Sainted Women* (1992) pp. 279–88.

Life of Chlothild. *Vita sanctae Chrothildis.* Ed. Bruno Krusch. *MGH, SRM* II (1888), pp. 341–48.
Life of Eligius of Noyon. See Audoin.
Life of Gertrude of Nivelles. *Vita sanctae Geretrudis.* Ed. Bruno Krusch. *MGH, SRM* II (1888), pp. 447–64. Trans. F&G *LMF*, pp. 301–26.
Life of Gertrude: Miracles: *De virtutibus, quae facta sunt post discessum beate Geretrudis abbatissae.* Ed. Bruno Krusch. *MGH, SRM* II (1888), pp. 464–74.
Life of Lantbert of Lyon. *Vita Lantberti abbatis Fontanellensis et episcopi Lugdunensis.* Ed. W. Levison. *MGH, SRM* V (1910), pp. 606–12.
Life of Philibert of Jumièges. *Vita Filiberti abbatis Gemeticensis et Heriensis.* Ed. W. Levison. *MGH, SRM* V (1910), pp. 568–606.
Lives of Radegund. See Venantius Fortunatus and Baudonivia.
Luminais, Évariste-Vital. "Les Énervés de Jumièges." Oil on canvas. 1880. Also known as "The Sons of Clovis." Art Gallery of New South Wales, Australia. Acquisition #712.
Luminais, Évariste-Vital. "Les Énervés de Jumièges." Oil on canvas. After 1880. Accession # D.912.1 Musée des-Beaux-Arts, Rouen.
Malitourne, Pierre (Pierre-Armand). "La sculpture en 1848." *L'Artiste: Revue de Paris.* Paris: Ferdinand Sartorius, 1848, pp. 141–45.
Mansi, Joannes Dominicus *Sacrorum conciliorum nova et amplissima collection,* 31 vols. Florence and Venice, 1758–98.
Mézeray, François Eudes de. *Abrégé chronologique, ou Extrait de l'historie de France,* vol. 1 Paris: Thomas Iolly, 1668.
Mézeray, François Eudes de. *Histoire de France depuis Faramond jusqu'au règne de Louis le juste: enrichie de plusieurs belles & rares antiquitez & de la vie des reynes.* Paris: Denys Thierry, Jean Guignard, Claude Barbin, 1685.
Miracle de sainte Bautheuch. Ed. Gaston Paris and Ulysse Robert. *Miracles de Notre Dame, par personages. Publiés d'après le ms. de la Bibliothèque nationale,* vol. 6. Paris: F. Didot, 1876, pp. 79–167.
Miracles of Austreberta. *Austreberthae abbatissae Pauliacensis.* Ed. J. Mabillon. AASS, OSB, III, i (1639). Trans. Jo Ann McNamara *Sainted Women,* pp. 318–25.
Montfaucon, Bernard de. *Les monumens de la monarchie Françoise.* Paris: Gandouin & Giffart, 1729.
Navery, Raoul de (= Marie-Eugenie Chervet). *Les mystères de Jumièges.* Paris: Librairie Ch. Delagrave, 1883.
Obituaries for Victor Thérasse. "Nécrologie artistique de 1864." *Le Courrier artistique: beaux-arts, expositions, musique, théâtre, arts industriels, ventes.* Paris: Louis Martinet. Jan. 15, 1865, p. 132. E. B. De L. "Nécrologie: Thérasse (Victor)." *La Chronique des arts et de la curiosité: supplément à la gazette des beaux-arts,* Oct. 10, 1864, pp. 253–54.
Old-Irish Penitential. Trans. D. A. Binchy. *The Irish Penitentials.* Ed. Ludwig Bieler. Dublin: Dublin Institute for Advanced Studies, 1975, pp. 258–77.
Orléans, Marie Louise Adélaïde. *Élévations sur la concorde des Évangiles,* and *Méditations sur la règle de Saint-Benoît.* BnF Arsenal. Cote 2556.
Orléans, Marie Louise Adélaïde. *Les confessions de Mme l'abbesse de Chelles, fille du duc d'Orléans.* BnF Arsenal. Cote 6108.
Paban, Gabrielle de. *Année des dames, ou Petite biographie des femmes célèbres pour tous les jours de l'année,* 2 vols. Paris: Crevot, 1820.
Pactus Legis Salicae (Lex Salica). Trans. Katherine Fischer Drew. *The Laws of the Salian Franks.* Philadelphia: University of Pennsylvania Press, 1991.
Passion of Leudegar of Autun. *Passio s. Leudegarii episcopi et martyris Augustodunensis.* Ed. Bruno Krusch. *MGH, SRM* V (1910), pp. 282–322. Trans. F&G *LMF,* pp. 193–253.
Passion of Praeiectus. *Passio Praeiecti episcopi et martyris Arvernensis.* Ed. Bruno Krusch. *MGH, SRM* V (1910): 212–48.
Penitential of Theodore. Trans. John T. McNeill and Helena M. Gamer. *Medieval Handbooks of Penance.* New York: Columbia University Press, 1938, pp. 179–217.

Pharr, Clyde. *The Theodosian Code and Novels and the Sirmondian Constitutions.* Princeton: Princeton University Press, 1952.
Prévault, H. *Les princesses de France, modèles de vertu et de piété.* Lille: L. Lefort, 1829.
Ronsard, Pierre de. *Les quatre premiers livre* [sic] *de la Franciade.* Paris: Gabriel Buon, 1572.
Rule of Columbanus. Ed. and trans. G. S. M. Walker. *Sancti Columbani Opera.* Dublin: Dublin Institute for Advanced Studies, 1957.
Saint-Ouen, Laure Boen de. *Histoire de France depuis l'établissement de la monarchie jusqu'à nos jours.* Paris: Louis Colas, 1827.
Ségur, Louis-Philippe, Comte de. *Histoire universelle, ancienne et modern.* Paris: Alexis Eymery, 1821–35.
Simons-Candeille, Julie. *Bathilde, reine des francs, roman historique,* 2 vols. Paris: Le Normant, Imprimeur-Librairie. Rue de Seine, No. 8. F.S.G., 1814.
Surius, Laurentius. *Concilia omnia tum generalia tum provincialis,* 4 vols. Cologne, 1567.
Testament of Burgundofara (Oct. 26, 633/634). Trans. Alexander O'Hara and Ian Wood. *Jonas of Bobbio. Life of Columbanus, Life of John of Reome, and Life of Vedast.* Liverpool: Liverpool University Press, 2017, pp. 311–14.
Thérasse, Victor. "Letter to the Director of the Beaux-Arts." Feb. 13, 1846. *Archives Nationales.* Cote F/21/57.
Thierry, Augustin. *Récits des Temps Mérovingiens,* 2 vols. Paris: Garnier Frères, 1840.
Venantius Fortunatus. *Vita s. Radegundis.* Ed. Bruno Krusch. *MGH, SRM* II (1888): 358–77. Trans. Jo Ann McNamara, *Sainted Women,* pp. 60–86.
Venantius Fortunatus. *De domno Sigiberctho rege et Brunichilde regina.* Venanti Fortunati Opera Poetica. ed. Fridericus Leo, MGH, Auctores Antiquissimi, vol. 1V. 1. Berlin, 1881.
Whitby Life of Gregory the Great. Text, translation, and notes by Bertram Colgrave. *The Earliest Life of Gregory the Great.* Cambridge: Cambridge University Press, 1968.

2. Modern Sources

Aali, Heta. "Merovingian Queenship in Early Nineteenth-Century French Historiography." PhD thesis, University of Turku, 2016.
Aali, Heta. *French Royal Women during the Restoration and July Monarchy: Redefining Woman and Power.* London: Palgrave Macmillan, 2021.
Altet, Xavier Barral I. "Le décor des monuments religieux de Neustrie." *La Neustrie,* pp. 209–24.
Ajot, José and Nadine Berthelier-Ajot, "Les fouilles de l'abbaye royale Notre Dame de Chelles." *Archeologia* 234 (1988): 56–66.
Aupest-Conduché, Dominique. "De l'existence du concile de Nantes." *Bulletin philologique et historique (jusquà 1610) du Comité des travaux historiques et scientifiques* Paris: 1973): 29–60.
Bailey, Lisa Kaaren. "Handmaids of God: Images of Service in the Lives of Merovingian Saints." *Journal of Religious History* 43.3 (2019): 359–79.
Barbier, Josiane. "Le système palatial Franc: Genèse et functionnement dans le nord-ouest du Regnum." *Bibliothèque de l'École des chartes* 148 (1990): 245–99.
Barbier, Josiane. "Testaments et pratique testamentaire dans le royaume Franc (VIe–VIIIe siècles)," in F. Bougard, C. La Rocca, and R. Le Jan, eds., *Sauver son âme et se perpétuer. Transmission du patrimoine et memoire au haut moyen age.* Rome: Publications de l'École française de Rome, 2005, pp. 7–79.
Bardiès-Fronty, Isabelle, Charlotte Denoël, and Inès Villela-Petit, eds. *Les temps Mérovingiens: trois siècles d'art et de culture (451–751).* Paris: Éditions de la Réunion des museés nationaux—Grand Palais, 2016.
Bathrellos, Demetrios. *The Byzantine Christ: Person, Nature, and Will in the Christology of St. Maximus the Confessor.* Oxford: Oxford University Press, 2004.
Becher, Matthias. "Der sogenannten staastsstreich Grimoalds. Versuch einer Neubewertung," in Jörg Jarnut, Ulrich Nonn, and Michael Richter, eds., *Karl Martell in seiner Zeit.* Sigmaringen: Jan Thorbeke, 1994.

Bellessort, André. *Sainte Bathilde: Reine de France*. Paris: Albin Michel, 1941.
Bengtsson, Anders. *La Vie de Sainte Bathilde. Quatre versions en prose des XIIIe et XVe siècles*. Lund: Lund University, 1996.
Berthelier, Nadine. "Chelles à l'époque mérovingienne," in *Saint Géry et la christianisation dans la nord de la Gaule, V–IX siècle*. Cambrai: Actes du Colloque, 1984. *Revue du Nord* 68.269 (1986): 345–60.
Berthelier, Nadine and José Ajot. "Chelles. Abbaye mérovingienne," in Nancy Gauthier, ed., *Les premiers monuments chrétiens de la France*, Vol. 3: *Ouest, Nord et Est*. Paris: Picard, 1998, pp. 184–87.
Besse, Jean-Marie. *Abbayes et prieurés de l'ancienne France: recueil historique des archevêchés, évêchés, abbayes et prieurés de France*, Vol. 7: *Province ecclésiastique de Rouen*. Paris: A. Picard, 1914.
Bitel, Lisa. *Women in Early Medieval Europe, 400–1100*. Cambridge: Cambridge University Press, 2002.
Bitel, Lisa. *Landscape with Two Saints. How Genevefa of Paris and Brigit of Kildare built Christianity in Barbarian Europe*. Oxford: Oxford University Press, 2009.
Bonde, Sheila and Clark Maines. "The Archaeology of Monasticism: A Survey of Recent Work in France, 1970–1987." *Speculum* 63 (1988): 794–825.
Bonner, Gerald, David Rollason, and Clare Stancliffe, eds. *St. Cuthbert: St. Cuthbert, his Cult and his Community to A.D. 1200*. Woodbridge: Boydell, 1989.
Bournazel, E. "Réflexions sur le rôle et la place de la reine dans le palais royal et le gouvernement aux temps Mérovingiens." *Le corti nell'alto Medioevo: Spoleto 24–29 aprile 2014*. Spoleto: Fondazione Centro italiano di studi sull'Alto Medioevo, 2015, pp. 385–428.
Brown, Peter. *Holy Treasure: The Holy Poor in Early Christianity*. Charlottesville, VA: University of Virginia Press, 2016.
Brubaker, Leslie and Julia H. Smith, eds. *Gender in the Early Medieval World: East and West, 300–900*. Cambridge: Cambridge University Press, 2004.
Busson, Didier. *Paris*. Carte archéologique de la Gaule, 75. Paris: Académie des Inscriptions et Belles-Lettres, 1998.
Caroli, M. "A Woman's Body for the Empire's Salvation: The *translatio* of Queen Balthild's Body and the Crisis of the Year 833," in M. Räsänen, G. Hartmann, and J. Richards, eds., *Relics, Identity, and Memory in Medieval Europe*. Turnhout: Brepols, 2016, pp. 91–113.
Charamond, Christian. "Chelles," in Jean-Noël Griffisch, Danielle Magnan, and Daniel Mordant, eds., *La Seine-et-Marne. Carte Archéologique de la Gaule* 77.1. Paris: Académie des Inscriptions et Belles-Lettres, 2008, pp. 416–34.
Charlier, Philippe et al. "Into the Wax: Forensic and Anthropological Analysis of Human Hairs in Merovingian and Carolingian Royal Seals (France)." *Forensic Science, Medicine and Pathology* 12 (2016): 220–25.
Chevalier, Pascale. "Merovingian Religious Ar chitecture: Some New Reflections." *OHMW*, pp. 657–92.
Clément, André. *Louise-Adélaïde d'Orléans, Abbesse de Chelles et son époque (1700–1750): 6 Octobre–27 Octobre*. Ville de Chelles: Musée Alfred-Bonno, 1963.
Coleman, Emily, "Infanticide in the Early Middle Ages," in Susan Mosher Stuard, ed., *Women in Medieval Society*. Philadelphia: University of Pennsylvania Press, 1976, pp. 47–70.
Coon, Lynda. *Sacred Fictions: Holy Women and Hagiography in Late Antiquity*. Philadelphia: University of Pennsylvania Press, 1997.
Couturier, M. J. *Sainte Bathilde, reine des Francs*. Paris: Pierre Téqui, 1909.
Crawford, Sally. "Overview: The Body and Life Course," in David A. Hinton, Sally Crawford, and Helena Hamerow, eds., *The Oxford Handbook of Anglo-Saxon Archaeology*. Oxford: Oxford University Press, 2011.
Crawford, Sally and Carenza Lewis. "Childhood Studies and the Society for the Study of Childhood in the Past." *Childhood in the Past* 1 (2008): 5–16.

Dailey, E. T. *Queens, Consorts, Concubines: Gregory of Tours and Women of the Merovingian Elite*. Leiden: Brill, 2015.
Davis, David Brion. *The Problem of Slavery in Western Culture*. Oxford: Oxford University Press, 1988.
D'Avery, David. *Papacy, Monarchy and Marriage, 860–1600*. Cambridge: Cambridge University Press, 2017.
de Jong, Mayke. "Monastic Prisoners or Opting Out? Political Coercion and Honour in the Frankish Kingdoms," in Mayke de Jong, Frans Theuws, with Carine van Rhijn, eds., *Topographies of Power in the Middle Ages*. Leiden: Brill, 2001, pp. 291–328.
de Jong, Mayke. "Queens and Beauty in the Early Medieval West: Balthild, Theodelinda, Judith," in C. La Rocca, ed., *Agire da donna. Modelli e pratiche di rappresentazione (secoli vi–x)*. Turnhout: Brepols, 2007, pp. 235–48.
de Maillé, Marquise. *Les cryptes de Jouarre*. Paris: A. & J. Picard, 1971.
Deloche, Maximin. *Étude historique et archaèologique sur les anneaux sigillaires et autres des premiers siècles du moyen age. Description de 315 anneaux, avec dessins dans le texte*. Paris: Ernest Leroux, 1900.
Depreux, Philippe. "Princes, princesses et nobles étrangers à la cour des rois Mérovingiens et Carolingiens: alliés, hôtes ou otages?" *Actes des congrès de la Société des historiens médiévistes de l'enseignement supérieur public, 30e congrès: L'étranger au Moyen Âge* 30 (Göttingen, 1999): 133–54.
Dérens, Jean. "Note sur la topographie religieuse de Paris à l'époque mérovingienne." *La Neustrie*, vol. 2, pp. 45–51.
Desthuilliers, Annick. "Chelles." *Notre Departement. La Seine-et-Marne* 20 (Aug.–Sept. 1991): 5–13.
Diem, Albrecht. *The Pursuit of Salvation: Community, Space, and Discipline in Early Medieval Monasticism with a Critical Edition and Translation of the Regula cuiusdam ad virgines*. Turnhout: Brepols, 2021.
Drews, Wolfram. "Migrants and Minorities in Merovingian Gaul." *OHMW*, pp. 117–38.
Dunn, Marilyn. *The Emergence of Monasticism from the Desert Fathers to the Early Middle Ages*. Oxford: Wiley-Blackwell, 2003.
During, Lisabeth. *The Chastity Plot*. Chicago: University of Chicago Press, 2021.
Duty, Claude. "Les Énervés de Jumièges" (short film). Court-métrage de Claude Duty (20 min), 1986. Avec Serge Giamberardino, Jean-Philippe Sarthou, Anne Le Guernec.
Duval, Noël, Patrick Périn, and Jean-Charles Picard, "Paris," in Jean-Charles Picard et al., eds., *Province ecclésiastique de Sens (Lugdunensis Senonia). Topographie Chrétienne des cités de la Gaule*, vol. 8. Paris: De Boccard, 1992, pp. 97–129.
Earenfight, T. *Queenship in Medieval Europe*. New York: Palgrave Macmillan, 2013.
Ebling, Horst. *Prosopographie der Amsträger des Merowingerreich von Chlothar II (613) bis Karl Martell (741)*. Munich: Wilhelm Fink Verlag, 1974.
Effros, Bonnie. "Symbolic Expressions of Sanctity: Gertrude of Nivelles in the Context of Merovingian Mortuary Custom." *Viator* 27 (1996): 1–10.
Effros, Bonnie. "Beyond Cemetery Walls: Early Medieval Funerary Topography and Christian Salvation." *Early Medieval Europe* 6.1 (1997): 1–23.
Effros, Bonnie. *Caring for Body and Soul: Burial and the Afterlife in the Merovingian World*. University Park, PA: Pennsylvania State University Press, 2002.
Effros, Bonnie. *Creating Community with Food and Drink in Merovingian Gaul*. New York: Palgrave Macmillan, 2002.
Effros, Bonnie. "Artistic, Scholarly and Popular Depictions of the 'Première Race' in Late Nineteenth-Century France," in Helmut Reimitz and Bernhard Zeller, eds., *Mittelalter und europäische Erinnerungskultur. Forschungen zur Geschichte des Mittelalters* 14. Vienna: Institut für Mittelalterforschung, Österreichische Akademie der Wissenschaften, 2009, pp. 71–91.

Effros, Bonnie. *Uncovering the Germanic Past: Merovingian Archaeology in France, 1830-1914.* Oxford: Oxford University Press, 2012.
Esders, Stefan. "The Merovingians and Byzantium. Diplomatic, Military, and Religious Issues, 500-700." *OHMW*, pp. 347-69.
Ewig, Eugen. "Das Privileg des Bischofs Berthefrid von Amiens für Corbie und die Klosterpolitik der Königin Balthild." *Beihefte der Francia* 1 (1973): 62-114.
Feffer, Laure-Charlotte. *Frédégonde Reine: Nouveaux récits des temps mérovingiens.* Arles: Actes Sud, 2014.
Flechner, Roy and Janel Fonataine. "The Admission of Former Slaves into Churches and Monasteries: Reaching beyond the Sources." *Early Medieval Europe* 29.4 (2021): 586-611.
Fleming, Robin. *Britain after Rome: The Fall and Rise, 400 to 1070.* London: Allen Lane, 2010.
Folz, Robert. "Tradition hagiographique et culte de sainte Bathilde, reine des Francs." *Comptes rendus des séances de l'Académie des Inscriptions et Belles-Lettres* 119.3 (1975): 369-84.
Fouracre, Paul. "Merovingian History and Merovingian Hagiography." *Past and Present* 127 (1990): 3-38.
Fouracre, Paul. "Why Were So Many Bishops Killed in Merovingian Francia?," in Natalie Fryde and Dirk Reitz, eds., *Bischofsmord in Mittelalter.* Göttingen: Vandenhoeck and Ruprecht, 2003, pp. 13-35.
Fouracre, Paul. "Balthild and 'her' Seal Ring, Text and Artefact," in Osamo Kano and Jean-Loup Lemaitre, eds., *Entre text et Histoire.* Paris: Boccard, 2015, pp. 129-42.
Fouracre, Paul and Richard Gerberding. *Late Merovingian France: History and Hagiography, 640-720.* Manchester: Manchester University Press, 1996.
Fox, Yaniv. *Power and Religion in Merovingian Gaul: Columbanian Monasticism and the Frankish Elites.* Cambridge: Cambridge University Press, 2014.
Gaborit-Chopin, Danielle. "Les trésors de Neustrie du VIIe au IX siècle d'après les sources écrites: orfèvrerie et sculpture sur ivoire." *La Neustrie,* pp. 259-93.
Gaillard, M. "Female Monasteries of the Early Middle Ages (Seventh to Ninth Century) in Northern Gaul: Between Monastic Ideals and Aristocratic Powers," in J. Burton and K. Stöber, eds., *Women in the Medieval Monastic World.* Turnhout: Brepols, 2015, pp. 75-96.
Ganz, David. *Corbie in the Carolingian Renaissance.* Beihefte der Francia 20. Sigmaringen: Jan Thorbecke, 1990.
Garipnazov, Ildar. *Graphic Signs of Authority in Late Antiquity and the Early Middle Ages, 300-900.* Oxford: Oxford University Press, 2018.
Gaudemet, Jean. "Le pseudo-concile de Nantes." *Revue de droit canonique* 25 (1975): 40-60.
Gauthier, Nancy, ed. *Les premiers monuments chrétiennes de la France, 3 Ouest, Nord et Est.* Paris: Picard, 1998.
Garver, Valerie L. "Childbearing and Infancy in the Carolingian World." *Journal of the History of Sexuality* 21.2 (2012): 208-44.
Gerberding, Richard. *The Rise of the Carolingians and the Liber Historiae Francorum.* Oxford and New York: Clarendon Press, 1987.
Glancy, Jennifer. *Slavery in Early Christianity.* Oxford: Oxford University Press, 2002.
Grubbs, Judith Evans. "Constantine and Imperial Legislation on the Family," in Jill Harries and Ian Wood, eds., *The Theodosian Code: Studies in the Imperial Law of Late Antiquity.* 2nd ed. London: Bloomsbury, 2010, pp. 120-42.
Guerout, Jean. "Le testament de Sainte-Fare: matériaux pour l'étude et l'édition critique de ce document." *Revue d'histoire ecclésiastique* 60 (1965): 761-821.
Hadjadj, Reine. *Bagues mérovingiennes: Gaule du Nord.* Paris: Éditions les Chevau-Légers, 2007.
Haydock, Hannah, Leon Clarke, Elizabeth Craig-Atkins, Rachel Howcroft, and Jo Buckberry. "Weaning at Anglo-Saxon Raunds: Implications for Changing Breastfeeding Practice in Britain over Two Millenia." *American Journal of Physical Anthropology* 151 (2013): 604-12
Halsall, Guy. "Gender in Merovingian Gaul." *OHMW,* pp. 164-85.

Hammer, Carl I. "Holy Entrepreneur: Agilbert, a Merovingian Bishop between Ireland, England and Francia." *Peritia* 22/23 (2011–12): 53–82.
Hannah, Emma L., T. Rowan McLaughlin, Evelyn M. Keaveney, and Susanne E. Hakenbeck. "Anglo-Saxon Diet in the Conversion Period: A Comparative Isotopic Study Using Carbon and Nitrogen." *Journal of Archaeological Science: Reports* 19 (2018): 24–34.
Harper, Kyle. *Slavery in the Late Roman World AD 275–425*. Cambridge: Cambridge University Press, 2011.
Harries, Jill and Ian Wood, eds. *The Theodosian Code: Studies in the Imperial Law of Late Antiquity*. 2nd ed. London: Bloomsbury, 2010.
Heidrich, Ingrid. "Les maires du palais neustriens du milieu du viie au milieu du viiie siècle." *La Neustrie*, pp. 217–29.
Hemmer, K. A., J. A. Evans, C. A. Chenery, and A. L. Lamb. "Evidence of Early Medieval Trade and Migration between Wales and the Mediterranean Sea Region." *Journal of Archaeological Science* 40 (2013): 2352–59.
Hen, Yitzhak. *Culture and Religion in Merovingian Gaul, AD 481–751*. Leiden: Brill, 1995.
Hen, Yitzhak. *Roman Barbarians: The Royal Court and Culture in the Early Medieval West*. New York: Palgrave Macmillan, 2007.
Hen, Yitzhak. "Changing Places; Chrodobert, Boba, and the Wife of Grimoald." *Revue Belge de Philologie et d'Histoire* 90.2 (2012): 225–43.
Hen, Yitzhak. "The Merovingian Polity: A Network of Courts and Courtiers." *OHMW*, pp. 217–37.
Hershenzon, Daniel. "Jews and the Early Modern Mediterranean Slave Trade," in Jessica Marglin and Matthias Lehmann, eds., *Jews and the Mediterranean*. Bloomington: University of Indiana Press, 2020, pp. 81–106.
Hillner, Julia. *Helena Augusta: Mother of the Empire*. Oxford: Oxford University Press, 2023.
Hofmann, Julia. "The Marriage of Childeric II and Bilichild in the Context of the Grimoald Coup." *Peritia* 17/18 (2003/4): 382–93.
Horden, Peregrine. "Public Health, Hospitals, and Charity." *OHMW*, pp. 299–319.
Hubert, Jean. Comments on Robert Folz, "Tradition hagiographique" *Comptes rendus des séances de l'Académie des Inscriptions et Belles-Lettres* 119.3 (1975): 383–84.
Huet, Gédéon. "La légende des Enervés de Jumièges: texte latin." *Bibliothèque de l'École des Chartes* 77 (1916): 197–216.
Hughes, Susan H., Andrew R. Millard, Sam J. Lucy, Carolyn A. Chenery, Jane A. Evans, Geoff Nowell, and D. Graham Pearson, "Anglo-Saxon Origins Investigated by Isotopic Analysis of Burials from Berinsfield, Oxfordshire, UK." *Journal of Archaeological Science* 42 (2014): 81–92.
Inrap (Institut national de recherches archéologiques préventives). "Paris retrouve sa première enceinte médiévale," at the rue Rivoli: https://www.inrap.fr/paris-retrouve-sa-premiere-enceinte-medievale-5044.
James, Edward. *The Franks*. Oxford: Basil Blackwell, 1988.
James, Edward. "The Merovingians from the French Revolution to the Third Republic." *Early Medieval Europe* 20.4 (2012): 450–71.
Jennings, Lawrence C. *French Anti-Slavery: The Movement for the Abolition of Slavery in France, 1802–1848*. Cambridge: Cambridge University Press, 2000.
Joye, Sylvie and Paul Bertrand. "Les 'testaments de saints' en Chrétienté occidentale," in Marie-Céline Isaïa and Thomas Granier, eds., *Normes et hagiographie dans l'Occident latin (Vie–XVIe siècle) Actes du colloque internation de Lyon 4–6 octobre 2010*. Turnhout: Brepols, 2014, pp. 293–307.
Kemp, Kathryn. "Where Have All the Children Gone? The Archaeology of Childhood." *Journal of Archaeological Method and Theory* 8.1 (2001): 1–34.
Langlois, Eustache-Hyacinthe. *Essai historique et descriptif sur l'abbaye de Fontanelle ou de Saint-Wandrille et sur plusieurs autres monuments des environs*. Paris: J. Tastu, 1827.

Langlois, Eustache-Hyacinthe. *Essai sur les Énervés de Jumièges et sur quelques décorations singulières des Églises de cette abbaye; suivi du miracle de Sainte Bautheuch, publiée pour la premiere fois.* Rouen: Edouard Frère, 1838.

Laporte, Jean-Pierre. *Le Trésor des saints de Chelles.* Ville de Chelles: Société archéologique et historique de Chelles, 1988.

Laporte, Jean-Pierre. "La reine Bathilde ou l'ascension sociale d'une esclave," in Michel Rouche and Jean Heuclin, eds., *La femme au moyen-âge.* Maubeuge: J. Touzot, 1990, pp. 147-69.

Laporte, Jean-Pierre and Raymond Boyer. *Trésors de Chelles: sepultures et reliques de la reine Bathilde († vers 680) et de l'abbesse Bertille († vers 704). Catalogue de l'exposition organisée au Musée Alfred Bonno, David Coxall, responsable du Musée.* Ville de Chelles: Société archéologique et historique: Les amis du Musée, 1991.

Le Forestier, Cyrille. *Archéologie des nécropoles mérovingiennes en Île-de-France. Rapport d'activité.* Programme collectif de recherche. Ministère de la Culture et de la Communication, 2013.

Le Jan, Régine Hennebicque. "Prosographica Neustrica: Les agents du roi en Neustrie de 639-840." *La Neustrie,* pp. 231-69.

Le Jan, Régine. *Femmes, pouvoir et société dans le haut Moyen Age.* Paris: J. Picard, 2001.

Le Jan, Régine. "Personal Names and the Transformation of Kinship in Early Medieval Society (Sixth to Tenth Centuries)" in George T. Beech, Monique Bourin, Pascal Chareille eds. *Personal Names Studies of Medieval Europe.* Kalamazoo, MI: Medieval Institute Publications, 2002, pp. 31-50.

Le Jan, Régine. "La sacralité de la royauté mérovingienne." *Annales. Historire, Sciences Sociales* 6 (Nov.-Dec. 2003): 1217-41.

Levillain, Léon. Review. "Maurice Lecomte, *Le Testament de Sainte Fare.*" *Bibliothèque de l'École des Chartes* 60 (1899): 95-100.

Levillain, Léon. *Examen critique des chartes mérovingiennes et carolingiennes de l'abbaye de Corbie.* Paris: A. Picard et fils, 1902.

Lin, Sihong. "The Merovingians and the Monothelete Controversy." *Journal of Ecclesiastical History* 71.2 (2020): 235-52.

Loseby, S. T. "The Role of the City in Merovingian Francia." *OHMW,* pp. 583-610.

Machemer, Theresa. "France Seeks Proposals for Memorial to Victims of Slavery." *Smithsonian Magazine,* July 15, 2020.

McAuley, James. "France Confronts Slavery: A Demon of its Past." *Washington Post,* May 28, 2016.

McCormick, Michael. *Origins of the European Economy: Communications and Commerce 300-900.* Cambridge: Cambridge University Press, 2002.

McLaughlin, Megan. *Consorting with Saints: Prayer for the Dead in Early Medieval France.* Ithaca: Cornell University Press, 1994.

McNamara, Jo Ann. *Sainted Women of the Dark Ages.* Durham and London: Duke University Press, 1992.

McNamara, Jo Ann. "*Imitatio Helenae*: Sainthood as an Attribute of Queenship," in S. Sticca, ed., *Saints: Studies in Hagiography.* Binghamton: Medieval and Renaissance Texts and Studies, 1996.

Merceron, J. E. "De l'hagiographie à la chanson d'aventures: l'image de sainte Bathilde reine de France," in Miren Lacassange, ed., *Ce nous dist li escris...che est la verite.* Aix-en-Provence: Presses universitaires de Provence, 2000, pp. 193-206.

Moreira, Isabel. "Provisatrix Optima: St. Radegund of Poitiers' Relic Petitions to the East." *Journal of Medieval History* 19 (1993): 285-305.

Moreira, Isabel. "Living in the Palaces of Love: Love and the Soul in a Vision of St. Aldegund of Maubeuge (c. 635-684)." *Quidditas* 19 (1998): 143-65.

Moreira, Isabel. "Dreams and Divination in Early Medieval Canonical and Narrative Sources: The Question of Clerical Control." *Catholic Historical Review* 89 (2003): 607-28.

Moreira, Isabel. *Heaven's Purge. Purgatory in Late Antiquity*. Oxford and New York: Oxford University Press, 2010.

Moreira, Isabel. "Hector of Marseilles Is Purged: Political Rehabilitation and Guilt by Association in the 7th Century *Passion of Saint Leudegar of Autun*." *Quaestiones Medii Aevi Novae* 17 (2012): 191–209.

Moreira, Isabel. "Purgatory's Intercessors: Bishops, Ghosts, and Angry Wives," in R. Pollard, ed., *Imagining the Medieval Afterlife*. Cambridge: Cambridge University Press, 2020, pp. 133–52.

Moreira, Isabel. "Visions and the Merovingian Afterlife." *OHMW*, pp. 988–1011.

Moreira, Isabel. "Rings on her Fingers: Merovingian Rings and Religion in Late Antiquity," in Mark D. Ellinson, Catherine Gines Taylor, and Carolyn Osiek, eds., *Material Culture and Women's Religious Experience*. London: Lexington Books, 2021, pp. 303–36.

Nelson, J. "Queens as Jezebels: The Careers of Brunhild and Balthild in Merovingian History," in Derek Baker, ed., *Medieval Women*. London: Basil Blackwell, 1978, pp. 31–77.

Nelson, J. "Writing Early Medieval Biography." *History Workshop Journal* 50 (2000): 129–36.

Nelson, J. "Gendering Courts in the Early Medieval West," in Leslie Brubaker and Julia Smith, eds., *Gender in the Early Medieval World, East and West, 300–900*. Cambridge: Cambridge University Press, 2004, pp. 185–97.

O'Hara, Alexander and Ian Wood. *Jonas of Bobbio. Life of Columbanus, Life of John of Reome, and Life of Vedast*. Translated Texts for Historians, vol. 64. Liverpool: Liverpool University Press, 2017.

Paxton, Frederick. *Christianizing Death: The Creation of a Ritual Process in Early Medieval Europe*. Ithaca: Cornell University Press, 1990.

Pelteret, David A. E. *Slavery in Early Medieval England from the Reign of Alfred until the Twelfth Century*. Woodbridge: Boydell, 1995.

Perez, Émilie. "Children's Lives and Deaths in Merovingian Gaul." *OHMW*, pp. 186–213.

Perkins, Charles C. "The Abbey of Jumièges and the Legend of the Enervés." *American Journal of Archaeology and of the History of the Fine Arts* 1.2/3 (1885): 131–37.

Pestell, Tim. "Das Baldehildis-Siegel," in E. Wamers and P. Périn, eds., *Königinnen der Merowinger. Adelsgraber aus den Kirchen von Köln, Saint-Denis, Chelles und Frankfurt am Main*. Regensburg: Schnell und Steiner, 2013, pp. 145–48.

Picard, Jean-Charles, Br. Beaujard, E. Dabrowska, Chr. Laplace, N. Duval, P. Périn, L. Piétri. *Province ecclésiastique de Sens (Lugdunensis Senonia)*, Topographie Chrétienne des cités de la Gaule, vol. VIII. Paris: De Boccard, 1992.

Pion, Constantin, Bernard Gratuze, Patrick Périn, Thomas Calligaro. "Bead and Garnet Trade between the Merovingian, and Indian Worlds." *OHMW*, pp. 819–859.

Pontal, Odette. *Histoire des Conciles Mérovingiens* Paris: Editions du Cerf, 1989.

Potter, David. *Theodora. Actress, Empress, Saint*. Oxford: Oxford University Press, 2015.

Prinz, Friedrich. *Frühes Mönchtum im Frankenreich*. 2nd ed. Darmstadt: R. Oldenbourg, 1988.

Rebillard, Éric. *In Hora Mortis: Évolution de la pastorale chrétienne de la mort au IVe et Ve siècles dans l'occident Latin*. Palais Farnèse: École Français de Rome, 1994.

Rio, Alice. "Self-Sale and Voluntary Entry into Unfreedom, 300–1100." *Journal of Social History* 45.3 (2002): 661–85.

Rio, Alice. *Slavery after Rome, 500–1100*. Oxford: Oxford University Press, 2017.

Quevilly, Laurent. "Les Énervés de Jumièges." Jumieges.free.fr.

Rollason, D. W. *The Mildrith Legend: A Study of Early Medieval Hagiography in England*. Leicester: Leicester University Press, 1982.

Samson, Ross. "The Merovingian Nobleman's Home: Castle or Villa?" *Journal of Medieval History* 13 (1987): 287–315.

Sanders, Gabriel. "Le remaniement carolingien de la 'Vita Balthildis' mérovingienne." *Analecta Bollandiana* 100 (1982): 411–28.

Santinelli, Emmanuelle, *Des Femmes éplorées? Les veuves dans la société aristocratique du haut Moyen Âge*. Lille: Septentrion, 2003.

Santinelli, Emmanuelle, "Les reines Mérovingiennes ont-elles une politique territoriale?," in Rita Compatangello-Soussignan and Emmanuelle Santinelli, eds., *Territoires et frontières en Gaule du Nord et dans les espaces septentrionaux francs*. Revue du Nord 85.351 (2003): 631–53.

Sarti, Laury. "The Digression on Pope Martin I in the Life of Eligius of Noyon," in Stefan Esders, Yaniv Fox, Yitzhak Hen, and Laury Sarti, eds., *East and West in the Early Middle Ages: The Merovingian Kingdoms in Mediterranean Perspective*. Cambridge: Cambridge University Press, 2019, pp. 149–64.

Sarti, Laury. "The Military and its Role in Merovingian Society." *OHMW*, pp. 255–77.

Senate Website. http://www.senat.fr/lng/en/the_luxembourg_palace/a_republican_palace.html.

Schroeder, Caroline T. "Francia as 'Christendom': The Merovingian *Vita Domnae Balthildis*." *Medieval Encounters* 4 (1998): 265–84.

Sicard, Damien. *La liturgie de la mort dans l'église latine des origines à la réforme carolingienne*. Aschendorff Verlag: Münster, Westfalen, 1978.

Simon, Clélia. "Les statues du péristyle de l'église Sainte-Marie-Madaleine à Paris (1837–1841): Le premier programme romantique religieux?" *Livraisons d'histoire de l'architecture* 12 (2006): 111–20.

Sivan, Hagith. *Galla Placidia: The Last Roman Empress*. Oxford: Oxford University Press, 2011.

Smith, J. *Europe after Rome: A New Cultural History, 500–1000*. Oxford: Oxford University Press, 2007.

Sommar, Mary E. *The Slaves of the Churches: A History*. Oxford: Oxford University Press, 2020.

Sortir à Paris. "The Memorial to the Victims of Slavery Moves to the Trocadero Gardens." https://www.sortiraparis.com/en/news/in-paris/articles/301043-the-memorial-to-the-victims-of-slavery-moves-to-the-trocadero-gardens. Sept. 22, 2023.

Squatriti, Paolo. "Good and Bad Plants in Merovingian Francia," *OHMW*, pp. 718–737.

Stafford, P. *Queens, Concubines and Dowagers: The King's Wife in the Early Middle Ages*. Athens, GA: University of Georgia Press, 1983.

Tatum, S. "*Auctoritas* as *Sanctitas*: Balthild's Depiction as 'queen-saint' in the *Vita Balthildis*." *European Review of History* 16 (2009): 809–34.

Theuws, Frans. "Long-Distance Trade and the Rural Population of Northern Gaul," *OHMW*, pp. 883–915.

Tinterow, Gary. "Paintings: Catalogue, 119–149," in Gary Tinterow and Philip Conisbee, eds., *Portraits by Ingres: Image of an Epoch*. New York: Metropolitan Museum of Art, 1999, pp. 398–401.

Torchet, Clément. *Histoire de l'abbaye royale de Notre-Dame de Chelles*, 2 vols. Paris: Retaux-Bray, 1889.

Tys, Dries. "Maritime and River Traders, Landing Places, and Emporia Ports in the Merovingian Period in and around the Low Countries," *OHMW*, pp. 765–796.

Urban, Elizabeth. *Conquered Populations in Early Islam: Non-Arabs Slaves, and the Sons of Slave Mothers*. Edinburgh: Edinburgh University Press, 2020.

Vieillard-Troiekouroff, May. "La sculpture en Neustrie." *La Neustrie*, pp. 225–57.

Vierck, H. E. F. "La 'chemise de Sainte-Bathilde' à Chelles et l'influence byzantine sur l'art de cour mérovingien au viie siècle." *Actes du Colloque International d'archéologie, Rouen, 3–4 Juillet 1975*. Rouen: Musée départemental des antiquités de Seine-Maritime et la Circonscription des antiquités historiques de Haute-Normandie, 1978, pp. 521–64.

Wamers, E. and P. Périn et al., eds. *Königinnen der Merowinger: Adelsgräber aus den Kirchen von Köln, Saint-Denis,Chelles und Frankfurt am Main*. Regensburg: Schnell & Steiner, 2013.

Wemple, Suzanne Fonay. *Women in Frankish Society: Marriage and the Cloister, 500–900*. Philadelphia: University of Pennsylvania Press, 1981.

Whitelock, Dorothy Whitelock, ed. *English Historical Documents c.500–1042.* London: Eyre and Spottiswoode, 1955.

Wickham, Chris. *Framing the Early Middle Ages: Europe and the Mediterranean, 400–800.* Oxford: Oxford University Press, 2005.

Wieczorek, Alfried, Patrick Périn, Karin V. Welck, and Wilfried Menghin, eds. *Die Franken: Wegbereiter Europas,* 2 vols. Mainz: Verlag Philipp von Zabern 1996.

Wilton, David. "What Do We Mean by Anglo-Saxon? Pre-conquest to the Present." *Journal of English and Germanic Philology* 119.4 (2020): 425–54.

Wikiphidias, *L'Encyclopédie des sculpteurs français* (accessed June 14, 2019). http://www.wikiphidias.fr/

Wood, Ian. *The Merovingian North Sea.* Alingsås: Viktoria Bokförlag, 1983.

Wood, Ian. "Frankish Hegemony in England," in Martin Carver, ed., *The Age of Sutton Hoo: The Seventh Century in North-Western Europe.* Woodbridge: Boydell, 1992, pp. 235–41.

Wood, Ian. *The Merovingian Kingdoms 450–751.* London: Longman, 1994.

Wood, Ian. *The Modern Origins of the Early Middle Ages.* Oxford: Oxford University Press, 2013.

Yorke, Barbara. "Queen Balthild's 'Monastic Policy' and the Origins of Female Religious Houses in Southern England." *Anglo-Saxon Studies in Archaeology and History* 20 (2015): 7–16.

Yvinec, Jean-Hervé and Maude Barme. "Livestock and the Early Medieval Diet in Northern Gaul." *OHMW,* pp. 738–62.

Index

For the benefit of digital users, indexed terms that span two pages (e.g., 52–53) may, on occasion, appear on only one of those pages.

'abolition,' terminology of xviii–xxi, 152
'Anglo-Saxon' terminology, use of xix
Acts of Aunemund 126–127, 131
Adalard, statutes of 119
Adalgisel 33–34
Aega, mayor of Neustria 29, 34, 55–56, 60
Aethelthryth (Etheldreda, Audrey) 111–112
Agilbert of Paris 110
Agnès de Villars 145–147
Agnes of Poitiers 100–101
Alfred-Bonno Museum, Chelles 151
Amandus of Maastricht 85
Andelys, convent 116–118
Anna, King of East Anglia 111
Anne de Clermont-Gessan de Chaste 147–149
Anonymous nun's history of the Abbey of Chelles 149
Anseflidis (his wife) 98
Anthimus 47–48, 104
Arnulf of Metz 33
Audoin of Rouen 56–57, 63–64, 74–76, 86–87, 125–127
Audoin of Rouen, *Life of Saint Eligius* 7–8, 18–19, 46–47, 50–51, 62–64, 85, 125–126, 128, 143–144
Aunemund of Lyon 7–8, 126–127, 130–131
Aurelianus of Arles 99–100

Baldehildis seal matrix 177–178
Balthild, queen, as abolitionist xx–xxi, 58, 70, 122, 136–137, 140–141, 151–153, 155, 157–158, 162–163, 175
  as Anglo-Saxon xix
  as Benedictine nun 93–97, 143–144, 150, 157–158
  as Jezebel 7–8, 129–132
  as Saxon 135–136, 143–144
  compassion and humanitarian concern, notion of xx–xxi, 57–58, 70, 73–74
  clothing 8–9, 45, 95–97, 108–109, 115–118
  education 52
  exhumation and 'translation' of body in 833 7–9, 102–103, 108–110, 114–115, 143–144
  gifts to Rome 84–86
  liturgy of Balthild 119–120
  personal appearance 21–22, 24–28, 95–97, 101, 109
  pregnancy (prophecy) 52–53, 126–127
  prohibition of infanticide 71–73
  regency 55–57, 84
  slave status versus royal descent 7–8, 14–15, 17–23
  statue of, *see* Thérasse, Victor
  vision 105–108
Basina, queen 50, 127
Baudonivia, *Life of Radegund* 4–6, 127
Bede 7–8, 81–82, 85–86, 90–91, 111–112
Bellessort, André xvii–xviii
Benedictine rule 76–77, 82–83, 91–92, 104–106, 141–143, 147–148, 150–151
Berchar 97–98
Berchild 33
Beretrude 41
Bertilla of Chelles 4–5, 81–83, 89–97, 102–106, 109–116, 118–121, 145–151, 161–162, 172–173
Bilichild, queen 19–21, 29, 41, 50, 53–54, 56–57, 97–98
Binet, Étienne (1569–1639) 143–144, 152
Bodilo 98
Bollandus, Johannes 170
Bonaparte, Alexandrine, Madam Lucien, Princessa Canino 166–167
Bonno, Alfred 8–9, 173–174
breastfeeding, in Anglo-Saxon England 12
Brun, Élisabeth 168–169
Burgundofara, 'testament' 79

Cardinal Richelieu, Armand Jean du Plessis, Cardinal 144–145
Catherine de Scoraille de Rouisille-Fontages 144–145

212　INDEX

Cavé, Hygin-Edmond-Ludovic-Auguste 159–160, 162, 165–166
Charles X 154–155
Chelles, convent 1, 57–58, 68–69, 80–83, 88, 141–143
Chervet, Marie-Eugenie (= Raoul de Navery) 174–175
Childebert I 41, 99–100, 102–103
Childebert III 29, 98
Childeric I 127
Childeric II xix, 1, 26, 29, 41, 54–57, 83, 97–98, 124–125, 127, 136
childhood, Anglo-Saxon England 4–5, 10–15
Chilperic I 41–42, 50, 80–81
Chilperic II (Daniel) 97–98
Chimnechild, queen 29, 54, 56–57
Chlothar I 19–20, 50
Chlothar II 32–33, 41–43, 55, 59, 74, 126–127
Chlothar II, their son 41
Chlothar III xix, 1, 52–53, 55–57, 70–71, 77–78, 97–98, 109, 124–127, 130–131, 161–162
Chlothar IV 98
Chlothild 1, 40–41, 50, 81–82, 99–100, 102–103, 124, 140, 150–151, 157, 163–164, 170–173
Chrodebert of Paris 56–57
Chrodechild 98
Church of Holy Cross, Chelles 81, 97, 99–103, 109–110, 150–151
Church of Notre Dame, Chelles 109–110, 114, 151
Church of Saint Vincent and the Holy Cross, Paris 41, 98–100
Church of Saint-Denis 40–41, 77
Church of St Andrew, Chelles 8–9, 150–151, 172
Church of St George, Chelles 1, 43, 81, 99, 102–103, 109–110, 141–143, 150–151
Church of the Holy Apostles 40–41
Ciperis de Vignevaux 136
Clichy 34, 42–43, 50–51, 59, 67–68, 127
Clovis I 1–3, 32, 40–41, 43, 50, 123–124, 127
Clovis II xix, 1–3, 7–8, 15, 23–26, 29, 31–36, 38–40, 43–44, 49–50, 52–56, 60–61, 66–67, 74, 76–78, 81–82, 85–87, 101–102, 123–126, 132–136, 140, 149, 161–162, 170–172, 174–175
Code Noir 153
Columbanus 31, 45, 76–77, 82–83, 91–92, 94, 104–105, 133, 170–172
Corbie, monastery 4–5, 77–78, 80, 102–103, 109, 113–115, 119–120, 122, 136, 145, 161–162

Council of Autun (663×680) 83
Council of Bordeaux (662×675) 83
Council of Chalon-sur-Saône 60–63, 71, 83–84
Council of Losne (673×675) 83–84
Council of Nantes (658×666) 83–84
Council of Rouen (650×655) 83–84
Couturier, Mathieu xvii–xviii
Cynifrid, physician 112

D'Andilly, Robert Arnaud xx–xxi, 144, 152–155
Dagobert I 2–3, 7, 29, 31–36, 39, 41–42, 50–51, 53, 55–56, 61, 67, 86–87, 126–127, 132–133, 136, 170–172
Dagobert II 97–98
Dalfinus of Lyon 129–130
De Gisors, Henri-Alphonse Guy 155–156, 159–161
Diem, Albrecht 82–83, 91–92
diet 47–49
diet, in Anglo-Saxon England 11–14
Dreux du Radier, Jean François (1714–1780) 161–162
Dreux, royal chapel 156–158
Duty, Claude 138–139

Ealdwulf, King of the East Angles 81–82, 90–91
Ebroin, Mayor of Neustria 32, 39, 54, 56–57, 93, 97–98, 125, 131–133
Ecgfrith of Northumbria 111–112
Eligius of Noyon 7–8, 18–19, 45–53, 56–57, 60–70, 74–76, 84–87, 93, 101–103, 114, 116–118, 120, 125–129, 132–133, 143–145, 150, 170–172
Erchinoald, mayor of Neustria 1–2, 4–5, 17, 21–25, 29, 32, 34–40, 51–52, 55–57, 66–67, 77–78, 97–98, 135–136
Esther, biblical queen 5–6, 21–23, 124
Ethelburga of Anglia 111–112

Faremoutiers 79, 81–82, 106, 110–112, 141
Fire at convent of Chelles in 1226 120–121, 150–151
Flaochad, mayor of Burgundy 39, 55–56
Fredegund, queen 41, 50, 80–81, 169–172

Galen, physician 104
Galswinth, queen 50, 170–172
Genesius of Lyon 37–38, 67, 74–76, 88, 101–103, 106–108, 114, 118, 120, 131, 150, 161–162
Genovefa 40–41, 140, 157

Gisela, abbess 7–8, 17–18, 30, 102, 114, 150–151
Gomatrude 33
Gregory I, Pope 85–86
Gregory, bishop of Tours 40–42, 80–81, 123–124, 127, 159, 169–172
Grimoald, mayor of Austrasia 7, 29, 39–40, 54
Guyonne Marguerite de Cosse de Brissac de Rousille 145

Hegilvid, abbess 102–103, 109, 114–115, 119
Helena, mother of Constantine 5–6, 101–102, 124
Hénault, Charles-Jean-François (1685–1770) 161–162
Hereswith 81–82, 90–91
Hild, abbess 81–82, 90–91
Holy Cross convent, Poitiers 82–83, 100–101

Ingres, Jean-Auguste Dominique 157–158, 163–164

James, Edward 170–172
Jennings, Lawrence 155
Jonas of Bobbio 82–83
Jonas of Bobbio, Life of John of Réomé 82–83, 106
Jouarre, convent 46, 79–81, 89, 102–103, 110, 114–115, 141, 172–173
Jumièges, monastery 7–8, 68–69, 77–79, 113, 119–120, 132–135, 137, 145, 174–175
Junot, Laure, Duchess of Abrantes 166–167

Langlois, Ésperance 137–138
Langlois, Eustache-Hyacinthe 137
Laporte, Jean-Pierre 10, 26, 102, 110, 113–121, 172–173
Lavisse, Ernest 170–172
Les énervés de Jumièges (legend of) 132–139, 174–175
Leudegar of Autun 7–8, 48–49, 75–76, 93, 102–103, 131
Leudesius, mayor of Neustria 32, 34, 97–98
Life of Austrebertha of Pavilly 68–69, 132–133
Life of Balthild I (Merovingian) 4–6, 17, 22–23, 37–40, 90, 99–100, 118–119, 124–126, 170
Life of Balthild II (Carolingian) 7–8, 17–18, 70–71, 84, 99–100, 103, 119–120, 143–144, 170
Life of Bertilla of Chelles 7–8, 20–21, 90–92, 109, 115
Life of Lantbert of Lyon 125

Logium, monastery 79
Louis the Pious 114, 119
Louis XIV 144–147, 153, 156
Louis XVIII 154–155
Louise-Adélaïde d'Orléans 140–141, 145–149, 156
Louis-Philippe, King 140–141, 154–159, 162
Luminais, Évariste Vital, painting by 137–139, 174–175
Luxeuil, monastery 66–67, 79–80, 93

Madeleine de la Porte de la Meilleraye 144–145, 149, 151–152
Madeleine-Elisabeth Delphine de Sabran 149
Malitourne, Pierre-Armand xv, 164
Marie de Lorraine (1583–1627) 143–145
Martin I, pope 85
Mazarin, Giulio, Cardinal 144–145
Mézeray, Eudes de 167, 170–172
Mildreth 90–91
Montfaucon, Bernard de 170

Nantechild 7, 23, 29, 31, 33–36, 39–40, 50, 55–56, 61, 116–118
Napoleon I, emperor 153–155, 166–167

Oribasius, physician 104

Philibert of Jumièges and Noirmoutier 7–8, 68–69, 77–79, 132–135
Philippe II, Duc d'Orléans 145–147, 156
Pierre de Ronsard 136–137
Pippin, mayor 33
Pius IX, pope 172–173
Pontal, Odette 84

Radegund, queen 19–20, 46, 50, 91–94, 99–101
Raedwald, king of Mercia 4
Ragnetrude 33–34
Ragnoberta 39, 55–56
Regula cuiusdam ad virgins 82–83, 91–94, 100–101, 104–105
Relic collection at Chelles 101–103, 112–118
Rule of Caesarius of Arles for nuns 82–83, 91–92, 95–97, 104–105
Rule of Columbanus 92, 94, 100–101

Saint-Germain-des-Prés, monastery 41, 99–100
Saint-Ouen, Laure 170–172
Saint-Wandrille, monastery 79, 132–133
Sarti, Laury 49–50
Schoelcher, Victor 175

Sigibert III, king of Austrasia 29, 33–34, 54, 85
Sigobrand of Paris 75–76, 88, 131
Simons-Candeille, Julia 166–167
Simony 75–76, 84
slavery in late antiquity xix–xx, 16
Stephen of Ripon's Life of St Wilfrid 7–8, 50–51, 122–123, 129–132

Theodechild of Jouarre 110
Theodora, Empress xvi–xvii, 19–20, 70, 116–118, 122–123
Thérasse, Victor 140–141, 155–165, 167–168, 170, 175
Theuderic III xix, 1, 55, 97–98, 124–125, 127
Theutlinda of Jouarre 81

Thierry, Augustin 137–138, 169–172
Torchet, Clément 141, 148–150, 172–174

Ultrogotha, queen 41, 99–100, 102–103, 124

Venantius Fortunatus 100–101, 127
Victoria, queen 156–157, 163–164
Viking raids 42, 120–121, 133, 150–151
Ville de Chelles 24, 43, 102–103, 120–121, 168–169, 172–173

Waratto, mayor of Neustria and Burgundy 98
Wilfrid of Ripon, Bishop of York 50–51, 111
Wulfegund 33
Wulfoald, mayor of Austrasia 97–98